Young Adult Literature Adolescent Identity across Cultures and Classrooms

Taking a critical, research-oriented perspective, this exploration of the theoretical, empirical, and pedagogical connections between the reading and teaching of young adult literature and adolescent identity development centers around three key questions:

- Who Are the Teens Reading Young Adult Literature?
- Why Should Teachers Teach Young Adult Literature?
- Why Are Teens Reading Young Adult Literature?

All chapters work simultaneously on two levels: each provides both a critical resource about contemporary young adult literature that could be used in YA literature classes or workshops *and* specific practical suggestions about what texts to use and how to teach them effectively in middle and high school classes.

Theorizing, problematizing, and reflecting in new ways on the teaching and reading of young adult literature in middle and secondary school classrooms, this valuable resource for teachers and teacher educators will help them to develop classrooms where students use literature as a means of making sense of themselves, each other, and the world around them.

Janet Alsup is Associate Professor of English Education at Purdue University with a joint appointment in the College of Liberal Arts and the College of Education.

Young Adult Literature and Adolescent Identity across Cultures and Classrooms

Contexts for the Literary Lives of Teens

Edited by Janet Alsup
Purdue University

Routledge
Taylor & Francis Group

NEW YORK AND LONDON

First published 2010
by Routledge
711 Third Avenue, New York, NY 10017

Simultaneously published in the UK
by Routledge
2 Park Square, Milton Park, Abingdon, Oxon OX14 4RN

Routledge is an imprint of the Taylor & Francis Group, an informa business

© 2010 Taylor & Francis

Typeset in Minion
by Keystroke, Tettenhall, Wolverhampton

Library of Congress Cataloging-in-Publication Data
Young adult literature and adolescent identity across cultures and classrooms:
contexts for the literary lives of teens / edited by Janet Alsup.
p. cm.
Includes index.
1. Young adult literature–Study and teaching. 2. Young adult literature–Stories,
plots, etc. 3. Ethnicity in literature–Study and teaching. 4. Identity (Philosophical
concept) in literature. 5. Characters and characteristics in literature. I. Alsup, Janet.
PN1008.8.Y68 2010
809'.892830712–dc22
2009045561

ISBN10: 0–415–87698–2 (hbk)
ISBN10: 0–415–87699–0 (pbk)
ISBN10: 0–203–85313–X (ebk)

ISBN13: 978–0–415–87698–8 (hbk)
ISBN13: 978–0–415–87699–5 (pbk)
ISBN13: 978–0–203–85313–9 (ebk)

Contents

Preface

For all of us contributing to this volume, young adult literature is a fascinating, though sometimes troublesome, genre. While we have a respect and appreciation for YAL, we do not accept its usefulness as a classroom text without question—instead, we consider, reconsider, ask questions, reflect, and read many examples of YA books before deciding what might be best for 21st-century teens in the English classroom. Many of us are past or present secondary school English teachers with experience teaching YA literature to adolescents. And while we focus primarily on American teenagers as readers of YAL, we don't stop there, as we also consider the literacy needs of students from diverse ethnic backgrounds, including Chinese American, Arabic, and Hispanic students. In short, our goal in this book is to theorize, problematize, and reflect upon the teaching and reading of YA literature in secondary school classrooms—all with the primary intent of assisting teachers who choose to teach young adult literature. We also hope that by subjecting the genre to serious scholarly study, our work might prompt additional academic respect for YAL.

Part I, "Who Are the Teens Reading YAL?" explores the various subjectivities of teen readers currently reading young adult literature. This section begins with Chapter 2, Joy Dangora's "African American Young Adult Literature and Black Adolescent Identity: Developing a Sense of Self and Society through Narrative." Joy's chapter examines the work of Mildred Taylor, Walter Dean Myers, and Jacqueline Woodson through the lens of current pedagogical and psychological research theorizing African American teenage identity development.

Chapter 3, "Depictions of Chinese Americans in Young Adult Literature: *American Born Chinese* and Beyond," by Nai-Hua Kuo, continues the emphasis on YA books about diverse adolescents; however, Nai-Hua focuses on Chinese American teens. She looks at four contemporary young adult novels and memoirs about Chinese Americans and examines how they depict Chinese American youth.

Chapter 4, "Composing Themselves: The Discursive (De)Construction of Queer Identity in Six Young Adult Novels," by James R. Gilligan, describes the depiction of queer teens in six YA novels and analyzes how their character-ization is often associated with artistic or purposeful discourse such as poetry writing, diary writing, or letter writing. James theorizes this phenomenon and discusses how such a discursive process might mirror the sexual identity development of adolescents.

Chapter 5, "Teaching through the Conflict: Examining the Value of Culturally Authentic Arabic Young Adult Literature," by Nisreen Anati, explores what Nisreen labels "Arabic young adult literature," and argues for its inclusion in schools both in the Arabic world and in the United States. This chapter summarizes and critically analyzes several quality YA novels about Arabic teens and provides suggestions for teachers in various settings for using these novels with students.

The linked Chapters 6 and 7, "Funds of Knowledge and Mexican American Cultural Values in MA YAL" and "Mestizaje: Forging Identity through Hybridity," by William J. Broz and René Saldaña, Jr., take a thoughtful and informed look at the often fractured cultural identities of Mexican American teens and how reading selected YA texts about the Mexican American experi-ence might help them value and retain their cultural heritage in contemporary America.

Part II, "Why Should Teachers Teach YAL?" explores various arguments for and against the inclusion of YAL in the secondary literature curriculum. Chapter 8, "Engaging and Enchanting the Heart: Developing Moral Identity through Young Adult Fantasy Literature," by Aliel Cunningham, moves from an examination of the depiction of individual teenagers in literature to a more theoretical analysis of the uses of YA books as pedagogical tools—in Aliel's case, she focuses on fantasy young adult literature. Aliel argues that, contrary to the belief that fantasy literature is morally inappropriate or even dangerous, it can actually help teens cultivate a sense of right and wrong in an often complicated modern world.

Chapter 9, "Beyond the Comics Page: Pedagogical Opportunities and Challenges in Teaching Graphic Novels," by Lisa Schade Eckert, continues to theorize the YA novel, this time by focusing on graphic novels written for young adults. Lisa explores why teachers assign graphic novels (or don't assign them) and how such novels might be particularly appropriate for adolescent readers. Chapter 10, "Pedagogues and Demigods: Captivity, Pedagogy, and Young Adult Literature in an Age of Diminished Expectations," by Jeff Spanke, takes the discussion of the teaching of the young adult novel to a new dimension. By comparing the YA book to the early American captivity narrative, Jeff argues that perhaps whole-class teaching of YA novels is not appropriate when trying to promote healthy teenage identity growth. However, he provides ideas for ways young adult novels might effectively be included in the English language arts curriculum.

Chapter 11, "Perspective Giving and Taking in the Secondary English Class: Considering the Case of Erin Gruwell," by Jeanne Smith Muzzillo, examines the practice of asking students to take on the perspectives or identities of others when teaching literature. Jeanne problematizes this relatively common pedagogical strategy by examining *The Freedom Writers Diary*, in which she worries that the teacher, Erin Gruwell, encourages color blindness and the trivialization of difference among her students. Jeanne ends her chapter by providing suggestions for how perspective-taking activities can be mindfully done in an English classroom.

Part III, "Why Are Teens Reading YAL?" explores why teenage readers are attracted to the genre and what teachers can learn from a study of their interest. Chapter 12, "The Appeal of Young Adult Literature in Late Adolescence: College Freshmen Read YAL," is one of two empirical studies in the book. In this chapter, Gail Zdilla reports on a small empirical study she conducted with students in her university "teaching reading in the content areas" course. Through surveys and interviews with her students, Gail learns about their reading habits and how and why they read young adult literature, even though they are currently 18–20 years old.

Finally, Chapter 13, "1 Female Reader Reading YAL: Understanding Norman Holland's Identity Themes Thirty Years Later," my chapter, is also the report of a small, mixed-method study. In this chapter, I analyze what I learned about the reading habits of female readers of young adult books. Drawing upon the 1975 text by Norman Holland entitled *5 Readers Reading*, I examine how the young readers in my study connect their individual subjectivities to their reading habits and processes.

I invite you to engage with this fascinating collection of chapters exploring the genre of young adult literature and its potential for changing the lives of teen readers living across various cultures and within diverse classrooms.

Acknowledgements

I wish to thank Naomi Silverman, Senior Editor at Routledge, an imprint of the Taylor & Francis Group, for her support of this project.

I also thank Purdue University for supporting my work through a College of Liberal Arts Center for Humanistic Studies fellowship (2007) and a faculty fellowship for "Study in a Second Discipline" (2009).

Finally, I thank my husband, Keith Alyea, for his constant love and support.

Chapter 1

Introduction

Identification, Actualization, or Education: Why Read YAL?

Janet Alsup

Young adult literature (YAL), or literature written for readers between the ages of 12 and 20, has been taught in American schools since the 1970s and read by teens since the late 1960s, when books such as S.E. Hinton's *The Outsiders* (1967), Ann Head's *Mr. and Mrs. Bo Jo Jones* (1968), and Robert Lipsyte's *The Contender* (1967) were first published. Today, Newbery, Michael Printz, Coretta Scott King, Pura Belpre, and Américas Award-winning books are regularly taught in middle and high school English classes, and many more young adult novels are available in school libraries. YA books appear on district-approved reading lists, and teachers can either buy or find online multitudes of instructional materials to complement their teaching of books such as Lois Lowry's *The Giver* (1993) and Louis Sachar's *Holes* (2000). Many books have been published about the teaching of YAL and how teachers can best integrate it into their classrooms, notably those written by Donald Gallo, Virginia Monseau, John and Kay Parks Bushman, and Joan Kaywell. Many more articles by these and other scholars of young adult literature have been published in journals for teachers such as the *English Journal*, the *Journal of Adolescent & Adult Literacy*, and the *ALAN Review*. One could argue that YA literature has finally achieved a sort of acceptance and respect for which it has been searching since the advent of the genre as a viable publishing category in the 1960s.

However, what has *not* occurred with YA literature in the past 35 years is a systemic and scholarly examination of the literary and pedagogical effectiveness of the genre. There continues to be a great need for educational and literary scholars to study the genre from a critical, research-oriented perspective. While many articles and books assume the effectiveness of YAL as a genre to be read by young adults to improve both their reading skills and their self-concepts, very few studies or analyses support these assumptions. (Notable exceptions include works by John Noell Moore and Roberta Seelinger Trites.)

As English educators, we work in an inherently multidisciplinary world. As my co-authors and I wrote in the July 2006 issue of *English Education* (Alsup et al., 2006), "Historically, English education has been defined as an interdisciplinary field of academic inquiry focused on the preparation of English language arts teachers, and, by association, the teaching and learning of all aspects of English studies" (p. 279). The article goes on to list "English studies, education, the scientific study of human behavior, and related fields" as disciplinary bodies upon which English education draws in order to "transform theory and research in these fields into pedagogical-content questions as a basis for enhancing the understanding of the teaching and learning of English in all of its manifestations" (p. 279). In other words, we look to many different disciplines and ways of knowing to understand our students, our research, and our teaching practice. This multidisciplinary point of view serves us well as we try to understand the uses of literature and the effects of literature teaching on adolescent minds, bodies, and emotions. In this book, the contributors and I certainly assume this eclectic stance, drawing upon knowledge from various fields of study, including literary study, psychology, sociology, education, African American studies, feminist studies, and biological science, in order to understand better the effective use of YAL and to address effectively the interests and concerns of our target audience: teachers of young adult literature and English teacher educators.

In this chapter, I introduce the four major themes or ideas around which the book revolves: teenage identity growth and young adult literature; reader response approaches to teaching and reading young adult literature; the connections between psychological and educational theories of identification and young adult literature; and socio-cultural theories linking literacy to social change. Of course, in the chapters that follow, these themes are not discussed in mutually exclusive ways; the authors often discuss them as overlapping ideas, highlighting connections between, for example, teenage identity growth and brain research or social justice and critical reading.

Teenage Identity Growth

The idea of teenage identity formation as it relates to YA literature is central to the ideas explored in this book. I first became interested in theories of identity when I was working on my previous book, *Teacher Identity Discourses: Negotiating Personal and Professional Spaces* (Alsup, 2006). In that book, I explored the identity development of young teachers of English, not teen readers of YA texts. But many of the theories I discussed are useful to this book as well: discourse as an identity spark; narratives or storytelling as central to identity growth and self-perception of identity; and the connection (or disconnection) between discourses, subjectivities, and identity strands. As I state in *Teacher Identity Discourses*, one of the major theorists of discourse as identity is James P. Gee (see Gee, 1990/1996, 1999). In Gee's definition of discourse, the individual brings certain subjectivities to a discursive act, while, at the same time, the discourse affects the individual engaging in it. Therefore, discourse has a very real-world effect—what one says or does affects not only others but oneself. To simplify even further: how one communicates determines the person one becomes.

When thinking about reading literature and why a teacher of English might choose to teach literature, I returned to Gee's theory and began to narrow it to focus on narrative discourse, and, even more particularly, on narrative discourse that one *reads*. In other words, I switched my focus to stories or novels. I began to wonder if reading a novel might cause a person to change. And, more specifically, could reading a *young adult* novel cause a teenager to change in some internal way? As we know, teenagers are knee-deep in a particularly volatile time of life. They are rife for change and sometimes seem to change both physically and emotionally before our very eyes, as many developmental psychologists from Piaget to Erickson to Kegan have theorized and researched. As developmental psychologist Jane Kroger (1996) writes, "Although the foundations of 'I' are formed in infancy through the interactions of care-takers and child, adolescence does seem to be a time, at least in contemporary, technologically advanced western cultures, when one is confronted with the task of self-definition" (p. 18). The teenage years are also a time of tremendous activity in the frontal lobes of the brain, as scientists have recently discovered (Strauch, 2003). The prefrontal cortex is the part of the brain which inhibits actions that might be culturally or personally inappropriate; during the teen years these segments of the brain are not yet fully developed. As scientist Chuck Nelson writes,

> A lot of teenagers just don't see consequences of actions. They don't think ahead. They don't see that getting good grades today, for instance, makes a big difference to the person they will be later on. When they get older, they start to get that. And I think it has to do with development of the brain, particularly the prefrontal cortex, the part that controls working memory, inhibition, impulse control.
>
> (Quoted in Strauch, 2003, pp. 32–33)

Other brain researchers can shed light on what happens during the adolescent reading experience, which might differ from an adult reader's experience. First, brain researchers such as Mark Solms and Oliver Turnbull (2002) also tell us that the adolescent brain is in a critical and fast-paced time of development. During puberty, as during infancy, the teen brain is rapidly developing additional synaptic connections—whether or not these synapses are nurtured depends largely upon the richness of a teenager's environment. Second, Canadian researcher David S. Miall (1995) writes prolifically about connections between emotional response to reading and the prefrontal cortex of the brain which enables a reader to anticipate the future direction of a narrative and fill in the "gaps" in a text's meaning, as described by reader response theorist Wolfgang Iser (1978). According to Miall, when the prefrontal cortex is undeveloped (as in teens) or damaged, an individual has a more difficult time processing rapidly changing conditions or stimuli and responding to them appropriately. When reading a novel, processing various subplots, character

changes, and developing themes might be more difficult for a teenage reader—
at least without the guidance of a more skilled, mature reader, such as a teacher
or parent. Furthermore, Miall argues that the foregrounding of literary
elements or narrative structures in literary texts triggers emotional responses in
the frontal cortex of the brain; these emotional responses draw upon a reader's
personal experiences and memories. However, this emotional response does
not necessarily result in a one-way, simplistic transmission from the novel to
the reader's mind. Instead, readers are

> invited to reassess the feelings and memories they bring to such a story; the
> story may impel them to place their first feeling within the context of a
> second that modifies or limits the first in some way. As a result, an affective
> marker that, prior to the act of reading, guided a reader's understanding
> may be transformed or replaced as a result of reading.
>
> (Miall, 1995, pp. 11–12)

In other words, critical reading results, and readers may understand their
emotions in a new way.

An aspect of identity formation of great interest to my work on young adult
literature and teen identity development is the notion of narrative identity.
Jerome Bruner (2002) has written that "it is through narrative that we create
and re-create selfhood, that self is a product of our telling and not some essence
to be delved for in the recesses of subjectivity" (pp. 85–86). Other narrative
theorists agree. Dan P. McAdams, Ruthellen Josselson, and Amia Lieblich
(2006, p. 3) write:

> The stories we tell about our personal experiences grow in complexity and
> detail as we move through childhood and into the adolescent and young
> adult years. It is not until adolescence, some researchers and theorists have
> argued, that we are able and motivated to conceive of our lives as full-
> fledged, integrative narratives of the self (Habermas and Bluck, 2000;
> McAdams, 1985).

So, given the focus on identity development during adolescence, and the importance of building narratives of the self, might not adolescence be the perfect
time to read and explore literary narratives that encourage critical reflection?
Perhaps literature teaching might be key to positive identity growth and development for teen readers. And taking this argument a step further, could YAL,
literature written specifically for an audience of teen readers about teen
characters having life-like problems, be the ideal genre to prompt and support
such positive identity growth? If YAL has a unique tendency, based on general
characteristics it possesses, to assist teen readers in positive identity growth,
the teacher is led to ask some hard questions about its classroom use. To what

extent is the job of the literature teacher to effect personal change among students? Are English teachers qualified to elicit purposefully the identity change or growth of their students? Is it ethical to teach a book because a teacher believes it will make her students "better," "more moral," or "more empathetic" people? If literature can result in such deep, personal change, doesn't that make it especially dangerous, as many censors already argue? When English teachers themselves defend books they teach based on their enormous power to change readers' lives, how can they deny the censor's anger at the very same possibility? It then becomes a matter of whose values are taught and whose values are right—a battle that is surely futile.

However, something everyone seems to recognize is that literature *is* indeed powerful. It does do something to the reader, especially when the reader is engrossed in the reading process, or, as Victor Nell (1988) writes, "lost in a book," as his book-length work is titled. Readers can change through vicarious experience; they can grow, develop, ask new questions, think new thoughts, and even feel new emotions. All from reading a book—particularly, Nell argues, a fictional narrative. Total engagement in a narrative world is powerful and can create internal, personal narratives of self that, some argue, might guide a reader's behavior in the future.

These questions of literature and literature teaching are not new. Plato recognized the power of literature and feared it. He banished the poets from his ideal republic, arguing that they ruled by affect and imagination, not logic or analytical thought, and hence distorted reality and corrupted their audience. Since that time, it seems that "poetry" or other types of imaginative literature, such as fiction, have been simultaneously revered and detested as pedagogical forms. Today, some argue that literature is being pushed out of the language arts curriculum by the teaching of reading strategies and comprehension skills, which seem much less muddy or morally unclear. So what can we as literature teachers do to defend literature teaching and reaffirm the benefits of reading literature, benefits that we, as readers, have experienced many times? Northrop Frye in *The Educated Imagination* (1964) writes about how the so-called educated reader can overcome the fissure between intellect and emotion with which teachers often struggle and can even connect the two in a seamless synthesis of lived-through experience and critical analysis. He also makes the point that the reader with the educated imagination can tell the difference between convention and reality; he or she knows the difference between fiction and fact and can, therefore, learn from fiction without risk of losing touch with reality or making rash life decisions simply to mimic a character in a novel.

However, Richard Gerrig in *Experiencing Narrative Worlds* (1993) agues that fiction has the power to change behavior every bit as much as nonfiction. For example, if a reader reads a newspaper article about an upcoming particularly bitter storm season, he or she might do something about it: go to the hardware store to buy wood to board up windows, for example. Gerrig uses the example of the movie *Jaws* to argue for the similar power of fictional narratives: *Jaws* is a fictional movie—everyone knows that, no one has ever disputed that fact. However, Gerrig tells stories of individuals who would not go swimming for months after seeing the film, out of fear of a great white shark. Why? Perhaps, Gerrig argues, because the emotions we feel when reading or viewing fiction are the same emotions we feel when we read or view non-fiction—or experience real events. And these emotions, particularly when they resonate with our experience and we can identify with them, may lead to behavior change. So, bringing together Frye's and Gerrig's theories, while, yes, fiction *may* change behavior, it perhaps won't cause a reader to lose touch with reality or disregard his or her life experiences and situational realities—*if* the reader is properly educated.

In this so-called "me generation," when adolescents in our schools are more "confident, assertive, entitled, and more miserable than ever before" according to author and psychology professor Jean M. Twenge (2006), perhaps attending to the emotional and psychological needs of our students through literary study is more important than ever. However, for the teacher of YAL, the questions of what to teach, why, and how are complex and require much consideration, even if he or she is an unwavering fan of YA books.

Reader-Response Approaches to Teaching and Reading

Many teachers of middle and high school English teach literature through the pedagogical lens of reader-response theory, as espoused by Louise Rosenblatt and Robert Probst, among others. Reader-response criticism, as a way of reading and interpreting texts, has a long and somewhat varied history among literary scholars and literacy theorists and researchers. It can be said to have begun with the work of I.A. Richards in the 1920s (*Practical Criticism*, 1929) or with the writings of Louise Rosenblatt in the 1930s. Rosenblatt's work (1938/1978; 1938/1983) is particularly important to this volume, however, since she tends to maintain a pedagogical focus throughout her work. Her trans-actional theory of reading, whereby text and reader function in a kind of symbiotic relationship to produce meaning from a text (what Rosenblatt calls the "poem"), is a useful concept for secondary teachers of literature, who are often concerned with motivating resistant young readers. If a teacher believes that the reader brings knowledge to a text and that his or her responses are mostly valid products of personal experience in combination with textual representation, then the teacher develops an inherent respect for student response to texts, personal response that can lead to more distanced, critical responses with careful teaching.

Such personal, or "lived-through," response is an essential component of reading and understanding literary texts, according to Rosenblatt's theories of reader-response. Other reader-response scholars agree, although their theories vary slightly. For example, Wolfgang Iser (1974, 1978) also writes about the interaction of reader and text, but in his version of reader-response the reader is actively supplying implied information left out by the author, as he or she reads the text line by line. Therefore, the reader is constantly filling in "gaps" as he or she reads by making decisions about what is only implicitly referred to in a text. Less holistic than Rosenblatt's approach, Iser similarly values the input of the reader in making meaning. David Bleich's "subjective criticism" (1981) also values the input of the reader, but to a greater extent than either Rosenblatt's or Iser's approaches to reader-response. Bleich argues that instead of using the text to understand a reader's (or a student's) responses, one can use the reader's responses to understand the text. The response of the reader is not simply part of a transaction with the written word; it *transforms* the written word into something meaningful. Norman Holland, a reader-response theorist with a more psychological bent, theorizes that a reader's reading is based on a static "identity theme" which underlies the reader's personality and influences how a reader makes meaning from a text. His classic *5 Readers Reading* (1975) is referenced in my final chapter, "1 Female Reader Reading YAL: Understanding Norman Holland's Identity Themes Thirty Years Later."

Secondary teachers have gravitated toward reader-response theories of teaching and reading because of the nature of their audience: adolescents who are often unmotivated to read and who don't see books as relevant to their lives. When they are allowed to read books that do focus on characters, settings, or situations familiar to them (such as in much YA literature), and when they are allowed to respond personally to these texts prior to engaging in any critical analysis, teens often respond more positively to reading. Additionally, many contemporary English teachers believe that education is more than the accumulation of facts and discrete bits of knowledge. It is also about the growth and development of human psyches that are thoughtful, empathetic, and open-minded, in addition to intelligent. Consequently, for many middle and high school English teachers, teaching literature becomes more than teaching a body of classic texts or teaching students to define literary terms or identify examples of figurative language. Teaching literature is about teaching their students to become better human beings. Therefore, reading literature suddenly becomes a very personal act—perhaps even a type of therapeutic experience (i.e., bibliotherapy), as readers come to terms with developmental problems and challenges through vicarious experience of the trials and tribulations of teen protagonists.

However, again, these opinions are not without debate. Not all teachers see literature and literature teachers as assistance for young readers in coming to terms with their fledgling identities through personal response. Some teachers I've taught in graduate courses argue that they are not qualified to act as "therapists," and that they really don't want to know all the deepest secrets of their students' personal development, details which sometimes arise in class discussions or response journal writings if students are encouraged to read YA books and respond personally to them. So again, just as with the issue of literature and identity development, using reader-response theory as a framework for teaching YAL is complicated. Should teachers teach literature in order to support the identity growth and development of teens, or even to provide a sort of bibliotherapy? Or is this type of approach inappropriate, ineffective, or even dangerous?

Deanne Bogdan (1992; and Bogdan and Straw, 1993) explores issues of reader-response in the contemporary literature classroom at both the secondary and the post-secondary levels. Harkening back to Plato's banishment of the poets, Bogdan explores how literature has always been seen by some as a dangerous influence on readers, particularly young readers, who might more easily identify with characters and change their behavior based on narrative experience. She describes the "paradox" (1992, p. xxii) of the contemporary literature teacher who is expected to teach for both "enculturation into a collective worldview" and "personal growth and development." She notes that literature teachers have accepted reader-response pedagogies wholeheartedly, and that they routinely encourage students to have personal, aesthetic, "lived-through" experiences with texts they read for class assignments. While Bogdan agrees that reader-response approaches are valuable and appropriate for holistic, student-centered literature curricula, she worries that such approaches also leave teachers vulnerable to accusations that they are teaching values and morals, or otherwise indoctrinating students into a particular way of thinking or being. She cites the earlier work of Northrop Frye to argue that the literature teacher must encourage and allow personal response, but must also teach students to be critical readers who can step back and detach themselves from a narrative in order to understand and experience it fully. She writes:

> Identification as a form of psychological projection is inseparable from literary knowing engendered by emotional engagement with the text, but so is withdrawal of that projection through critical detachment. That is why students need both the experience of literature as life and the aesthetic awareness that distances literature from life. The enjoyable reading of literature and the study of its craft, historicity, and ideology does give with one hand and take away with the other. But it is just this capacity of literary language to work against itself that justifies its educational significance as perhaps the best pedagogical tool we have for both individual growth and social criticism.
>
> (Bogdan, 1992, p. 94)

The individual growth to which Bogdan refers is brought under the heading of the "actualization contract" for teaching and responding to literature in her later book, co-edited with Stanley B. Straw, *Constructive Reading: Teaching Beyond Communication* (1993). This contract, according to Bogdan and Straw in their introduction, is set up in opposition to the so-called "communication contract," which, they argue, used to be the dominant model readers accepted when reading. In other words, in the past, readers read in order to communicate with authors and ideas; now they read to come to realizations or gather information they can use to improve their personal lives. Consequently, according to Bogdan and Straw, reading has become more of a stimulus for practical action leading to individual growth and less of a way to communicate with other people or times. If this is the case, then reading literature has become primarily an opportunity for self-actualization for many readers, both young and old. YAL seems optimally positioned to be such a tool for young readers, since it provides characters and settings with which teens can readily identify and plotlines they can easily mine for clues about how to live.

Psychological and Educational Theories of Identification

The concept of literary identification becomes even more central when we discuss books written specifically for teenagers. Young adult authors often state they write books about teens for teens just for this purpose: so teen readers can identify with the main characters and their struggles and hence learn about themselves. Teachers often teach young adult novels for a similar reason: they believe their teenage students can relate to the characters and situations and hence will be more interested in the books and become more engaged readers—readers who react emotionally to books and who allow books to affect them.

There are many ways of defining "identification," but in its essence it is, as Gary Woodward (2003) writes, "the conscious alignment of oneself with the experiences, ideas, and expressions of others" (p. 5). Should teachers encourage such identification among their students, as is often done with response-based literature pedagogies? Can a reader learn and grow through vicariously experiencing a character's trials and tribulations? Or can a reader be encouraged to act in dangerous and irresponsible ways after identifying with an antisocial character? Deanne Bogdan argues that identification with a character or set of characters in fiction might be inevitable, especially if the reader is skilled and can become engrossed in a text. She also argues that such emotional, and even physical, engagement with a text is not bad—it is, in fact, quite satisfying. However, it is equally important that readers should be able to step back and distance themselves from the text—recognize it as a fiction built with and through narrative conventions. Then readers can both experience the narrative world and step back from it, setting it in the context of their lives, other reading they have done, and other knowledge they have obtained. The reader becomes what Bogdan calls a "holistic" or "autonomous" reader (similar to a reader exhibiting Frye's "educated imagination") who can merge response, analysis, and eventually social criticism (Bogdan, 1992, pp. 123–124).

One difficulty young adult literature presents when discussing theories of identification is that it is often explicitly trying to create a world very similar to that of the adolescent; the young adult author attempts to speak from and even through the teen discourse community so that the teen reader can have an unmediated experience with the text and closely identify with the characters and events. Often, young adult authors will say this is so that young people can learn about themselves and get over difficult problems in their lives through vicarious experience. I believe these intentions are mostly good, and I don't doubt that sometimes such bibliotherapy happens, even though increasing book sales must be part of the equation as well.

However, I wonder how readers can learn more about themselves by reading about characters just like them. How exactly does persistent textual identification lead to individual growth? Woodward argues that true identification is not a simplistic, one-to-one correspondence. Rather, when you truly identify with a character there are enough similarities to make the connection, but you are also given the opportunity to see differences and potentially even choose to be unlike the character in some ways. Hence, the process of identification is a critical exercise in self-exploration. Norman Holland in *The Dynamics of Literary Response* (1968/1975, p. 278) conceptualizes literary identification in a similar way when he writes, "Thus, our so-called 'identification' with a literary character is actually a complicated mixture of projection and introjection, of taking in from the character certain drives and defenses that are really objectively 'out there' and of putting into him feelings that are really our own, 'in here.'"

So, identifying or relating to a character involves a mental and emotional grappling with what the character represents—an ongoing interaction between the reader's lived experience and the narrative with which he or she is engaging. While reading can and does evoke emotion and memory, the reader uses the narrative experience to reconsider these personal responses in a new, vicarious context. This very active literary identification differs greatly from the Aristotelian idea of catharsis, which views the literary text as an avenue for eliminating negative emotions, rather than rethinking them. Interestingly, such cognitive grappling is often what English teachers strive to do through literary discussion and writing in the classroom.

Recent young adult literature for girls exemplifies some of the potential challenges when a teacher opts for a pedagogical focus on identification. The widely popular series novels *Gossip Girl* (Von Ziegesar, 2002), *The A-List* (Dean, 2003), and *The Clique* (Harrison, 2004) depict female teen characters whose happy endings are related to the acquisition of goods and people, rather than the growth of the self. When I read these novels I tend to ask myself what these narratives might be teaching adolescent girls about being a teenage girl in the 21st century. If female teen readers are identifying in a pure and unmediated way with these main characters, could these contemporary young adult novels affect their identity development and burgeoning self-concepts? Could such identification result in potentially dangerous or personally destructive behavioral change?

According to many psychological and educational researchers, girl-on-girl "relational aggression" such as occurs in the *Gossip Girl* series is a fact of life for many young girls, who "often have difficulty achieving a sense of belonging and often resort to methods which exclude others in order to feel they have a place for themselves" (Parker, 2005, p. 117). Teen chick lit is rife with "girl-fighting"—backbiting, name-calling, and stereotypically female aggressive behavior that some say is fed by media representations of girls that urge them to strive for perfection, often through battling their female peers. So perhaps the *Gossip Girl* novels are simply reflecting reality in a way that might make a teen reader feel vindicated or not quite so isolated in her struggles. In this way, there could be a psychological benefit to the reading process—a sort of bibliotherapy. On the other hand, the books could be creating a confrontational reality for girls that they otherwise would not choose.

It's true that literature teachers often strive to help students learn about themselves through texts, and reader-response pedagogies and response-based literature curricula often encourage them to use literature for such biblio-therapeutic, affective reasons. However, literature teachers also see themselves as teachers of literary criticism, literary history, and a body of canonical texts, which can make easy reader identification a challenge. This dual purpose of literature teaching can cause frustration—especially, I argue, for secondary school teachers who have been exposed to more response-based pedagogical methods and tend to embrace them because of their need to motivate recalcitrant students. Literature teachers may indeed be experiencing a sort of identity crisis: are they objective teachers of a body of work, or does their job include an emotional, moral, or even therapeutic component?

I believe when we teach literature to adolescents it is important to work with students to recognize both the similarities and the differences between the text and their own experiences. The recognition of these differences, or the so-called "gap" between the reader's real life and the world created in the text, is essential—I argue every bit as essential as recognizing the similarities. Without this gap, and without study of the gap, it is difficult to create the so-called educated imagination or the holistic reader—the reader who is able both to *experience* a textual world and to *view* it with distanced aesthetic awareness as a creation of the author's imagination.

Instead, the teacher might select texts, young adult or otherwise, which are different in some ways from the teen students' real worlds. So perhaps when teaching young adult literature in the classroom, we need to avoid books like the *Gossip Girl* series, which try so hard to mimic teen discourse and life situations, and instead should choose books that create some dissonance in the teenage world: for example, *Dairy Queen* (2006) by Catherine Gilbert Murdock, about a girl who joins the local football team; *Tree Girl* (2004) by Ben Mikaelsen, about a teenage girl in Guatemala who hides in a tree while her family is massacred in a brutal military coup; or *Chanda's Secrets* (2004) by Allan Stratton, about an adolescent girl in Africa whose life is changed for ever by the AIDS epidemic. Or even science-fiction, fantasy, or graphic novels that create a generic or formal separation between the narrative and the reader, even if there are conceptual points of connection between the main character and the adolescent student.

In conjunction with this suggested change in book selection methodology, teachers might change how they teach literature in their classrooms so that adolescents have a larger repertoire of critical lenses through which to read (and hence learn from) literary texts, whether they are reading them independently or for school. In recent years, numerous scholars in English education have advocated the direct teaching of literary theory to adolescents to enhance student responses to texts, including Lisa Schade Eckert (2006) and Deborah Appleman (2000).

So how, specifically, should we teach young adult literature? In which classroom practices should we engage? Bogdan and Straw provide some ideas:

> Learning situations that require students to work in groups, to identify their own background knowledge, to use that knowledge in constructing meaning, to take on other communities' interpretive strategies, to explore how other interpretive communities come to make meaning with literature, to take on alternatively the roles of authors and readers, to negotiate the interpretive strategies with one another, appear to result in students with the most highly developed and educationally discursive imaginations.
>
> (Bogdan and Straw, 1993, p. 5)

I don't believe that the emotionally driven process of identification can be our main pedagogical impulse when teaching literature—young adult or otherwise. While essential to the literary experience, individual actualization cannot be all we attempt to give our students. In order to promote real growth, the cognitive *and* emotive must be tapped in tandem. The reading of literature is a combination of direct experience and distanced analysis; a merging of emotional, personal response and socio-cultural criticism.

Literacy and Social Justice

Many educators have argued for the importance of literacy for personal freedom and social justice (see Freire, 1970/1993; Apple, 1993; Shor, 1987; hooks, 1994; among others). Only when individuals are critical readers and effective communicators can they make a difference in the quality of their own lives and the lived conditions of those around them. English teachers believe in the power of literacy and, furthermore, that through the study of literature students can become more effective and critically aware language users.

Therefore, the study of literature, and perhaps especially young adult literature, has the potential to change students' lives, particularly those who might be disenfranchised by dominant society. Many of the chapters in this collection, predominately those in Part I, address the power of reading young adult literature not only to help teens grow individually but to help them understand how they can gain agency in a culture which too often discriminates against those who are un-white, un-Protestant, and un-heterosexual. Teens whose subjectivity is not consistent with those who control society's economic and cultural structures have an even more difficult time creating a sustainable identity than teens who belong to dominant social, ethnic, or racial groups.

The "achievement gap" is a topic of much lively conversation in education with various theories being floated to help "close" it. This gap often exists in test scores, including reading scores, between students of color and white students, as well as between students of poverty and those from middle- and upper-class families (NAEP, 2008). Additionally, when national high school completion rates are calculated, 91 percent of whites complete high school, while only 85.6 percent of blacks and 65.7 percent of Hispanics do so (NCES, 2001). James Gee calls this disparity not a literacy crisis but an "affiliation crisis," whereby non-mainstream students are choosing not to affiliate with the institution of school, with their teachers, and with the reading they are assigned (cited in Lewis, 2001, p. xviii). Perhaps young adult literature, with its settings, events, and characters which attempt to mirror the "real" lives of students, might encourage disenfranchised teen readers to enter narrative worlds when much anachronistic, classical literature leaves them feeling disconnected from school reading. As I've argued earlier in this introduction, reading young adult literature can precipitate important identity work on the part of teen readers; working through the complex cognitive-emotional process of char- acter identification, for example, can help young readers understand their own experiences more clearly and critically. What happens during this transaction between a reader and a text might also assist teens in thinking about how their individual experiences fit into a larger socio-cultural context, often rife with racism, sexism, and homophobia.

Seeing one's personal subjectivity as part of a larger system of social relation- ships which often become politicized, thereby seeming to disconnect individual identity from the objectives of the larger social group, is an important, and sometimes difficult, part of maturation. Kohlberg might characterize this time of life as that of post-conventional morality, when the individual recognizes the overriding importance of a fair and just society that respects the rights of all over the individual needs of one. Kohlberg (1981) places most teens in the stage prior to post-conventional morality, what he terms "conventional morality," whereby individuals act in ways that live up to others' expectations and preserve the social order. Just as reading young adult literature with its resultant emotional and cognitive effects might bolster a teen reader's under- standing of self in a complex world, perhaps thoughtful reading might also deepen a teen's awareness of the larger socio-cultural matrix in which he or she lives, leading to the type of self-actualization described by Straw and Bogdan. In a time when global literacies and citizenship are becoming goals for educators, it seems appropriate to view reading literary texts as a pathway to cross-cultural understanding and heightened awareness of the goals of social justice.

In a draft CEE (Conference on English Education) position statement outlining beliefs about social justice in English education, sj Miller writes:

> The United States' first belief statement, *The Declaration of Independence*, asserts that all men [*sic*] are created equal; however, this promised ideal has failed and not all people are treated fairly. Manifestations of power and privilege have oppressed and marginalized people based on ethnicity, age, gender, ability, social class, political beliefs, marital status, size [height and/or weight], sexual orientation, gender expression, spiritual beliefs, language, and national origin. While the American educational system is supposed to mediate differences and provide equal opportunities for ALL students, schools often reinforce and reproduce injustice. Through a sustained commitment to social justice in all its forms, English education can disrupt these inequitable hierarchies of power and privilege.
>
> (Miller, 2009, p. 1)

Teachers of young adult literature should keep these powerful words in mind when inviting their remarkably diverse and varied students into new literary worlds.

I now invite the reader to begin experiencing the various chapters of this text, which taken together provide a fascinating and wide-ranging examination of the genre of young adult literature and the literary lives of its teen readers.

References

Alsup, J. (2006). *Teacher identity discourses: Negotiating personal and professional spaces.* Mahwah, NJ: Erlbaum/NCTE.

Alsup, J., Emig, J., Pradl, G., Tremmel, R., Yagelski, R.P., with L. Alvine, G. DeBlase, M. Moore, R. Petrone, and M. Sawyer. (2006). The state of English education and a vision for its future. *English Education,* 38(4), 278–294.

Apple, M. (1993). *Teachers and texts: A political economy of class and gender relations in education.* New York: Routledge.

Appleman, D. (2000). *Critical encounters in high school English: Teaching literary theory to adolescents.* New York: Teachers College Press.

Bleich, D. (1981). *Subjective criticism.* Baltimore, MD: Johns Hopkins University Press.

Bogdan, D. (1992). *Re-educating the imagination: Toward a poetics, politics, and pedagogy of literary engagement.* Portsmouth, NH: Boynton Cook.

Bogdan, D. and Straw, S.B. (Eds.). (1993). *Constructive reading: Teaching beyond communication*, Portsmouth, NH: Boynton Cook.

Bruner, J. (2002). *Making stories: Law, literature, life*. New York: Farrar, Straus and Giroux.

Dean, Z. (2003). *The A-List*. New York: Little, Brown.

Eckert, L.S. (2006). *How does it mean? Engaging reluctant readers through literary theory*. Portsmouth, NH: Heinemann.

Freire, P. (1970/1993). *Pedagogy of the oppressed*. New York: Continuum.

Frye, N. (1964). *The educated imagination*. Bloomington: Indiana University Press.

Gee, J.P. (1990/1996). *Social linguistics and literacies: Ideology in discourses* (2nd edn). New York: RoutledgeFalmer.

Gee, J.P. (1999). *An introduction to discourse analysis: Theory and method*. London: Routledge.

Gerrig, R. (1993). *Experiencing narrative worlds: On the psychological activities of reading*. New Haven, CT: Yale University Press.

Habermas, T. and Bluck, S. (2000). Getting a life: The emergence of the life story in adolescence. *Psychological Bulletin*, 126, 748–769.

Harrison, L. (2004). *The clique: A novel*. New York: Alloy.

Head, A. (1968). *Mr. and Mrs. Bo Jo Jones*. New York: Signet Press.

Hinton, S.E. (1967). *The outsiders*. New York: Viking Press.

Holland, N. (1968/1975). *The dynamics of literary response*. New York: Norton.

Holland, N. (1975). *5 Readers reading*. New Haven, CT: Yale University Press.

hooks, b. (1994). *Teaching to transgress: Education as the practice of freedom*. New York: Routledge.

Iser, W. (1974). *The implied reader: Patterns of communication in prose fiction from Bunyan to Beckett*. Baltimore, MD: Johns Hopkins University Press.

Iser, W. (1978). *The act of reading: A theory of aesthetic response*. Baltimore, MD: Johns Hopkins University Press.

Kohlberg, L. (1981). *Essays on moral development*, Vol. 1: *The philosophy of moral development*. San Francisco, CA: Harper & Row.

Kroger, J. (1996). *Identity development: Adolescence through adulthood*. Thousand Oaks, CA: Sage.

Lewis, C. (2001). *Literary practices as social acts: Power, status, and cultural norms in the classroom*. Mahwah, NJ: Lawrence Erlbaum Associates.

Lipsyte, R. (1967). *The contender*. New York: HarperCollins.

Lowry, L. (1993). *The giver*. New York: Bantam.

McAdams, D.P. (1985). *Power, intimacy and the life story: Personological inquiries into identity*. New York: Guilford Press.

McAdams, D.P., Josselson, R., and Lieblich, A. (Eds.). (2006). *Identity and story: Creating self in narrative*. Washington, DC: APA Books.

Miall, D.S. (1995). *Anticipation and feeling in literary response: A neuropsychological perspective*. Toronto: Elsevier Science Publishers.

Mikaelsen, B. (2001). *Touching spirit bear*. New York: HarperTeen.

Miller, sj (2009). Beliefs about social justice. Elmhurst, IL: Conference on English Education.

Murdock, C.G. (2007). *Dairy queen*. New York: Graphia.

National Assessment for Educational Progress (NAEP). (2008). *The nation's report card:*

Trends in academic progress (NCES 2009-479). Washington, DC: US Department of Education Office of Educational Research and Improvement.

National Center for Education Statistics (NCES). (2001). *Dropout rates in the United States: 2000.* Washington, DC: US Department of Education Institute of Educational Sciences.

Nell, V. (1988). *Lost in a book.* New Haven, CT: Yale University Press.

Parker, R.M. (2005). *An exploration of the experience of friendship, jealousy, and relational aggression in preadolescent girls.* Ann Arbor, MI: ProQuest Information and Learning Company.

Richards, I.A. (1929). *Practical criticism.* London: Kegan Paul, Trench, and Trubner.

Rosenblatt, L. (1938/1978). *The reader, the text, the poem: The transactional theory of the literary work.* Carbondale: Southern Illinois University Press.

Rosenblatt, L. (1938/1983). *Literature as exploration* (4th edn). New York: MLA.

Sachar, L. (2000). *Holes.* New York: Scholastic.

Shor, I. (1987). *Critical teaching and everyday life.* Chicago: University of Chicago Press.

Solms, M. and Turnbull, O. (2002). *The brain and the inner world: An introduction to the neuroscience of subjective experience.* New York: Other Press.

Stratton, A. (2004). *Chanda's secrets.* Toronto: Annick Press.

Strauch, B. (2003). *The primal teen: What the new discoveries about the teenage brain tell us about our kids.* New York: Anchor.

Twenge, J.M. (2006). *Generation me: Why today's young Americans are more confident, assertive, entitled—and more miserable than ever before.* New York: Free Press.

Von Ziegesar, C. (2002). *Gossip girl.* New York: Little, Brown.

Woodward, G. (2003). *The idea of identification.* New York: SUNY Press.

Part I

Who Are the Teens Reading YAL?

Young adult literature is literature written for adolescent or "teen" readers, typically defined as between the ages of 12 and 18. While we know the approximate ages of YA readers—the readers for whom the authors ostensibly write the books and the publishers publish them—what do we really know about who they are? And what do we know about how and why they might read these books?

The six chapters that follow explore this question in more depth—who are these teen readers of YAL, particularly in the United States? While much early young adult literature seemed to be written for the white, middle-class, suburban teen, this trend has slowed in the last two decades. We now see young adult literature written for and about African American, Mexican and Hispanic American, Chinese American, Arabic American, and Native American teens, in addition to books about gay and lesbian teens and teens living amid poverty and violence. These diverse books for diverse teen audiences raise many questions for the scholar and teacher of YA literature. How do we determine the cultural authenticity and resultant quality of these books? Why and how do we teach them to students both from these marginalized groups and from dominant ones? How might these books affect their intended readers? These questions, among others, are explored in the section that follows.

Chapter 2

African American Young Adult Literature and Black Adolescent Identity

Developing a Sense of Self and Society through Narrative

Joy Dangora

I spent the summer of 2006 dissecting a fifth-grade history text for cultural representation and found it to be an eye-opening experience. The principal of the small rural school where I had been teaching fourth grade for the past three years requested that I take a fifth-grade teaching position in the fall, requiring me to become familiar with a somewhat new curriculum. I found that the underrepresentation of women, blacks, Native Americans, and other major cultural contributors to American history stood as substantial proof that outside resources would be necessary truly to educate my students. However, textbooks are just one example of the underrepresentation of diverse cultures in American society. As anyone who turns on the television or frequents the movies knows, diverse cultures are absent, underrepresented, and/or mis-represented in media outlets as well. Creating a more accurate and complete historical picture for history's sake is vitally important, as is the inclusion of black literature in the English language arts curricula in order to impact identity development positively.

Mildred Taylor's *Roll of Thunder Hear My Cry* (1976) is based largely on the experiences of Taylor's father during the late 1920s and 1930s. The story is set during the economic hardships of the Great Depression, experienced by all Americans, and during the continuation of deeply rooted racial abuse known collectively as Jim Crow, specifically aimed at blacks. It is important to note that although many suffered during the Depression, life was hardest for rural African Americans (Wormser, 2003, p. 138). Having been laid off or replaced by white workers, about half of all African Americans found themselves out of work by 1932 (Library of Congress, 2002, p. 1). Objectification surfaced as a way in which Americans, both white and black, could define and/or redefine their self-identities.

Several of Taylor's characters display an obsession with material objects. In *The American Counterfeit* (2006), Mary McAleer Balkun discusses how material possessions objectify personal identities within culture and suggests how economic conditions and cultural aspirations are represented in literature written at a particular time. Specifically, Balkun investigates literature written between 1880 and 1930 for its social and racial implications. She describes mainstream American society as one "obsessed with authenticity," and says, "The appearance of the counterfeit (or counterfeits) in a text serves as a locus for exploring some of the energies and anxieties that emerged at the turn of the twentieth century" (p. 14). The most obvious case of an objectified identity in *Role of Thunder Hear My Cry* is found in Taylor's depiction of Uncle Hammer. Throughout the text, Taylor gives examples of Hammer's fascination with materialism, including his ornate clothing and shiny new Packard. In fact, Hammer is immediately described upon his emergence into the scene in a materialistic way. Taylor writes, "Instead of Mr. Granger, a tall, handsome man, nattily dressed in a gray pin-striped suit and vest, stood by the fire with his arm around Big Ma" (p. 119). Later, Taylor reveals the significance of Hammer's desire to own a Packard, when Big Ma inquires about the car's similarity to Granger's vehicle, and Uncle Hammer answers, "Well, not exactly like it Mama. Mine's a few months newer" (p. 120). Hammer seems to believe that objects reflect respect and power, and he utilizes material possessions to get the respect he wants for himself and his family.

William E. Cross (1995) has suggested a cognitive developmental model of racial identity that can be used when analyzing the thoughts and behaviors of several of Taylor's characters. According to Cross, African Americans potentially pass through a series of five stages in their development of black identity. These stages include Preencounter, Encounter, Immersion–Emersion, Internalization, and Internalization–Commitment. Cross argues that the environment in which an individual is raised greatly determines how, when, and if they will pass through each stage. Generally speaking, Cross suggests that because African Americans have been born in the United States, they begin without positive black identities that can be transformed later in their lives within their lived experiences. He argues that miseducation and Eurocentric cultural perspectives have played large parts in African American identity development (Cross, 1995, pp. 53–55). Cross's observations reflect American cultural history.

The first of Cross's five stages, Preencounter, is characterized in American society by one holding low salience, social stigma, or anti-black attitudes towards blackness. Typically, African Americans experience only dominant cultural-historical perspectives within public education, and they thus internalize these historical perspectives. Cross's second stage, Encounter, results when an individual witnesses or is directly involved in a life-changing racial experience, causing that person to see the world and black Americans differently. For instance, Cross says the death of Martin Luther King, Jr. was an event that caused many African Americans to progress negatively to stage two. Other examples include, but are not limited to, run-ins with the law, violent racial incidents, and subtle racial (or racist) occurrences directly experienced by African Americans. Many feelings, including "guilt, anger, and general anxiety"

(p. 62), result from these encounters. The third stage, Immersion–Emersion, allows the person to be totally involved in the black community (p. 63). During this stage, one's old beliefs from earlier stages and new black identities conflict, stirring up much emotion and confusion for the individual. This conflict can positively create a new self-identity or cause personal regression due to frustration. The fourth and fifth stages, Internalization and Internalization–Commitment, allow the individual to achieve an overall clarity of self-identity, causing a personal recognition of both the place where she or he resides and a personal affirmation of where she or he wants to be. In the fifth stage, the individual looks beyond her or his own predicament and attempts to make a difference in the larger society (pp. 53–67). Taylor reflects these stages in her writing through the fictional experiences of her characters.

For instance, Hammer's actions, including his need to objectify himself, suggest that he is in a transition between Immersion–Emersion and Internalization. His fascination with material objects is not a consequence of rejecting African American culture in a pro-white or anti-black manner. As in Cross's first stage of development, his belief that he and his family are entitled to these commodities as a result of his capability, hard work, and success is grounded in the ideals he has heard within the larger society:

> "You sure giving folks something to talk 'bout with that car of yours, Hammer," Mr. Granger said in his folksy dialect as he sat down with a grunt across from Papa . . . "What they got you doing up North? Bootlegging whiskey?"
>
> Uncle Hammer, leaning against the fireplace mantel, did not laugh. "Don't need to bootleg," he said sullenly. "Up there I got me a man's job and they pay me a man's wages for it."
>
> (p. 166)

In addition to the higher wages Hammer is earning working in the North as a part of the Great Migration, he has served in World War One, and this has influenced his self-concept. He believes he has earned his American citizenship. Hammer speaks of his involvement in the war several times. His response to Mama's request that he avoid a violent confrontation with the white man who caused Cassie to be treated as a lesser person without equal rights is especially powerful. Taylor writes, "'Unnecessary trouble! You think my brother died and I got my leg half blown off in their German war to have some red-neck knock Cassie around anytime it suits him? If I'd've knocked his girl down, you know what'd've happened to me?'" (p. 122)

Hammer's beliefs about his rights as an American citizen show that once he left the South and entered the war, he internalized a different identity than the one his relatives have. The Southern Logan family fears for Hammer's life when he goes out to confront the white man who pushed Cassie into the road. Hammer's aggression while the rest of the family remains passive deeply worries the Logan elders because their regional Immersion–Emersion has been affected by continual racism. When Cassie tells Big Ma what happened, the older woman realizes that Cassie's encounter can get Hammer into trouble. Taylor writes:

> "—and he twisted my arm and knocked me off the sidewalk!" I exclaimed, unwilling to muffle what Mr. Simms had done. I glanced triumphantly at Big Ma, but she wasn't looking at me. Her eyes frightened and nervous were on Uncle Hammer.
>   His eyes had narrowed to thin, angry slits. He said: "He knocked you off the sidewalk, Cassie? A grown man knocked you off the sidewalk?"
>
> (p. 122)

Hammer's reactions show that his Immersion–Emersion has placed him outside the lived experiences of Cassie's family. While his intentions are not directly stated, Taylor suggests that Hammer, having taken his gun with him, would have shot Mr. Simms if it were not for Mr. Morrison bringing him back home. Hammer believes he deserves respect for serving in World War One. Although Hammer is progressing to Cross's fourth stage of development (Internalization), his actions demonstrate that his experiences displace him from the Southern black community of this era. Rather than challenging Mr. Simms's actions in a thoughtful but non-confrontational manner, Hammer lashes out. Cross explains that once individuals recognize their importance as members of the larger community in the internalization stage, they are "calmer, . . . and at ease" (p. 68). At the same time, Taylor has purposely placed Uncle Hammer in her story to show her readers that Internalization for black men was especially difficult in the 1970s, the period when she was writing the story.

Roll of Thunder Hear My Cry was published immediately after the approximate end of the Black Power Movement (1966–1975). During this time, Martin Luther King, Jr.'s non-violent movement began to give way to a more militant resistance as black Americans faced a "state of constant terror" (Finlayson, 2003, p. 73). Ignited by the replacement of John Lewis by Stokely Carmichael, the Student Nonviolent Coordinating Committee (SNCC) called for African Americans to gain the power they deserved by whatever means necessary, and to do it without the help of whites (Finalayson, 2003, pp. 3–74).

During the March Against Fear in 1966, James Meredith began a journey from Memphis to Jackson on foot, determined to free the African American community of fear. After a sniper ambushed Meredith, several Civil Rights organizations, including the SNCC, stood up for this young student's rights. Martin Luther King, Jr. pleaded for a non-violent response, but Carmichael stated that he would not "beg the white man" and declared the need for black power. As a result, marchers began defiantly singing lyrics such as "freedom got a shotgun." Meredith became a symbol of self-worth, and Carmichael's militant actions in defense of his people and family allowed black Americans to reach a new sense of self-identity. Taylor's portrayal of Hammer depicts the attitudes and actions characteristic of these African Americans during the Black Power Movement (Finlayson, 2003, pp. 73–74). *Roll of Thunder Hear My Cry* reflects black frustrations which seem to provide adequate impetus for blacks to move toward Cross's stage of Internalization–Commitment.

Taylor also uses T.J. to demonstrate other uses of objectification in self-identity. Instead of having a positive effect on his self-image and way of life, his worldview causes disaster. T.J. is first introduced as a friend of Stacey Logan. Using the word "emaciated" to describe his physical appearance, Taylor suggests that he is economically malnourished because his family is share-cropping (p. 8). T.J.'s actions immediately illustrate his need for attention and suggest that he has identity insecurities. He frequently bullies and insults younger children, including Little Man and his younger brother Claude, taking delight in their misfortunes. He allows Claude to take his blame and receive a severe beating for his visiting of the Wallace Store, a place he and the Logan children have been forbidden to enter because of the Wallaces' racist actions. T.J.'s moral character is further called into question when he advocates cheating on Mrs. Logan's exam, and eventually plants his cheat-sheet on Stacey, thus making Stacey another innocent victim who Taylor shows must take the blame for T.J.'s wrongdoing.

T.J. proudly dangles information regarding the frequent, gruesome racial incidents characteristic of the South over the Logan children's heads. The elders of the Logan household attempt to shield the children from the details of such events, but T.J., well aware of this, enjoys getting attention from reporting them. At one point, he recalls an incident involving night men who tar and feather two innocent black men. As T.J. drags out the story for effect, Cassie explains, "Our faces were eager question marks; we were totally in T.J.'s power" (p. 73). As the Logan children are left speechless, T.J. laughs at the event, illustrating his lack of compassionate understanding of the plight faced by his own race.

Materialism is a negative aspect of T.J.'s character. His goal is to obtain material objects so that he can then gain attention and power. He persuades Stacey to accompany him to the Barnett Mercantile where they can see the pearl-handled pistol he so covets. T.J. comments, "I'd sell my life for that gun" (p. 108), foreshadowing his fate and the novel's tragic ending. When Stacey questions the high price of the pistol and points out that it cannot be used for hunting, T.J. remarks, "Ain't s'pose to hunt with it. It's for protection" (p. 108).

According to Cross, T.J.'s behavior is characteristic of "low salience" attitudes within the Preencounter stage of black identity development. Furthermore, although one is aware that she or he is black, for low salience blacks, skin color plays "an insignificant role in their everyday life" (p. 54). Cross describes low salience blacks as placing value in "things *other* than their blackness" and lists religion, lifestyle, and social status as some possible outlets (p. 54). For T.J., commodification is necessary to gain the social status without which he is lost.

Events described earlier involving T.J.'s mistreatment of his brother Claude and best friend Stacey, as well as his lack of compassion in regard to the local lynchings, prove that he places little if any importance on the ideas of black brotherhood, African American self-worth, and equality. Cross concludes that low salience attitudes are often reinforced, if not created in part, by unavoidable societal factors, specifically "miseducation," which leads to poor self-efficacy and the absence of essential cultural knowledge. He comments:

> The most damning aspect of miseducation is not necessarily poor mental health, but the development of a worldview and cultural-historical perspective which can block one's knowledge about, and thus one's capacity to advocate and embrace, the cultural, political, economic, and historical interests of Black people.
>
> (p. 56)

T.J. attempts to rectify his self-identity by attaining material possessions throughout the novel. While the pearl-handled pistol is the first and final object T.J. desires and pursues, Taylor includes several other instances in which he attempts to acquire specific items. The first occurs when T.J. manipulates Stacey out of the new wool coat Uncle Hammer has given him for Christmas by suggesting that the coat makes him look like a "fat preacher" (p. 136). In a similar fashion, T.J. attempts to acquire a flute Jeremy Simms has given Stacey as a gift, claiming that it is not favorable because it has come from a white child. Determined not to make the same mistake twice, Stacey refuses to hand over the flute. However, he continues to befriend T.J. It is only when T.J. gets Mrs. Logan fired from her job as a schoolteacher that Stacey finally casts T.J. aside, recognizing him as the selfish, insecure person that he is. When the rest of the school realizes what T.J. has done, they shun him as well (pp. 189–192).

With nowhere else to turn and desperate for acceptance, power, and commodities, T.J. becomes reliant on Melvin and R.W. Simms, neighboring white boys, who use him for their amusement. In this new relationship, he learns that he can acquire much of what he wants simply by complying with R.W. and Melvin's demands. To ensure that T.J. remains a constant source of entertainment, R.W. and Melvin appease him by helping him steal the items he desires. What T.J. does not realize, but later comes to find out, is that the consequences for such actions vary greatly according to skin color.

In a final attempt to prove his worth to himself and his black peers, T.J. shows up with the Simms brothers at the local African American church dressed in a suit jacket and tie. He shows off his clothing and refers to the Simms brothers as his best friends, hoping to elicit a reaction from Stacey and the others. Upon receiving no such reaction, he naïvely follows R.W. and Melvin to the Barnett Mercantile, like a hopeless drug addict (pp. 239–241). Thinking of nothing but the pistol, T.J. has no idea that his actions will dramatically change his life. The three break into the mercantile and steal the pistol, waking Mr. and Mrs. Barnett. Although it is R.W. who kills Mr. Barnett, the boys are masked and T.J. is left to bear the burden of the murder (pp. 244–248).

In a fashion similar to the lynching of 14-year-old Emmett Till in 1955, T.J. is taken from his home in the middle of the night and unjustly accused and tortured by several white men for a crime he did not commit. Although T.J. (unlike Till) survives the attack, life as he knows it is over. These similarities, along with the common Mississippi setting and Taylor's probable familiarity with the Till case, lead one to believe that she was foreshadowing that event in her narrative.

By the end of Taylor's novel, T.J.'s attempt to establish his self-worth, like that of Emmett Till, has completely backfired. Again as in Cross's model, T.J.'s actions suggest that, although he has spent his life in the Preencounter stage, he will now begin a new phase in his quest for black identity as a result of first-hand experience with unjust racial violence. The changing events that Taylor forces T.J. to endure challenge his concept of black identity. According to Cross, however, an encounter does not always ensure that one will continue toward the final stages that lead to achieving a positive black identity. Cross remarks, "It can be a very painful experience to discover that one's frame of reference, worldview or value system is 'wrong,' 'incorrect,' 'dysfunctional,' or, more to the point, 'not Black or Afrocentric enough'" (p. 62). Unfortunately for T.J., he will not get the chance to progress past the Encounter stage, as he is convicted of murder and sentenced to death in Taylor's sequel, *Let the Circle Be Unbroken* (1981).

Roll of Thunder Hear My Cry is a powerful novel not only as historical fiction depicting the unjust, race-related crimes faced by African Americans beginning in Taylor's father's era and spanning her own life, but as a significant depiction of racial identity and events that have impacted black America. While Taylor surely aims to heighten the awareness of black youth and ignite social change through her novel, she takes her writing one step further, alluding to past occurrences without specifically recreating history for her young audience. In her novels, she exposes her audience to violent racial climates without specifically relying on historical events. In the end, she forces her youthful audience to experience the socio-political economics of black America, suggesting that black identity relies on a communal environment of internalization–commitment.

Though Taylor's novels promote both positive African American identity development and more accurate portrayals of history, a powerful argument can be made for the inclusion of African American young adult literature in the classroom on the basis of black identity development alone. Alfred Tatum

(2006) is a well-known advocate of the need for educational reform better suiting the needs of African American males. In his work, he often reminds readers of the numerous studies indicating the poor academic performance of adolescent African American males as compared to white adolescent males. More specifically, he comments, "National reading achievement data continues to indicate that as a group, African American males—particularly adolescents in middle and high school classrooms—are not performing well" (Tatum, 2006, p. 44). Tatum lists "self-concept" and "identity issues" as contributors to the poor academic performance of African American males. He also points out that research has posed several solutions over the last decade that include "providing culturally responsive literacy instruction that links classroom content to student experiences" (p. 44).

Similarly, Violet Harris (1992), in her article "African-American Conceptions of Literacy: A Historical Perspective," recommends the "advocacy of curricular materials that provide authentic portraits of African-American culture and history, develop race consciousness and race pride, and inspire an adherence to the goal of 'uplift'" (p. 277). She offers this as one of the four prevalent themes found in bodies of literature written by African Americans. The three other themes mentioned include literacy as a valuable commodity, literacy as an emancipator and an oppressor, and the belief that European Americans do not fully support literacy instruction for African Americans (p. 277).

All of these themes can be found in educational theorist and critical pedagogue bell hooks' writing as well. In the first chapter of her book *Teaching to Transgress* (1994), she recalls her negative experiences with school integration:

> Attending school then [during segregation] was sheer joy . . . School changed utterly with racial integration. Gone was the messianic zeal to transform our minds and beings that had characterized teachers and their pedagogical practices in our all-black school. Knowledge was suddenly about information only. It had no relation to how one lived, behaved.
>
> (hooks, 1994, p. 3)

For hooks, much of her schooling was not the emancipatory experience she choruses and has spent her life creating for her own students. She reiterates her point, commenting, "For black children, education was no longer about the practice of freedom" (p. 3).

In support of advocating outside curricular materials that promote blackness and include accurate depictions of African American life and history for the sake of identity development, Harris cites the work of Alice Howard. Howard was an elementary school teacher who felt it essential that African American boys and girls see themselves and their self-worth in literature at an early age. In response to her beliefs, she created *ABC for Negro Boys and Girls*. The book was not published alone, but as a supplement to Silas Floyd's *Charming Stories for Young and Old* in 1925. The first verse of Howard's book (also included in Harris's article) echoes the strong racial pride themes found in Taylor's *Roll of Thunder Hear My Cry*:

> A Stand for Afro-American
> The Race that proved its worth;
> One more noble
> Cannot be found on earth.

(Quoted in Harris, 1992, p. 278)

Similarly, Taylor uses the character of Uncle Hammer to portray the ideas expressed in Howard's first verse. Hammer, being a Northerner, has come down to Mississippi to stand up for and to support his family against harsh racism. As previously mentioned, Hammer believes he has proved himself as an American citizen, worthy of respect, by fighting for his country in the war. Unlike Howard, Taylor implicitly suggests Hammer's strong sense of self-worth and racial pride through his actions. However, both authors convey a similar message.

Scholars such as William Cross, Violet Harris, and Alfred Tatum all suggest that themes of racial pride and self-worth are crucial for healthy adolescent African American male identity development that precedes academic success. These themes are strongly represented throughout the genre of young adult African American literature. In summary, after reading the works of hooks, Harris, and Tatum, as well as becoming familiar with district-adopted curricular materials, and recognizing the plight of today's African American males, I believe the argument for the inclusion of diverse literature is stronger than ever.

Two more young adult books, in addition to *Roll of Thunder Hear My Cry*, that I believe have a strong positive impact on all students, but especially black adolescent males, are Walter Dean Myers's *Scorpions* (1988) and Jacqueline Woodson's *Miracle's Boys* (2000). In combination with themes that support racial pride and self-worth, good African American young adult novels portray believable settings, characters, and events. Myers and Woodson often place their characters in realistic settings, such as the city, where adolescents deal with real-life problems faced by contemporary African American teens. Complex plots often include gang violence, the loss of loved ones, academic issues, and being jailed, often unjustly.

For example, in Myers's *Scorpions*, 12-year-old Jamal, the main character and middle child, finds himself in a bind when he takes his imprisoned brother's place in a local gang, in an attempt to raise money for that brother's judicial appeal and to toughen his own reputation. Jamal battles serious identity insecurities and an infatuation with a gun that eventually places him and his best friend, Tito, directly in harm's way. Tito warns Jamal several times throughout the novel of the consequences of getting involved with the Scorpions. Even after Jamal fails to heed Tito's warnings, Tito remains by his side until the end. A final battle for control with members of the gang results in Tito shooting two of the gang members, killing one and injuring another to save Jamal's life. Both boys are left emotionally scarred. Myers describes the emergence of Jamal's post-encounter identity at the end of the novel:

> Jamal walked home slowly. There were other things he had wanted to say to Tito. He had wanted to say something about being sorry about the gun, about not throwing it away when Tito had said they should. But he hadn't been able to bring the words to his mouth. They had lain in the bottom of his stomach like rocks weighing his whole life down.
>
> (p. 213)

Although Tito is found to be a juvenile delinquent and does not face a prison sentence, he is sent to Puerto Rico to live with his father, leaving Jamal to deal with the events on his own. Myers centers *Scorpions* on the dangers of gang membership, as it is a problem faced by many African American males in their adolescent years. He also uses Tito's self-sacrifice as a symbol for the ideals of friendship and black brotherhood that he wishes to instill in his audience.

Jacqueline Woodson's *Miracle's Boys* contains similar messages for readers. The story takes place in New York City, where three brothers are unexpectedly orphaned after the death of their mother due to a diabetic coma. Ty'ree, the oldest, is left in charge and sacrifices a scholarship to MIT to raise his two younger brothers. The only way the boys are permitted to stay together is under the condition that they stay out of trouble. This proves to be an especially difficult task for Charlie, the middle child, who has already been sentenced to juvenile detention for holding up a convenience store.

For the greater part of the novel, the three boys deal with feelings of loss, guilt, and anguish over the death of their mother. The story climaxes when Charlie is beaten up by gang members and then picked up by the police for having been in a stolen car (pp. 97–102). In this scene, Woodson uses the remarks of a policeman to convey the importance of black brotherhood:

> "Mr. Bailey knows the rules. He knows he breaks his parole, he goes to jail. He knows you go to an initiation, you're going to have to fight . . ." He shook his head and turned back to Ty'ree. "Last thing I want to do is send another young brother to jail. I'm going to let you take him home this time, but I don't want to see him in this precinct again."
>
> (p. 102)

Although Charlie had no knowledge that the car was stolen or that he was going to a gang initiation, he does admit to considering gang membership and provides a rationale for his thoughts. Several times he comments on his poor reputation with his family and his longing to "be someone." More specifically, he comments, "I'm always the one . . . the bad one. The loser.

That's me. The one who always messes up. Ain't it always been that way?" and "I ain't never gonna be anything . . . so why even try?" (p. 103). In regards to the benefits of gang membership, he remarks, "It makes you somebody. It gives you people" (p. 106).

All three boys are affected by the situation. Ty'ree and Lafayette, the youngest brother, are thankful and elated that Charlie is alive and not in serious trouble. Having feared that their brother was dead or more seriously injured, and having lost both parents, they are extremely relieved but also somewhat angry at the situation Charlie has created:

> "I don't want to see Aaron nowhere near our place," Ty'ree said. "You hear me?" New Charlie nodded and wiped rain off of his face. "I didn't want to fight nobody," he kept whispering. Ty'ree put his arm around New Charlie's shoulder. His other hand was still clenching in and out of a fist. "C'mon," he said. "Let's get out of this rain."
>
> (p. 107)

For Charlie, the event serves as a life-saving encounter that will positively alter his identity. It is evident by the end of the book that he recognizes the love of his brothers and feels a sense of membership in his family. It has taken him the entire novel to understand that his family must rely on one another in order to survive. The family is now able to begin moving on healthfully from the death of their mother.

African American literature is vital to the healthy development of black adolescent identity. Taylor, Myers, and Woodson are only three authors of many committed to this cause. Their applicable plots, settings, and characters aim at encouraging black males and females not only to read but to learn and apply newfound knowledge. They provide a safe way for students to explore dangerous situations such as gang membership and violence vicariously, without actually becoming involved. Furthermore, in addition to illustrating African American culture, novels such as Taylor's provide an accurate depiction of black history that is often omitted from curricular materials.

It is the responsibility of the teacher to reach all students to the best of his or her ability. As Tatum and others point out, too many African American adolescent males are being left behind. I believe that schools are not doing enough to foster positive black identity development, and as a result many black adolescent teens are not succeeding in public schools. After researching and discovering the many benefits of reading multicultural literature, I have begun to create a more diverse classroom library and to incorporate a variety of literature into my teaching. It is my sincere hope that students in my classroom will not become victims of underrepresentation and will experience rich and satisfying identity growth as they enter young adulthood. I believe African American young adult literature can help my hopes to be realized.

References

Balkun, M.M. (2006). *The American counterfeit: Authenticity and identity in American literature and culture.* Tuscaloosa: University of Alabama Press.

Cross, W.E. (1995). In search of blackness and Afrocentricity: The psychology of black identity change. In *Racial and ethnic identity.* Ed. Herbert W. Harris, Howard C. Blue, and Ezra E.H. Griffith. New York: Routledge.

Finlayson, R. (2003). *We shall overcome.* Minneapolis, MN: Learner.

Floyd, S. (1925). *Charming stories for young and old.* Washington, DC: Austin Jenkins.

Harris, V.J. (1992). African-American conceptions of literacy: A historical perspective. *Theory into Practice,* 31 (4) (Autumn), 276–286.

hooks, b. (1994). *Teaching to transgress: Education as the practice of freedom.* New York: Routledge.

Library of Congress. (2002). *Great Depression and World War II, 1929–1945: Race relations in the 1930s and 1940s.* Online: http://memory.loc.gov/learn//features/timeline/depwwii/race/race.html.

Myers, W.D. (1988). *Scorpions.* New York: HarperTrophy.

Tatum, A.W. (2006). Engaging African American males in reading. *Educational Leadership,* 63 (5) (February), 44–49.

Taylor, M.D. (1976). *Roll of thunder hear my cry.* New York: Puffin.

Taylor, M.D. (1981). *Let the circle be unbroken.* New York: Puffin.

Woodson, J. (2000). *Miracle's boys.* New York: Penguin Group.

Wormser, R. (2003). *The rise and fall of Jim Crow.* New York: St. Martin's Press.

Chapter 3

Depictions of Chinese Americans in Young Adult Literature

American Born Chinese and Beyond

Nai-Hua Kuo

Described as everything from a melting pot to a mosaic, America has long been viewed as a land of opportunity by immigrants from diverse ethnic backgrounds. Over the past 20–25 years, an increase in multicultural populations in the United States has resulted in a dramatic change in student demographics in schools. Currently, approximately 40 percent of the US K–12 school population is composed of students of color (NCES, 2003), and this number is growing annually. Teachers and educators are now more consciously aware than ever of the importance of introducing multicultural knowledge to their students from culturally, ethnically, and socially diverse backgrounds who might otherwise seem disengaged from academic content. Furthermore, to prepare our next generation for a more globalized world, students should not only gain awareness of their own cultural backgrounds but learn to understand and appreciate the cultural experiences of other ethnic groups; that is to say, they should be encouraged to "cross the borders" from their known cultures into the less familiar cultures of others (Noel, 2008; Stewart, 2008; Van Dongen, 2005). English language arts teachers have long argued that literature depicting varying cultural groups may serve as an important resource to meet such educational needs in secondary classrooms.

Although there are more than 13.5 million Asian Americans in the US population (US Census Bureau, 2007), the literary representation of people from this community is limited, particularly within the genre of young adult literature. Being a Chinese woman who is also a literacy educator, I decided to explore how the largest ethnic group among Asian Americans—the Chinese Americans (comprising more than three million individuals)—is depicted in readily available, contemporary YA books.

I focused my study on young adult books prominently featuring Chinese American characters and themes. It was not until I started searching for such books that I realized the paucity of YA novels representing the lives and experiences of Chinese Americans (Cai, 1994; Loh, 2006; Louie, 1993). Not only did the university and local library search results connect me to merely a handful of titles among the entire book collection about Asian Americans, but books written by and about people of color are disproportionately low in the publishing market overall (CCBC, 2009; Yokota, 1993). Take the 2008 data presented by the Cooperative Children's Book Center, for example. Multicultural literature occupied less than 20 percent of the market share of all children's literature published that year. Literature by and about Africans/ African Americans, American Indians, Asian Pacifics/Asian Pacific Americans, and Latinos are all included in this diminutive percentage of books published in the year. Based on the statistics, it is not hard to envision such lack of attention also extended to literature by and about Chinese Americans, particularly since the category is apparently so small it is not even included in the data.

In addition to the limited availability of any YA literature by and about Chinese Americans, the search for books more specifically focusing on *contemporary* Chinese American people and themes was an even greater challenge. First and foremost, the majority of the storylines of YA books I discovered center on Chinese people's US immigration experiences around the time of the American Gold Rush (mid-19th century), a time when Chinese men left their families at home and sailed across the ocean to seek a better life (this goal, of course, was rarely realized). The second most popular theme is the adjustment or assimilation to American life of new immigrants who entered the United States after the passage of the Immigration and Nationality Act of 1965. In brief, depictions of contemporary Chinese Americans remain relatively rare in the body of YA literature.

However, there is a small body of works depicting the lives of contemporary, young Chinese Americans living in mainstream American society. From these works, I selected four YA books for discussion in this chapter: two works of fiction (*Millicent Min, Girl Genius* (2003), by Lisa Yee, and *April and the Dragon Lady* (1994), by Lensey Namioka), a memoir (*The Lost Garden* (1991), by Laurence Yep), and an award-winning graphic novel (*American Born Chinese* (2006), by Gene Luen Yang). Taking these four texts as examples, this chapter aims to identify general features of quality multicultural literature, examine the specific messages expressed about contemporary Chinese Americans within these narratives, and explore how these texts might be important reading for Chinese American teens trying to bridge the gap between two often distinct cultures as they move into adulthood.

Discerning Quality Multicultural Literature

Of utmost concern for educators, especially when it comes to introducing literature about other cultures, is the selection of quality texts. In the following sections of this chapter, I provide suggestions for choosing quality multicultural literature as identified by multiple literacy educators and researchers (Cai, 2002; Landt, 2006; Louie, 2006; Loh, 2006; Pang et al., 1992) and discuss the extent to which the four books examined in this chapter might be good choices for classroom use.

Suggestion 1: Consider the Background of the Author

There are often debates about who has the authority to write stories about a particular cultural or ethnic group. Should only members of a group be encouraged to write about their own experiences? Or should anyone be encouraged to research and write a story set in any context, regardless of the identity of the author? For the most part, readers and scholars of multicultural literature judge the cultural authenticity of a text, at least in part, by the extent to which the author is a member of a specific group or is affiliated with the racial, ethnic, or cultural groups about whom the story is told. Loh (2006) writes that cultural insiders are believed to have access to special knowledge that allows them to represent themselves accurately. Regardless of the author's background, it takes considerable knowledge and experience within a culture for one to interpret and present its values, beliefs, and customs sensitively and accurately. Therefore, often one who is a member of an ethnic group is awarded more credibility when telling the story of individuals within the group.

The four authors of my selected YA texts are all either second- or third-generation Chinese Americans or immigrants who came to the United States at a young age. Despite their varying Chinese language competence, all acknowledge that a reflection of their Chinese American life and experience is present in their work. Nevertheless, these contemporary Chinese American writers are differentiated from earlier authors of Chinese immigrant narratives by a more self-evident sense of "Americanness," or what it means to be an American (Yin, 2000).

Lisa Yee, the author of *Millicent Min, Girl Genius*, claims that she did not set any ethnic agenda in making her protagonist a Chinese American girl. It just happened that the main character reflected who she was herself. Hence, after the release of her first book, she felt strange when people asked her to talk about being a Chinese American author (Smith, 2005). Quoting Lisa, "It wasn't until I became an author that anyone really took notice of my DNA. At first it sort of bothered me. What does what I look like have to do with what I write like?" However, as she started to travel around the country for book talks and conferences, she became more aware of the lack of books featuring Asian American characters. This gap made her want to demonstrate through her work that while race and religion could be different, people share many internal traits. To her, the characters' cultural–ethnic–religious backgrounds are just parts of the fabric of the story, not the crux of it (Yee, 2007).

Growing up wanting to be as American as possible but becoming very interested in his Chinese heritage in his early twenties, Laurence Yep—the author of *The Lost Garden*—is a prolific Chinese American YA author. His confusion and self-questioning since childhood have been revisited in many of his novels. What does it mean to be Chinese *and* American? What is it like to live the life of an outsider in an alien world or culture? Can one who belongs to two cultures ever feel at home anywhere? The transformation of his ethnic identity is interesting. Speaking only English, living in a black neighborhood outside of Chinatown, and having no quality books about Chinese Americans to read, Laurence did not see much Chineseness in himself as a child. Years later, when he became interested in his Chinese roots, he positioned himself as a Chinese American writer who tried to bridge two cultures. However, more recently, he became unsure whether the two cultures could ever be blended. In his view, Asian cultures are family and cooperation oriented, while American culture emphasizes the individual and competition. Therefore, he now sees himself as someone who will always be on the border between two cultures—never a full member of either. This identity split works to Yep's benefit as a writer because this outsider quality allows him to be a better observer of others. In addition, Yep does a great deal of research before he composes his narratives, because "I feel a responsibility as a Chinese-American not to make up facts about the past" (quoted in Marcus, 2002).

Gene Luen Yang is the author of *American Born Chinese*, the first graphic novel honored with the Michael L. Printz Award in 2007. Within the book's three storylines, Yang tackles several thematic elements common in Chinese American YAL: transformation, what it means to be an Asian American, and prejudice and acceptance (Margolis, 2006). With the exceedingly rare existence of nonwhite characters in the graphic novel market, Yang chose to compose a book reflecting his own experience as an Asian American. Yang claims that Jin Wang's story is a reflection of his own, albeit with some significant differences. First, Yang's appearance as a teen was more similar to Jin's friend, who wears huge eyeglasses and sports an evenly cut bang. Second, unlike the protagonist in his story, Yang did have some white friends in elementary school. Third, the true face of racism in the San Francisco Bay area, where Yang grew up, was more complex than what is portrayed in the novel. Nevertheless, when Yang shows his work to Chinese American friends, he reports that they claim the story resonates with them and reflects their life experiences.

Lensey Namioka, author of *April and the Dragon Lady*, immigrated into the US with her family when she was nine. Due to immersion in both Chinese and American societies, Lensey has profound knowledge of both Eastern and Western cultures, their diverse lifestyles, and their conflicts in values. Her first-hand Chinese American life experience and her intercultural marriage have provided authentic material for her literary works.

Suggestion 2: Look for Well-Developed Plots and Complex Portrayals of Character

This fundamental rule for choosing any quality reading is also applicable to multicultural literature. Although many successful children's novels follow a typical plot pattern—home, departure from home, adventure, and home-coming (Nikolajeva, 2002)—this formula does not have to be a restriction. An appealing storyline may come in different forms and contain diverse themes, but it usually includes multidimensional characters and a mature development of complications. Moreover, the emergence of conflict usually results in internal or external transformation of characters. It is not uncommon to find stereotyped or flat characters in YA literature. However, powerful characters exhibit many faces, including varying emotions, strengths and weaknesses, personality features, distinct capabilities and much more. These individual and realistic traits are what make the characters relatable to audiences of all backgrounds. Characters representing diverse cultural backgrounds should likewise be found empowered and demonstrating problem-solving skills, not playing subservient or clichéd roles.

The protagonists in each of the four books have a problem of their own to solve. April in *April and the Dragon Lady* struggles making choices between her Chinese home culture and the American values she has adopted. With a traditional and manipulative grandma on one hand and her Caucasian boyfriend and college dream on the other, April fearlessly confronts her dilemma and brings changes to everyone involved in her life.

Millie in *Millicent Min, Girl Genius* has her own troubles and concerns. Many Chinese American parents would be proud of this grade-skipping, academically successful preteen who matches the "model minority" (Lee, 2009) stereotype, but her distress lies in her social ineptitude. Realizing that her all-knowing attitude is an obstacle to friendship, Millie decides to pretend she's just a normal teenager when she has a chance to make a new friend. However, she finds that pretending to be someone she's not only leads to new problems.

Laurence Yep's vivid descriptions of his early years allow readers to travel back in time. As a young child, Laurence sees himself as incompatible with the Chinese world and describes himself as "obnoxious" (p. 51). He takes actions to be as little Chinese as he can: for instance, he uses a fork instead of chopsticks, drinks cola instead of tea, and becomes a Catholic instead of practicing Chinese religions. It is not until he leaves home for college and starts his writing career that he begins to research his cultural roots and embrace his heritage.

A similar transformation is evident in the character of Jin Wang in *American Born Chinese*. Trying to assimilate to the American culture, Jin has lost himself and thinks he can become someone he is not. After many trials and tribulations, he finally realizes that only his acceptance of his identity can set him free.

Both being born in the United States but living a Chinese lifestyle, Yep and Wang have always found it difficult to identify as part of either culture. Preoccupied with self-doubt and feelings of detachment, their characters, Jin and Laurence, are on a quest of self-exploration, seeking answers to their identity questions.

Suggestion 3: Seek Texts That Present Social Issues without Oversimplification

When versions of real-world events are included and carefully presented in literary works, readers may contemplate these events on a deeper level. Themes and issues that the four novels present, such as racism and cultural stereotypes, are problems many teens may encounter today, particularly youths with a multicultural background. Though Yang chooses to portray such unjust treatment within the genre of the graphic novel through the actions of the satirical character Chin-Kee, readers at all levels can easily understand his intention—to expose stereotypes of Chinese Americans and the related identity struggles of Asian American teens. In *The Lost Garden,* Laurence Yep also shares his unpleasant experience of racism. As a child, while he was walking in Golden Gate Park with a friend, a group of white boys approached them. After the name calling, noise making, and spitting, Laurence and his friend miserably fled the scene (p. 42). That was no singular incident, either; similar episodes occurred over the years. Such vivid portrayals, though not further commented on by Yep, enable readers to perceive how significant racism is in the lives of Chinese American teens, and its possible connection to a character's cultural identity struggle.

The topic of interracial relationships might also resonate with readers. April's conventional grandma is highly biased toward April's Caucasian boyfriend and refers to him as "foreign devil" (Namioka, 1994, p. 117). However, refusing to give up, April and her boyfriend eventually find their way into Grandma's heart. April's struggle is neither romanticized nor simplified.

Penned in a brisk and upbeat style, Lisa Yee's fiction presents a major problem that is equally significant to teenagers' lives: forming social connections. Being highly academic, enthusiastic, and the "brainiac," Millie's social antenna does not always seem to function in the ordinary way and receive the right signals. However, instead of shying away from the world, she builds friendships with same-age peers and changes her life, but only after much trial and error.

Suggestion 4: Choose Texts That Illustrate Cultural Features and Icons Accurately

One additional value of reading multicultural literature is exposure to people of other cultures through both text and illustrations. Unlike in children's literature, illustrations are few in YA literature, unless the book is a graphic novel. Sometimes, the picture on the front cover can be the only illustration present. However, even though the use of visual representation is not the focal point of YA literature, it is never negligible in conveying messages to the audience, particularly about multicultural characters. Cover images can be key factors for readers as they decide whether to pick up the book at all. More importantly, illustrations are expected to complement the text with an accurate representation of characters and plot (Pang et al., 1992).

The cover illustrations of the four chosen novels make their own connections to the text with different tactics. In *Millicent Min, Girl Genius*, the photo of a girl with Asian facial features makes it easy for readers to expect the story to be about a girl of Asian heritage. The bright pink and blue background colors also foreshadow the story's upbeat tone and suggest that it will be about female concerns.

In *The Lost Garden*, a portrait of an Asian boy appears in the center of the front cover. Embedded in the middle of the book are black-and-white photos of Laurence Yep's family—his parents, brother, grandma, and American wife. These photos are an added bonus to his memoir for they enable readers to visualize the characters' dress, appearance, residences, and lives.

In *April and the Dragon Lady*, the cover image of a dark-haired, oval-faced girl and a dragon with piercing eyes aptly reflects the title. The dragon has always been a symbol of power and prestige in Chinese culture, and Lensey Namioka juxtaposes the dignified grandma character with the dragon to demonstrate the unshakeable status a grandmother holds in a Chinese family.

Finally, the graphic novel *American Born Chinese* provides a considerable visual representation of Chinese figures and icons. The book cover illustrations alone include many Chinese cultural components. In the golden-yellow background, Yang sketches the eponymous character from the Chinese folk tale "The Monkey King," who is buried under a pile of rocks, inspecting the results of his behavior. In the center foreground there is a seemingly worried Chinese boy deep in thought and holding tight to a Transformer robot. Further left is a small illustration of an egregiously sardonic Chinese comic figure standing as the most stereotyped image of a Chinese boy. The sketches represent the key characters in the three storylines of the novel and pique readers' curiosity as to how such seemingly distinct Chinese figures could be related in the plot. Of course, the images throughout the graphic novel continue to represent visually the struggles of the Asian American teen trying to bridge two cultures, through such devices as depictions of contemporary classrooms and scenes from ancient Chinese folklore.

Messages for Teens in Chinese American Young Adult Literature

Now that I have described how a teacher might go about selecting quality multicultural, and more specifically Chinese American, YA literature for classroom use, I'd like to look more specifically at how the four texts I've chosen portray contemporary Chinese American adolescents, and how these portrayals might encourage thought and reflection on the part of today's teen readers from similar ethnic and cultural backgrounds. There are several contemporary themes of importance to Chinese American teens which these texts explore, including stereotypes of the "model" minority and women, and struggles when assimilating to American culture while maintaining ties to family traditions. In the sections that follow, I summarize these contemporary themes and motifs that are included in the texts and describe how reading and discussing such themes might be transformative for today's Chinese American youth.

Images of Contemporary Chinese Americans in YA Literature

The "Model Minority" Stereotype

In the American Gold Rush era, Chinese Americans were equated with poverty, ignorance, and weakness. However, the term "model minority" was coined in the mid-1960s by William Peterson to describe today's Asian Americans, particularly Chinese and Japanese Americans, who are viewed as hard-working, uncomplaining, and successful (Lee, 2009). Chinese American students and teens are often seen in this way as well, since they have the reputation of being academically motivated and successful.

This model minority stereotype is present in Chinese American YA literature. Take Millie, for example, in Yee's novel: she is presented as an intelligent "overachiever and a compulsive perfectionist" (p. 1). Because of her intelligence, she skips grades, becomes a high school junior at age 11, takes a summer poetry class in a college which she aces, and tutors a college student in psychology. She represents the type of student who might be more popular among teachers than her fellow students:

> "Well . . . guess what?" I exclaimed. "I'll bet I am the only one lucky enough to get every teacher's signature!" My favorite was from Coach Frank . . . Coach had written:
>
> *Millicent,*
> *You are the pride of our Math Bowl team. Can't wait to have you back next year when we sweep at Nationals!*
> *Coach Frank*
>
> (p. 5)

Although excelling in academic performance does not always correlate with social awkwardness, it does for Millie, which might ring true for many children with high IQs who communicate better with adults than their same-age peers: "I overheard one of my fellow students mutter, 'Nothing like being the teacher's pet. Just who does little Miss Smarty-Pants think she is?' To which another student replied, 'Well, she's certainly not one of us'" (p. 66).

When investigating reasons for the existence of this model minority stereotype, cultural factors become significant. In Chinese culture, education and the pursuit of knowledge have always been valued. Scholars are ranked among the highest in social stratification, better than businessmen and other professionals. Such emphasis on education is entrenched in many Chinese families even today. It is not uncommon to see parents stress their children's academic performance more than anything else.

Similar episodes and themes can be found in *The Lost Garden*: "My parents always put studies before anything else and always showed deep respect for any of my teachers" (p. 56). While Chinese American family values can partially explain the existence of this model minority stereotype, teachers should take care to avoid depictions and discussions of Asian American characters which represent this stereotype in simplified or unproblematized ways. While stereotypes might have a core of truth, they do not substitute for thoughtful and sensitive understandings of others, and at their worst they can stunt cross-cultural empathy.

The "Weak Women" Stereotype

Women in literature have long been given a subordinate and subsidiary role, and Chinese literature is no exception. However, depictions of Chinese women, young and old, have been changing in contemporary Chinese American YA literature. A fine example can be found in *April and the Dragon Lady*, in the characterizations of April and her grandma. Each is a strong and independent individual. However, their diverse views on life often lead to clashes because of cultural discrepancies between East and West. They disagree most about the role of women, inside and outside the home. Grandma is the head of the house and she holds very traditional Chinese beliefs. She disapproves of April's dream of going away to college to major in geology and maintain an inter-racial relationship. However, being determined and persistent, April finds a way to challenge Grandma and change her attitude. This back-and-forth battle between two strong-willed women is an important aspect of the book's plot and undermines the stereotype of Asian women as weak and without voice.

Another example subverting the weak women stereotype occurs in *Millicent Min, Girl Genius*. When Millie reprimands a boy who makes fun of a girl in the cafeteria, she humiliates the boy in public. Thereafter, the boy starts to bully Millie at lunchtime by throwing food at her and threatening to make her life miserable. One would think that, as a minority and unpopular female student, Millie would silently walk away and swallow the humiliation, but she doesn't. With her intelligence and knowledge of science, she makes a saltshaker bomb with which she can attack her tormentor. In short, contemporary Chinese American female characters such as Millie are far more empowered than their forebears.

Challenges of Contemporary Chinese Americans in YA Literature

Racism and Stereotyping

Even though our modern world is more globalized than ever—due, in part, to converging media such as the Internet and cell phones as well as more frequent travel—racism still finds its way into our daily lives, especially those of ethnic minorities. Being different from the typical "American" look, Asian Americans are often seen as exotic and foreign, no matter how long they have resided in the United States. Lee (2009, p. 5) comments, "while European immigrants are accepted as authentic Americans soon after their arrival in the United States, 3rd, 4th, and even 5th-generation Asian Americans are often perceived to be foreign." Hostility toward Asian Americans can result from such attitudes.

In *American Born Chinese*, Yang demonstrates how the protagonist Jin Wang suffers from racial stereotyping in various episodes. For instance, when he was transferred to a new school in the third grade, his teacher introduced him as a new immigrant moving to the United States "all the way" from China, while, in fact, his family was from San Francisco (p. 30). Later, when one of his classmates comments, "My momma says Chinese people eat dogs" (p. 31), the teacher's response does not help to rectify the stereotype but rather enhances it: "Now be nice, Timmy! I'm sure Jin doesn't do that! In fact, Jin's family probably stopped that sort of thing as soon as they came to the United States!" (p. 31). A simple misunderstanding or comment about another ethnic group could easily result in social aversion among peers. In real life, many immigrant descendants are still treated with similar prejudice, especially in areas with less diverse populations.

The issue of racism also troubled Laurence Yep in his younger days. But when he got to high school, being placed in honors classes seemed to alleviate this pain. According to his memoir, students in honors classes were ambitious to achieve good academic performance, so "good grades were a means of earning respect" (p. 84). Thus, in addition to those Asian American students who live up to the model minority standard receiving praise and acknowledgement from their teachers, their academic success might shield them from racial discrimination.

Identity Struggles

For those who have duel or multiple ethnic backgrounds, self-identity is a troubling issue, particularly in the teen years, when self-questioning occurs most often for all teens moving into adult roles. Chinese American young adults are no exception. Living in two worlds, often they could find their Eastern values clashing with or even challenging Western beliefs. Therefore, they may feel stuck between worlds, a feeling expressed by protagonists in much Chinese American YA literature. The experience of these protagonists can be represented by the "path of growth" model below (see Figure 3.1).

Identity Struggle ←——→ Self-Questioning ——→ Transformation

Figure 3.1 Path of Growth

These seemingly linear stages of growth are not as clear-cut as one might assume. Stages 1 and 2 (identity struggle and self-questioning) can be recursive, depending on the stimulus protagonists receive from outside and the degree of their self-reflection. Living across two cultures, Chinese American teen characters observe and experience things differently. They might find themselves torn between two cultural and social traditions, and, thus, the struggle begins. At the early stages of identity growth, they regard the two cultures and identities as exclusive of each other, so it seems to be an either/or choice for them. Then, inevitably, when they become comfortable "belonging" to one cultural or social group, incidents occur which cause them to doubt. Which world do I really belong to? Who am I? What does it mean to be Chinese? What does it mean to be American?

Take April, in Namioka's novel, as an example. When she is reasoning with her very traditional grandma, she believes, like other American girls, she has the right to be independent and fulfill her own dreams. However, when she is with her American boyfriend, she feels that her Chinese family bond is too entrenched for her just to walk away from her grandma. The dilemma leaves April struggling with her developing identity, asking questions of herself and others, trying to figure out how to integrate the two aspects of her life.

Nevertheless, after many trials and tribulations and deep reflection, the teenage protagonists finally reach stage 3, transformation. Then they realize the two cultural identities should not be split at all, but share a balance. They can never be purely one or the other because they are both—they are living across the two worlds (see Figure 3.2).

It is at stage 3 that the protagonists become mature characters. They start off uneasy, eager to assimilate to the mainstream society and be accepted like everyone else, which does not happen readily. When they try to imitate others, they forget who they really are and disregard their own cultural heritage. Only when they fully accept themselves, strengths and weaknesses, can they earn respect from others and own their dual identities. Quoting Yep:

> It took me years to realize that I was Chinese whether I wanted to be or not. And it was something I had to learn to accept: to know its strengths and understand its weaknesses. It's something that is a part of me from the deepest levels of my soul to my most common, everyday actions.

(p. 43)

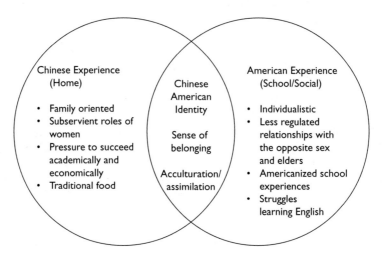

Figure 3.2 Cross-Cultural Identity

This could be a long and painful journey for teens living between cultures, but it is also a necessary one for their personal enlightenment and happiness.

Connections to the "Old World" in Chinese American YA Literature

Linking the Old and New

One very interesting and indispensable element in Chinese American YA literature is the presence of an icon or figure that introduces the old Chinese world to the lives of young Chinese Americans. The grandmothers in *April and the Dragon Lady*, *The Lost Garden*, and *Millicent Min, Girl Genius* all play this significant role; while in *American Born Chinese*, the satirical cousin Chin-Kee shoulders this responsibility.

All three grandmas have their distinct ways of adding Chinese components to the lives of the young protagonists. April's grandma is a stern and dignified woman; she is the head of the family and forces all members to practice and follow her conventional value system. Laurence Yep's grandma is different. She indirectly introduces the Chinese culture to Yep by living a traditional life-style, wearing Chinese costumes, having a Chinese diet, and speaking Chinese. This soft infiltration undeniably integrated Chinese elements into Yep's daily life:

> She [my grandmother] represented a "Chineseness" in my life that was as unmovable and unwanted as a mountain in your living room . . . As

much as I tried to deny my ethnic background, I was unable to escape completely from being Chinese because of my grandmother, Marie Lee.

(pp. 46–47)

Millie's grandma is a very close friend of hers and a humorous character. They share secrets, happiness, and worries. Though in some ways their grandmother/granddaughter relationship is more Western than Chinese, many of Millie's grandma's actions remind the readers of her Chinese origin. When Millie enters high school at the age of nine, her classmates make fun of her and call her names. To warn her naughty classmates, Millie's grandma shows she knows kung fu and is not afraid to use it. She does "a series of complicated moves involving low blocks, high kicks, and several impressive jump spins" (p. 12). Besides her knowledge of the martial arts, Millie's grandma is also very fond of Chinese traditions and wisdom. She recites Chinese poetry, quotes words of wisdom from Confucius in her conversations, gives jade as a parting gift to Millie, consults tea leaves before making decisions, and studies feng shui—the 6000-year-old Chinese art of balancing wind over water to create harmonious environments.

Without the presence of these grandmas, there would be a noticeable gap in the lives of the young Chinese American characters between their contemporary American existence and their ancient heritage.

Yang's presentation of "Chineseness" comes through an entirely different tactic. Through the most stereotyped character, Chin-Kee, Yang presents an amalgamation of all the negative images mainstream people could hold toward a Chinese person. This slant-eyed, buck-toothed, wax-yellow-skinned, and braided Chinese figure not only speaks poor English but seems to think with a different logic than others in the dominant culture. Yang's intention when including such a character is to force readers of all kinds to ponder underlying racial stereotyping of Asian Americans. Stereotypes are often consequences of misunderstandings or prejudice based on outdated information. To promote mutual understanding, it is important to pinpoint and discuss such confusion—particularly for young adults, of both Western and Eastern origin. Reading and discussing YA literature such as the books I've described in this chapter is one way to build such understanding.

Conclusion

For Chinese American teens, a lack of belonging can sometimes be overwhelming. They might undergo self-denial of their ethnic identity, cultural disapproval, or even fear of being regarded as "less American" if they behave in more Chinese-like ways in their daily activities. Reading quality contemporary YA literature about Chinese Americans could help Chinese American teens develop a satisfying personal identity integrating the various aspects of their selves. Via vicarious experiences with the characters, they might be able to explore problems Chinese American teens might face and share in the protagonists' personal identity transformations. Since, unfortunately, Chinese American teens might experience stereotyping and racism in their real lives, literary role models who have the courage to cope with such predicaments could be invaluable.

With the available choices of quality, contemporary Chinese American young adult literature as introduced in this chapter, teen readers might not only appreciate and enjoy literature by and about Chinese Americans but gain knowledge about and empathy for the Chinese culture and those individuals who identify with it. Adolescents who are not Chinese American might learn about others who are unlike themselves. Meanwhile, for Chinese American teens, these texts could provide opportunities to reflect on their heritage and on why being "American" does not have to mean not being Chinese.

References

Cai, M. (1994). Images of Chinese and Chinese Americans mirrored in picture books. *Children's Literature in Education*, 25 (3), 169–191.

Cai, M. (2002). *Multicultural literature for children and young adults.* Westport, CT: Greenwood Press.

Cooperative Children's Book Center (CCBC). (2009). *Children's books by and about people of color published in the United States.* Online: http://www.education.wisc.edu/ccbc/books/pcstats.asp.

Landt, S.M. (2006). Multicultural literature and young adolescents: A kaleidoscope of opportunity. *Journal of Adolescent & Adult Literacy*, 49 (8), 690–697.

Lee, S.J. (2009). *Unraveling the "model minority" stereotype.* New York: Teachers College Press.

Loh, V.S. (2006). Quantity and quality: The need for culturally authentic trade books in Asian American young adult literature. *The ALAN Review*, 34 (1), 36–53.

Louie, A.L. (1993). Growing up Asian American: A look at some recent young adult novels. *Journal of Youth Services in Libraries*, 6 (2), 115–127.

Louie, B.Y. (2006). Guiding principles for teaching multicultural literature. *The Reading Teacher*, 59 (5), 438–448.

Marcus, L. (2002). Interview with Laurence Yep. Online: http://www.papertigers.org/interviews/archived_interviews/lyep.html.

Margolis, R. (2006). *American Born Chinese*: Gene Yang's remarkable graphic novel grapples with racial prejudice. *School Library Journal*, 52 (9), 41.

Namioka, L. (1994). *April and the Dragon Lady.* New York: Harcourt.

National Center for Education Statistics (NCES). (2003). *Digest for Education Statistics, 2002* (NCES 2003-060). Washington, DC: US Department of Education.

Nikolajeva, M. (2002). *The rhetoric of character in children's literature.* Lanham, MD: Scarecrow Press.

Noel, J. (2008). *Developing multicultural educators* (2nd edn). Long Grove, IL: Waveland Press.

Pang, V., Colvin, C., Tran, M., & Barba, R. (1992). Beyond chopsticks and dragons: Selecting Asian-American literature for children. *The Reading Teacher*, 46 (3), 216–224.

Smith, C.L. (2005). Author feature: Lisa Yee: *Millicent Min, Girl Genius; Stanford Wong Flunks Big-Time*. Online: http://cynthialeitichsmith.blogspot.com/2005/11/author-feature-lisa-yee-millicent-min.html.

Stewart, S.L. (2008). Beyond borders: Reading "other" places in children's literature. *Children's Literature in Education*, 39 (2), 95–105.

US Census Bureau. (2007). The American community-Asians: 2004 (American Community Survey Reports). Online: http://www.census.gov/prod/2007pubs/acs-05.pdf.

Van Dongen, R. (2005). Reading literature multiculturally: A stance to enhance reading of some Hispanic children's literature. In D.L. Henderson & J.P. May (Eds.), *Exploring culturally diverse literature for children and adolescents: Learning to listen in new ways* (pp. 157–167). New York: Pearson Education.

Yang, G.L. (2006). *American born Chinese*. New York: First Second.

Yee, L. (2003). *Millicent Min, girl genius*. New York: Scholastic Press.

Yee, L. (2007). *A fish out of water?* Online: http://lisayee.livejournal.com/43917.html.

Yep, L. (1991). *The lost garden*. New York: Simon and Schuster.

Yin, X. (2000). *Chinese American literature since the 1850s*. Urbana and Chicago: University of Illinois Press.

Yokota, J. (1993). Literature about Asians and Asian Americans: Implications for elementary classrooms. In S.M. Miller & B. McCaskill (Eds.), *Multicultural literature and literacies: Making space for difference* (pp. 22–246). New York: State University of New York Press.

Chapter 4

Composing Themselves

The Discursive (De)Construction of Queer Identity in Six Young Adult Novels

James R. Gilligan

Literacy, Language, and Adolescent Identity

Of the many pressures and responsibilities confronting the contemporary adolescent, "the task of self-definition" (Kroger, 1996, p. 1) seems to cast a powerful shadow over all that he or she does. As Ritch C. Savin-Williams asserts, "According to psychoanalyst Erik Erikson, the unique developmental task of adolescence is to solidify a personal identity" (2005, p. 71). Once an adolescent understands—either consciously or subconsciously—that he or she must undertake the development of an identity, he or she must then decide how precisely this monumental and critical task is to be accomplished. Fortunately, for the teenager, adolescence is widely regarded within contemporary society as a time when one is expected to assume various guises and personae. No one truly expects an adolescent to select an identity and maintain it for very long, and various aspects of the culture surrounding the adolescent exert variable degrees of influence on his or her identity development.

One such aspect of that culture is literacy—the acts of reading and writing and, in particular, the creation of stories. This narrative approach to identity, as Jane Kroger explains, "suggests that language is a text out of which identities are constructed, justified, and maintained" (2000, p. 22). Language may serve as a focal medium for many aspects of the adolescent's surrounding culture and allow him or her to distill many elements of that culture into an intelligible story that he or she tells about him- or herself. In addition, in using language to construct stories, the adolescent can negotiate issues of power and self-empowerment, a salient theme in the development of one's identity. Roz Ivanič, addressing the "social struggles in which the self is implicated through the act of writing" (1998, p. 2), supports a social constructionist view of identity. She states that "identity is not socially *determined* but socially *constructed*" (p. 12; emphasis in original) and argues that "issues of power and power struggle are relevant to all aspects of the social construction of identity, among which language, literacy, and writing exist alongside other forms of social action and semiosis" (p. 13).

In a sense, using literacy and language to construct an identity is an attempt to impose some sort of order on the seeming chaos that surrounds the adolescent. Kroger asserts:

> Contemporary narrative psychologists . . . attempt to understand identity through the stories people tell about their lives in order to live, to bring many diverse elements together into an integrated whole, and to provide some sense of sameness and continuity to their life experiences. Identity, in narrative terms, does not exist until one's story is told.
>
> (2000, pp. 14–15)

Here Kroger introduces a new dimension in the use of narrative—it does not merely assist in the development of identity but is itself the means through which that identity is created. In other words, one's story *is* one's identity.

Problematizing the Development of Adolescent Identity

Although equating one's story with one's identity might overstate the case for the importance of narrative in the development of identity, James Collins and Richard Blot believe that "literacy practices such as reading and writing are integrally connected with the dynamics of identity, with the construction of selves" (2003, p. xviii). Additional factors, however, affect "the dynamics of identity" and complicate the connection between literacy and narrative on the one hand and identity development on the other.

An identity is always "in process." That is, no identity is ever fixed or stable. Jannis K. Androutsopoulos and Alexandra Georgakopoulou explain that

> [i]dentities are neither fixed nor categorical properties residing in people's minds; instead, they are emergent in the sequentiality of discourses, particularly in interactional sites, where they are dynamically (re)created . . . Identities can be actively reconstructed, reframed, and, even more or less consciously, transgressed and reconstituted.
>
> (2003, p. 1)

An important aspect of Androutsopoulos and Georgakopoulou's explanation is their characterization of identities as "emergent in the sequentiality of discourses." I understand this to mean that identities evolve and transform through the mediation of the discourses that create them. In other words, although no particular discourse will ever define an identity, every discourse that one uses in the development (or emergence) of one's identity will have an indelible impact on the ever-changing nature of one's identity.

Androutsopoulos and Georgakopoulou identify yet another issue that influences the already dynamic relationship between identity development and discourse: "Relationships between identities and their discursive constructions are complex, anisomorphic, and, to complicate matters even more, indirect, that is, mediated by various social attitudes, stances, values, etc." (p. 1). Acknowledging the unique nature ("anisomorphic," i.e., no two look alike) of the relationship between identity development and discourse in every individual's life, Androutsopoulos and Georgakopoulou also recognize the impact of social norms and principles on this relationship.

One aspect of emergent identity that is subject to the scrutiny of such social norms is the construction of a sexual identity or the development of sexual orientation within emergent adolescent identity development. The knowledge that an adolescent constructs is constantly in flux, as is his or her ever-evolving identity. Conceptualizing adolescent identity through the lens of queer theory—which subverts notions of fixed, essentialized identities—may enable language arts instructors to understand better the developmental processes in which their students are engaged. Such an understanding of adolescent identity development as a queer process can sensitize secondary language arts teachers to important issues that affect their students' literacy and can therefore enable them to design more relevant, purposeful reading assignments and writing opportunities for their students.

Queering Adolescent Sexual Identity Development

The qualities of instability, indeterminacy, and constant mutability characterize both Androutsopoulos and Georgakopoulou's theory of identity development and current conceptions of the term "queer." Will Letts, describing "the fluidity of queer" (2002, p. 124), explains that "[q]ueer is relational in reference to the normative rather than a fixed positivity . . . queer theories also shift concerns from an assimilationist politics of identity to a politics of difference" (p. 123). According to Letts, queer theory postulates "a shift away from identity politics to a view of bodies and identities as continually negotiated and always under construction" (p. 126). He concludes that "[i]dentity categories, then, are fluid and shifting and allow people to construct, deconstruct, reconstruct, and move more or less freely among them" (p. 125), thus elucidating the connection between queer theory and identity development.

Sexual identity development itself may in fact be understood as a queer experience insofar as it lacks any definitive stability. Marla Morris (2005, p. 12) suggests the difficulty involved in creating a stable identity: "The queer thing about gender and sexuality is that we don't really know what these categories are." Composing narratives is one way to attempt to bring clarity and stability to the ambiguity of sexuality and the instability of identity development. Dennis Sumara and Brent Davis identify narrative as a framing and unifying force in the development of sexual identity: "One's sexuality . . . is always structured by the various narratives and experiences of gender, race, ethnicity, access to resources, physical capacities, and so on" (1999, p. 196).

Variable developmental rates, however, further complicate the issue of identity. Erica M. Weiler mentions that "full assumption of one's sexual identity usually occurs around the age of 15 or 16, but this varies by individual" (2003, p. 11). And, as Margaret Rosario, Eric W. Schrimshaw, Joyce Hunter, and Lisa Braun have shown:

> even after youth's self-identify as gay/lesbian, a great deal of change may continue to take place in many aspects of sexuality. Thus, acceptance, commitment, and integration of a gay/lesbian identity is an ongoing developmental process that, for many youths, may extend through adolescence and beyond.
>
> (2006, p. 55)

Constructions and Deconstructions of Queer Identity in Six Young Adult Novels

Considering the numerous factors that affect the development of adolescent sexual identities and the intricacy and indeterminacy of these identities, an accurate fictional depiction of this phenomenon might seem nearly impossible. An analysis of six young adult novels, each of which features the construction of at least one character's emergent sexual identity, reveals a perhaps surprising correspondence to the ambiguities and shifting identities theorized and explicated in the aforementioned scholarship. The novels, published over a span of 24 years (the earliest, *Annie on My Mind*, was published in 1982; the most recent, *Is He or Isn't He?*, in 2006), also offer something of a historical perspective on the development of this subgenre within young adult literature. Interestingly, strategies of character development and motifs regarding the use of language—and its ultimate inadequacy—in the construction and deconstruction of queer identities remain strikingly similar throughout these six novels. In all six of the novels examined here:

1   Discourse—spoken, written, factual, or fictional—facilitates the development of a character's queer identity.
2   A character may utilize discourse in the successful construction of his or her own sexual identity, but attempting to utilize discourse to construct the sexual identity of another results in failure.
3   Discourse alone proves inadequate and cannot—in and of itself—accomplish the establishment of sexual identity; without accompanying action (and sometimes even with accompanying action), discourse can deconstruct sexual identity.

Annie on My Mind *(1982)*

In this quasi-epistolary novel, Liza Winthrop attempts to understand her attraction to her friend Annie by writing letters to her. Before she can communicate with Annie, though, she knows that she must "sort out what happened. [She has] to work through it all again" (Garden, 1982, p. 5). She recalls that she and Annie first met at the Metropolitan Museum of Art, where they pretended to be knights engaged in a joust. Their role-playing continues throughout their relationship, as they adopt various identities. Liza muses, "It felt a little as if we'd found a script that had been written just for us, and we were reading through the beginning quickly—the imaginative, exploratory part back in the museum, and now the factual exposition" (p. 58). Later, when she fumbles for the right thing to say to Annie, she worries that she'd "said something so dumb the whole friendship was going to be over with when it had only just started. *Finis*—end of script" (p. 73). Regarding their nascent relationship as a set of dramatic scenes driven by a script enables Liza to regard the development of her emerging sexual identity in terms of a familiar discourse.

Liza and Annie frequently engage in co-authoring fictional narrative quests in which they cast themselves as the *dramatis personae*, until one day Annie tells Liza, "'No, I don't want to do that with you so much any more . . . I don't want to pretend any more. You make me—want to be real'" (pp. 75–76). Later, however, when Liza gets angry at Annie, Annie lapses back into storytelling mode: "Will the Princess Eliza please to come for a ride in the magic wagon of the humble peasant? We will show her wonders—gypsies—seagulls—shining caves—the Triborough Bridge" (p. 90). Liza's anger quickly fades and she acknowledges "with relief that it was all right again between" them (p. 90). Reality, apparently, is a bit too strong for Liza and Annie to manage; they revert to fictional narratives to mediate their relationship—and their attraction to each other.

Once Liza utters the words "I think I love you" to Annie, she realizes, "I heard myself say it as if I were someone else, but the moment the words were out, I knew more than I'd ever known anything that they were true" (p. 94). The reality of her love for Annie is not apparent to her until she says the words; the very act of speaking her love for Annie constructs her identity as a girl who is in love with another girl. Liza repeatedly considers the power of the utterance: "Soon it wasn't hard any more to say it—to myself, I mean, as well as over and over again to Annie—and to accept her saying it to me" (p. 109); "'It scares me, too, Annie . . . but not because I think it's wrong or anything—at least I don't think it's that. It's—it's mostly because it's so strong, the love and the friendship and every part of it.' I think that was when I finally realized that—as I said it" (p. 121); and—talking to herself—"'But dammit,' she said aloud, 'you are gay, Liza, and something did happen in that house, and it happened because you love Annie in ways that you wouldn't if you weren't gay. Liza, Liza Winthrop, you are gay'" (p. 226).

After Liza receives a letter from Annie, in which Annie assures Liza that she understands if Liza is uncomfortable and that it's all right if she doesn't want to see Annie any more, Liza considers her identity:

> It was true I'd never consciously thought about being gay. But it also seemed true that if I were, that might pull together not only what had been happening between me and Annie all along and how I felt about her, but also a lot of things in my life before I'd known her—things I'd never let myself think about much.
>
> (p. 105)

Thinking about being gay, telling the story of her attraction to Annie, and writing letters to Annie (which she will never send) will help Liza "pull together . . . a lot of things" in her life; engaging in these discursive activities, in other words, helps Liza construct her identity as a lesbian.

The labels, however, are clumsy. Liza does not yet feel comfortable with the terms "gay" and "lesbian." Later, during an argument with Annie, Liza says, "Annie, I—I love you; it's crazy, but that's the one thing I *am* sure of. Maybe— well, maybe the other, being gay, having that—that label, just takes getting used to, but, Annie, I do love you" (p. 179). Clearly, speaking and writing are important components of Liza's identity development; she begins to create and understand her identity through the writing she does and through her conversations with Annie. Her discomfort with "that label" might even imply her unarticulated understanding that loving Annie does not necessarily make her gay—perhaps it makes her queer.

Liza's fondness for Plato's story explaining that lovers are actually two halves of the same person further illustrates the value she places in the power of narrative to construct identity: "I loved that story when I first heard it—in junior year, I think it was—because it seemed fair, and right, and sensible" (p. 116). The connection between stories and identity becomes apparent again later when Annie and Liza discover a collection of books about homosexuality hidden in the home of their lesbian teachers. Annie says,

> It's terrible . . . for us to have been so scared to be seen with books we have every right to read . . . Liza, let's not do that. Let's not be scared to buy books, or embarrassed, and when we buy them, let's not hide them in a secret bookcase. It's not honest, it's not right, it's a denial of—of everything we feel for each other.
>
> (pp. 153–154)

Annie's comments here solidify the connection both she and Liza have established between words, stories, and books and their emergent sexual identities.

Near the end of *Annie on My Mind*, Liza considers her reluctance to contact Annie and the impact it has had on their relationship: "Six months of not writing—that's a difference" (p. 197). The difference, of course, is the stagnation of her sexual identity development. In the absence of discourse, her sexual identity has remained static. She knows that she must recreate their relationship by writing or speaking it back into existence. Ultimately, Liza abandons the "long fragmentary letter" she is writing to Annie and takes action; she calls Annie instead (p. 233). Fittingly, the book ends with an affirmation of their mutual love: "'Annie—I'm free now. I love you. I love you so much!' And in a near whisper: 'I love you, too, Liza. Oh, god, I love you, too!'" (p. 234).

The World of Normal Boys (2000)

Robin, whose mother "encourages him to make up stories of his own" (Soehnlein, 2000, p. 25), considers a "thought he just had about boys—about liking boys instead of girls—that was a thought he'd never quite made into a sentence before, with a beginning, a middle and an end, even in his head" (pp. 52–53). Transforming a thought into a sentence—specifically a sentence that is structured like a story, with a beginning, a middle, and an end— precipitates Robin's coming out. He will later see himself as "a stranger to himself—a stranger he has not yet decided he wants to be" (p. 199) before eventually coming to terms with his gay identity.

Despite his mother's encouragement to create stories, Robin prefers to take action in his pursuit of a sexual identity. Of all the characters in the novels examined here, Robin is the most sexually active. He resists engagement in discursive activities, which might explain, at least in part, his inability to navigate the course of his sexual identity development. At the end of the novel, he leaves home, still searching for the world of normal boys, still unsure if he wants to become the stranger he sees in himself.

Empress of the World (2001)

Nicola (Nic) Lancaster, who sees herself as a writer and an artist as well as a budding archaeologist, attends a summer camp for gifted youth. Throughout the summer, she takes field notes in a notebook. She collects notes on the people she meets, and she uses these notes to help her construct identities for her friends. For example, Isaac "is funny . . . seems nice" and Kevin "is a bizarre combination of incomprehensibly smart and incomprehensibly stupid" (Ryan, 2001, p. 18). The book itself is structured as a series of Nic's field notes, each identified by the date, time, and place of the action she describes (e.g., "June 15, 7:30 a.m., My Room," p. 21). Nic also uses her field notes to contemplate her developing attraction to Battle, a girl she's met at camp, and the possibility that she might be a lesbian:

[T]hat feeling is nothing next to what I feel now about Battle.

And it's stupid, I can't believe how mind-numbingly, earth-shatteringly dumb it is. Dumber than my crush on André, even. At least with André, I had every reason to suspect that I was of an appropriate gender to be involved with him. It's so dumb I can't even cry. All I can do is sit here on the bed with my knees drawn up to my chin . . .

I've started to keep track of the number of times I hear someone mutter the word "dyke" in my direction—five so far . . .

What has changed about me, that makes these people now want to call me this name? Do I look different?

(pp. 72–73, 115)

Like Liza and Annie, Nic and Battle role-play to mediate their attraction to each other: "I am a lady-in-waiting, and she is the princess. No, the empress. The empress of the world" (p. 77). Again experiencing the same kind of semantic struggle in identifying themselves as Liza and Annie did, Nic asks Battle, "I don't know if that word fits . . . Do you think we're lesbians, Battle? . . . I'm just not sure it describes us completely accurately" (p. 119). During a conversation with her friend Katrina, Nic asks her:

"Why are you so *obsessed* with the whole lesbian thing? I've liked boys before, I probably will again, so I believe that the appropriate word is *bisexual*, since you're so desperate to give me a label."

"Why are *you* so obsessed with *not* being one? I believe that the appropriate word is *denial*."

I sigh. I don't know what I am.

(p. 139)

Nic struggles with labels and cannot comfortably identify herself as either a lesbian or not-a-lesbian; this dilemma exemplifies the queer process of adolescent identity development. Realizing that "words *don't* always work" (p. 126), the inadequacy of language becomes a kind of ironic mantra for Nic, as she soothes her inability to articulate her feelings and identity by repeating the phrase "words don't always work" (pp. 134, 192–193, 197).

Despite the inadequacy of language, Nic attempts to compose an identity for Battle just as she attempts to compose an identity for herself. Nic mentions wanting Battle "to have something that [she—Nic—has] actually created" (p. 122), and she tells Battle that she's created a picture of her and written about her: "You were so beautiful, I had to draw you. But I didn't admit to myself what I was feeling until I was trying to write this thing for class about you" (p. 131). The act of drawing Battle and writing about Battle enables Nic to create an identity for herself as a girl who is attracted to another girl, even if the label of "lesbian" doesn't accurately capture this newly discovered identity. Ultimately, Nic creates a puppet fashioned in Battle's likeness, using

Battle's "real hair" (p. 134). When she shows Battle the puppet, Battle resists Nic's attempt to construct an identity for her and exclaims, "'Stop—stop trying to *explain* me. I can't take this'" (p. 143).

Nic later realizes "that when Katrina doesn't know what's going on, she makes up a story to make all the things she doesn't understand make sense." She then admits, "I do the same thing" (p. 148), exemplifying Sumara and Davis's theory of narrative as a framing and unifying force in the development of sexual identity.

Bilal's Bread *(2005)*

Bilal Abu, a 16-year-old Iraqi refugee living in Kansas City, Missouri, "was interested in words—he wrote stories, poems, lyrics to songs. He had notebooks full of the stuff. It was an interest he kept quiet about, lest the other boys make fun of him" (X, 2005, p. 39). Discussing one of his compositions with his friend Muhammad, he says, "It's a song. It's called 'Killed by Love.' But maybe it's a poem. I don't know. You have to speak it—when you speak it, it has this sort of ring to it" (p. 40). As a poet, Bilal recognizes the power of utterance—speaking words imbues them with a "sort of ring," perhaps the ring of truth. Bilal's poem "My First Suicide," which he recites during a poetry competition, is a meditation on his struggles to reconcile his sexual orientation and his Islamic faith. At the conclusion of the poem, he proclaims,

> I am queer
> Yes, I am queer
> And let this be a suicide
> a death to lies and my deceit
> a death to all my furtive hiding
> a death to my dishonesty.
>
> (p. 230)

As he exults over the joy he felt in realizing that "the world was not going to end because he had just stood up and outed himself in front of the entire community" (p. 233), he offers his creative compositions as evidence that he's "trying to understand what's happening to [him]. And [he's] trying to be honest" (p. 235).

Written discourse in the form of Bilal's poetry certainly plays a pivotal role in the development and realization of his sexual identity. And although his words seem to embody his identity ("I am queer / Yes, I am queer"), the words alone do not possess the power to actualize his identity. As Bilal himself explains, the words must be spoken. In the act of speaking, the "ring" of truth emerges.

M or F? *(2005)*

Marcus, the male protagonist, narrates the odd-numbered chapters in this novel. His best friend, Frannie, narrates the even-numbered chapters. Together they tell the story of "their" online romance with Jeff, a young man of indeterminate sexual orientation. As they chat with Jeff, Marcus does the typing, although he assumes the identity of Frannie. Marcus, an aspiring film director, thinks of himself as "someone who knows a good story when he sees one" (Papademetriou & Tebbetts, 2005, p. 1). He frames much of his narrative as film scenes, describing the action with such terms as "Opening credits roll. Cameras track down the hallway" (p. 1); "Cue the flashback. The screen goes wavy and blurs out" (p. 12); "This next scene opens with a tracking shot. The camera moves slowly through my house" (p. 179); and "The camera zooms in on my face" (p. 248).

Characterizing Frannie and himself, he states, "If she was the star of the show, then I was the nervous director standing behind the camera and biting his nails" (p. 59). When Frannie reminds him that "This is real life, sweetie . . . not a movie," he argues, "it's the same thing" (p. 5). Marcus clearly sees himself as a director, creating scenes and constructing reality according to his preferences and desires. Each time Marcus chats as Frannie, he assumes a new screen name (NICENITE, HI_IT'S_ME, FRANNO), recreating himself as Frannie each time. He confesses, "I was kind of sort of *being* Frannie. It made perfect sense that I'd start to see [Jeff] the same way she saw him" (p. 76).

Marcus begins to contemplate the impact of this charade on his identity and on his sense of himself: "What did that say about me, if I felt like my own best self when I was pretending to be someone else?" (p. 150). Ultimately, Marcus, like Nic in *Empress of the World*, concludes that language alone is inadequate in the creation of an identity; he and Frannie discover that Jeff is straight. Moreover, they all discover that language has completely obfuscated their identities, since, while Marcus was chatting (as Frannie) with Jeff, Jeff's gay friend Glenn was chatting as Jeff. So, two gay men, unbeknown to each other, were chatting—one disguised as a girl and the other disguised as a straight guy. Discourse—encoded as online chat—has deconstructed their identities.

Marcus finally acknowledges that "words weren't going to do it" (p. 276), and, as Frannie mentions, Marcus now "just *said* stuff. Stuff that wasn't in code" (p. 290). Marcus comes to understand that in constructing an identity, neither the creative medium of film nor the code of language is adequate: "Sometimes using code just isn't good enough" (p. 296).

Is He or Isn't He? *(2006)*

Anthony, an aspiring screenwriter, attempts to determine the sexual orientation of Max, a young man to whom both he and his best friend Paige are attracted. He casts Max as "Michael" in his movie, a young man who falls in love with "Dominick," played by Anthony himself. Anthony hopes that assuming the fictional identity of Dominick will assist him in determining the sexual orientation of Max, as manifested in the fictional identity of Michael. After numerous delays in the rehearsal of their kissing scene (much to Anthony's frustration), the time finally arrives for them to rehearse: "They were no longer Anthony and Max, but Dominick and Michael. After forty-five minutes, they finally got to the kissing scene" (Hall, 2006, p. 245).

During the scene, when Anthony/Dominick and Max/Michael kiss, Anthony contemplates revising the scene as he tries to find the truth beneath the fiction:

> Anthony wrapped his arms around Max's shoulders, pulling him close. It felt so good having his arms around him! He wished he could press his head against Max's chest and just cuddle with him. But that wasn't in the script. Rats! Was there time for a rewrite? Maybe he could work it in. Until then, though, there was only the kiss.
>
> Anthony gazed into Max's eyes, hoping he could see inside him. Hoping he could see that the feelings reflected in his eyes weren't Dominick's feelings for Michael, but his own feelings for Max.
>
> (p. 245)

After convincing himself that Max was kissing him back, Anthony reprimands himself:

> *This does* NOT *mean anything. Max is not kissing you. It's Michael. Michael is kissing you back. And you're not Anthony, you're Dominick. This is a scene from your movie. It's not real. Keep reminding yourself of that. It's* NOT *real!!!*
>
> (pp. 246–247)

Nevertheless, Anthony—conflating fictional identities with actual identities and acting with reality—convinces himself that "the kiss had to be real" (p. 247). In the end, Max tells Anthony, "I was acting. My character, Michael, was into the kiss, but I wasn't . . . I was pretending I was kissing a girl" (p. 283). In attempting to construct a queer identity for Max, Anthony—like Nic in *Empress of the World* and Marcus in *M or F?*—falls victim not only to the inadequacy of words but to the unreliability of actions. Discourse and action assisted in Anthony's construction of a queer identity for Max, and they were equally responsible for its deconstruction.

Conclusions and Implications

Ivanič explains how a writer's "particular choice of words and structures" reveals that writer's attempt to affiliate him/herself with a particular discourse community and implies some "statement of identity" (1998, p. 45). She builds on the social aspect of identity development within literacy communities by modifying Norman Fairclough's use of the term "manifest intertextuality." Ivanič distinguishes between "actual intertextuality"—a writer's overt use of another writer's text, usually through quotations—and "interdiscursivity"— the unavoidable echo of a text type, genre, or set of conventions (p. 48). According to Ivanič, writers unconsciously select from available discourses as they construct their identities and position themselves "by the discourse types they draw upon" (p. 55).

The first four novels discussed here (see Table 4.1 for a summary comparison of the novels) make use of the "interdiscursivity" of the "coming out" story. As Patrick Merla explains, "coming out" is a significant event in the life of a gay person (although he limits his description to a gay man's "coming out"):

> "Coming out" is the central event of a gay man's life. It is at once an act of self-acknowledgement, self-acceptance, self-affirmation, and self-revelation intimately linked to how he views himself and how he interacts with the world. It can happen in stages, or be an instance of illumination in which a gay man recognizes who he is. It can be interior, a psychological sorting of facts and feelings, or an external act of identification to another person or persons. For most gay men, coming out involves all of these in one way or another. Because the individual's very identity is involved, and society in general makes such an issue of sexuality . . . the event is intimately linked to how the person views himself and how he responds to other people and the world.
>
> (1996, p. xvi)

Annie on My Mind and *Empress of the World,* each of which features the protagonist's "coming out," also examine those protagonists' attempts to co-construct a sexual identity for another. As the last two novels illustrate, depictions of the (de)construction of queer identities are not limited to "coming out" stories. *M or F?* and *Is He or Isn't He?,* as their titles suggest, focus not so much on a protagonist's coming out or the sexual identity development of the narrator but on whether it is possible to construct a sexual identity for a specific object of desire—in both cases, a young man of indeterminate sexual orientation. These two novels represent a shift in focus from one's own sexual identity construction to the attempted construction—and ultimate deconstruction—of the sexual identity of another.

Conceptualized as "literacy performances"—that is, discourse in conjunction with action—the discursive activities of these fictional characters might have real-world implications for young adult readers. If, as Elizabeth Birr Moje and Mudhillun MuQaribu argue, "reading and writing matter for how one identifies and is identified" (2003, p. 204), these fictional narratives, which

Table 4.1 Discursive (De)Constructions of Queer Identity in Young Adult Novels

Novel	Year of Publication	Character	Discursive Medium	"Other"	Theme(s)
Annie on My Mind	1982	Liza	Letters	Annie	• Inadequacy of language • Inaccuracy of labels (e.g., lesbian)
The World of Normal Boys	2000	Robin	Stories	—	• Action without discourse is ineffective
Empress of the World	2001	Nic	Field notes	Battle	• Inadequacy of language • Inaccuracy of labels (e.g., lesbian)
Bilal's Bread	2005	Bilal	Poetry	—	• Words embody identity • Speaking produces "ring" of truth
M or F?	2005	Marcus	Online chat Film	Jeff	• Inadequacy of language • Language deconstructs identity
Is He or Isn't He?	2006	Anthony	Screenplay	Max	• Inadequacy of language • Language deconstructs identity • Unreliability of actions

depict the various ways in which multiple discursive practices may be utilized in the development of sexual identity, may serve as models for young adult readers who are themselves in the process of developing sexual identities. Furthermore, engaging in this kind of discursive identity work may enable young adults to help bring about social change regarding attitudes toward queer youth. Mollie V. Blackburn's (2002/2003) study of Justine, a young lesbian who composed poetry in the development of her sexual identity, stands as one example of the power of a "literacy performance" to facilitate a young adult's identity development and effect social change.

Blackburn explores "the literacy performances and identity work of a young woman who challenges homophobia and heterosexism and their consequences for literacy learning and academic agency" (p. 314). Describing a poem that Justine wrote and shared with her out-of-school youth group, Blackburn explains how Justine, in a literacy performance, was able to construct a sexual identity and a world in which she was empowered:

> In the writing of the poem, her figured world was still a heterosexist and homophobic one, and her positionality was still characterized by a man's slur followed by her own silence. In her journal, however, she was safe. Here, she could author herself into the world . . . as a beautiful and powerful dyke who was "empowered by her sisters" and therefore rejected marginalization by not caring who watched her as she "kiss[ed]" and "fondl[ed]" her girlfriend. She went even further to author herself into the poem as someone who will eventually retaliate against, and thus have power over, those who marginalized her . . . in the poem, Justine created a new world in which lesbians were no longer victims of heterosexism and homophobia; indeed, they fought against such forms of hatred and oppression.
>
> (p. 317)

Justine constructs her identity "interdiscursively," by selecting the discourse of empowered lesbianism; engaging in "identity work in multiple contexts," she capitalized on her experience with the youth group "by using the poem in a project at school" (p. 320). Thus combining out-of-school literacy with (valued) school literacy, "Justine's literacy performances and identity work were for and about social change both in and out of schools" (p. 321). Analyzing the complex, recursive relationship between Justine's literacy performances in the two environments, Blackburn concludes that "the literacy performances that youth engage in at school help shape those in which they engage outside of schools" (p. 323).

The research regarding literacy instruction and the development of identity has specific implications for language arts teachers:

1   Literacy, language, and discourse play a significant role in the social construction of identity.

2   Language arts teachers need to develop strategies to cope with the ways in which literacy influences and is influenced by adolescent identity development.

3   In order to maximize the benefits of literacy instruction, language arts teachers should understand identity development as a queer, constantly evolving process that evinces transitory incarnations of identity.

We can make use of these ideas as we design instructional units and conduct further research into the increasingly complex relationship between literacy and the development of identity. James Moffett urges us to educate our students so that they will "heal and grow":

> If education is supposed to help people get better, that's not only in the sense of "get better *at* something," like writing, but in a second sense of "get well" and in a third sense of "become a better person." People want to *get better* in all senses at once. We don't just want our *writing* to come out right, *we* want to come out right.

> (1994, p. 29)

It is my hope that including these young adult novels, along with writing opportunities that facilitate the discursive constructions of identities, within English language arts curricula will foster important social change within schools and communities and will enable us to help our students "get better" in all three senses that Moffett describes.

References

Androutsopoulos, J. & Georgakopoulou, A. (2003). Discourse constructions of youth identities: Introduction. In J.K. Androutsopoulos & A. Georgakopoulou (Eds.), *Discourse constructions of youth identities* (pp. 1–25). Amsterdam: John Benjamins.

Blackburn, M. (2002/2003). Disrupting the (hetero)normative: Exploring literacy performances and identity work with queer youth. *Journal of Adolescent & Adult Literacy*, 46 (4), 312–324.

Collins, J. & Blot, R. (2003). *Literacy and literacies: Texts, power, and identity.* Cambridge: Cambridge University Press.

Garden, N. (1982). *Annie on my mind.* New York: Farrar, Straus and Giroux.

Hall, J. (2006). *Is he or isn't he?* New York: Avon.

Ivanič, R. (1998). *Writing and identity: The discoursal construction of identity in academic writing.* Amsterdam: John Benjamins.

Kroger, J. (1996). *Identity in adolescence: The balance between self and other.* New York: Routledge.

Kroger, J. (2000). *Identity development: Adolescence through adulthood.* Thousand Oaks, CA: Sage.

Letts, W. (2002). Revisioning multiculturalism in teacher education: Isn't it queer? In R.M. Kissen (Ed.), *Getting ready for Benjamin: Preparing teachers for sexual diversity in the classroom* (pp. 119–131). Lanham, MD: Rowman and Littlefield.

Merla, P. (1996). Introduction. In P. Merla (Ed.), *Boys like us: Gay writers tell their coming out stories* (pp. xv–xviii). New York: Avon.

Moffett, J. (1994). Coming out right. In L. Tobin (Ed.), *Taking stock: The writing process movement in the '90s* (pp. 17–30). Portsmouth, NH: Heinemann.

Moje, E.B. & MuQaribu, M. (2003). Literacy and sexual identity. *Journal of Adolescent & Adult Literacy*, 47 (3), 204–208.

Morris, M. (2005). Queer life and school culture. *Multicultural Education*, 12 (3), 8–13.

Papademetriou, L. & Tebbetts, C. (2005). *M or F?* New York: Razorbill.

Rosario, M., Scrimshaw, E.W., Hunter, J., & Braun, L. (2006). Sexual identity development among lesbian, gay, and bisexual youths: Consistency and change over time. *Journal of Sex Research*, 43 (1), 46–58.

Ryan, S. (2001). *Empress of the world*. New York: Speak.

Savin-Williams, R.C. (2005). *The new gay teenager*. Cambridge, MA: Harvard University Press.

Soehnlein, K.M. (2000). *The world of normal boys*. New York: Kensington Books.

Sumara, D. & Davis, B. (1999). Interrupting heteronormativity: Toward a queer curriculum theory. *Curriculum Inquiry*, 29 (2), 191–208.

Weiler, E. (2003). Making school safe for sexual minority students. *Principal Leadership*, 4 (4), 10–13.

X, S. (2005). *Bilal's bread*. Los Angeles, CA: Alyson.

Chapter 5

Teaching through the Conflict

Examining the Value of Culturally Authentic Arabic Young Adult Literature

Nisreen M. Kamel Anati

When I came to the United States from Palestine in 2002, I was amazed at the abundance of available books written expressly for children and young adults. While I was a graduate student, I took courses in both children's and young adult literature, and I discovered for the first time that certain books exist that are written solely for American adolescents. In one particular graduate class, we were required to read a number of novels addressing topics related to the lives of contemporary American young adults, such as teen friendships, romances, family relationships, drug use, and even school violence. Through these books and other assigned readings, the class explored the value of integrating young adult literature into the English language arts curriculum, primarily to motivate "reluctant" teen readers who have little interest in canonical texts.

Although I enjoyed reading all the assigned novels, ultimately I felt that they were not very relevant to me, an Arabic woman. Most of the books dealt with issues of importance to *American* young adults, not young adults in Palestine or the United Arab Emirates, where I would return after graduation. I began to wonder if literature existed written for and about *Arab* young adults, the children of my heritage. Having read so much YAL and having explored its usefulness with teens, I became very interested in integrating Arabic young adult literature into the English language arts curriculum in both Arabic and non-Arabic secondary schools for the same reason American teachers integrate YA literature: to motivate teen readers by giving them the opportunity to read stories that connect to their real-life experiences. Of course, non-Arab teen readers of Arabic young adult literature could also benefit from such reading by learning about an often stereotyped ethnic group, particularly post-9/11. Consequently, it became my goal to seek out quality Arabic young adult literature (AYAL) and explore its usefulness in both the American and the Arabic classroom. For the purposes of my search, I defined "Arabic young adult literature" as any literary piece written about Arab young adults, by either Arab or non-Arab authors, published in English or available in English translation. Since I wanted my work to be useful for teachers in both the United States and the Arab world, the availability of the text in English was important.

As my search began, I scanned information in what seemed like endless numbers of databases, websites, journals, magazines, and public and university libraries. Painfully, it was very obvious that there are relatively few books written that might be categorized as young adult literature for Arab young adults. In total, I found fewer than a hundred books about Arab young adults, and these were primarily written by non-Arab authors. Furthermore, I was unable to locate any studies or attempts to define or examine the main characteristics and categories of culturally authentic Arabic young adult literature. As I discovered that non-Arab authors were writing most of the novels, I became concerned with the textual authenticity of the books that were available. Was the available AYAL accurately representing the concerns and values of real Arabic teens? Were these books avoiding common stereotypes of Arabic people? Or were they just reinforcing simplified and discriminatory notions of Arabs as "camel riders" and terrorists?

Therefore, in addition to simply seeking out texts, my project took on a second, perhaps more important, goal: to critique the cultural authenticity of available AYAL and through wide reading and content analysis establish a teacher-friendly criterion of the key characteristics of "culturally authentic" texts. Additionally, I resolved to provide suggestions for teachers concerning the integration of AYAL into the English language arts curriculum in Arabic and non-Arabic speaking countries.

Where Is the Arabic Literature?

Arabic literature has long been a rich source of knowledge and entertainment in the Arab world. Perhaps the best known example is *One Thousand and One Nights* (often known to US readers as *The Arabian Nights*). However, there appears to be a shortage of readily available contemporary Arabic literature for modern readers of any age, including young adults, particularly in the genre of fictional prose. Traditionally, Arabic authors felt that literature should have a pedagogical function, having an overriding educative purpose rather than just existing for entertainment. This belief did not stop the traditional "hakawati," or storyteller, who would retell the entertaining parts of more educational works or one of the many Arabic fables or folk tales which were not usually transcribed. However, historically, there have been only a few fictional stories set down in writing for Arabic readers. A good example of the lack of popular Arabic prose fiction is that the stories of Aladdin and Ali Baba, usually regarded as tales from *One Thousand and One Nights*, were not originally parts of those tales. They were first included in a French translation of the tales by Antoine Galland, who heard them being told by a traditional storyteller, and they existed only in incomplete Arabic manuscripts before that time.

A revival took place in Arabic literature during the 19th century, along with many other aspects of Arabic culture. This reappearance of literary writing in

Arabic was confined mainly to Egypt until the 20th century, when it spread to other countries in the region. This renaissance was felt not only within the Arab world but beyond, with a growing interest in translating Arabic works into European languages. Also, the Western forms of the short story and the novel began to be preferred over the traditional Arabic storytelling and poetic forms. Many critics point to *Zaynab*, a novel written by Husayn Haykal in 1913, as the first true Arabic-language novel.

In an increasingly globalized world, literature in translation has an especially important role. Increasingly, writers, readers, and publishers are turning to literature as a bridge between cultures, particularly estranged Western and Arab societies. This growing interest is, in turn, driving a boom in translation. However, not surprisingly perhaps, most translations are from English into other languages, not from another language, such as Arabic, into English. Hence, the huge American market is seen as driving the imbalance (CTV, 2008). Bookstores in the United States, for example, rarely stock more than Nobel-prize-winner Naguib Mahfouz's *Cairo Trilogy* (1957), a masterful, realistic account of life in Cairo and of a merchant family in the mid-20th century. Western readers likely know little of Mahfouz's more experimental work, his political and religious allegories, or his historical dramas. The result is a kind of one-way mirror between America and the rest of the world.

"Culturally Authentic" Arabic Literature

Many critics are skeptical that currently available, contemporary texts about Arabic countries and people are authentic representations of Arabic culture, perhaps particularly those written by non-Arab authors. According to Landt (2006, p. 38), "Cultural authenticity—the accuracy of the language, customs, values, and history of the culture—can be difficult, if not impossible, to determine if one is not familiar with the culture depicted." In fact, there is a debate over whether only authors *from* a culture are qualified to write *about* their culture. This question seems simple, but its answer is quite controversial, especially when Arabic culture is at the core of the discussion. The Arab world consists of twenty-four countries with diverse political, geographical, historical, economic, social, religious, and cultural backgrounds. How can any one individual speak as an "insider" about the Arab world? Darwin Henderson (2005, p. 270) challenges us to think about this question of qualification in his essay "Authenticity and Accuracy: The Continuing Debate," when he asks, "What constitutes an authentic, accurate depiction of a culture? Are there criteria an author or illustrator must meet, qualities he or she must possess, that indicate how an individual could be qualified to write or illustrate a book outside his or her culture?"

The writer's cultural origin and perspective are not the only elements that make a good story. Henderson writes, "Authors who write outside their own cultural experiences often cite artistic freedom among their decisions to write such stories." Then he adds, "Some authors further defend their right to produce such texts by suggesting that if writers were only allowed to write from their own cultural experiences, their productivity and imaginative freedoms would be limited" (p. 267). Jacqueline Woodson, an award-winning African American young adult writer, also addresses this topic of people writing outside of their own experience, stating, "My hope is that those who write about the tears and the laughter and the language in my grandmother's house have first sat down at the table with us and dipped the bread of their own experiences into our stew" (quoted in Landt, 2006, p. 38).

Who, then, decides the level of cultural authenticity of a particular book? I have found that even when living within the same culture, people have differences of opinion about authenticity and cultural sensitivity when their own culture is portrayed in literature. I have found that even when a book is deemed "culturally authentic" by educators and scholars, there can be disagreements as to its sensitivity and accuracy by actual readers both inside and outside the culture.

After reading many of the available books written for and about Arab young adults, I believe that most of the young adult books written by non-Arab authors only report observable details with relatively low sensitivity to the lived experiences and complex cultural matrices of Arabic history, values, beliefs, and traditions. The authors of such books sometimes do not seem to make a true effort to understand, learn, or inhabit Arabic culture. For example, *A Stone in My Hand* (2002) by Cathryn Clinton is a story of Palestinian adolescents who seek their freedom. Clinton reports observable details with little sensitivity to or seeming awareness of the lived experiences of Palestinian people and the complex Palestinian history, values, beliefs, and traditions. For example, no single Arabic word is used in the entire story even though such inclusion is often an essential element of authentic multicultural literature. Other texts written by non-Arab authors spell Arabic words incorrectly (e.g., *Mahshi* instead of *MaHshi* in *Figs and Fate: Stories about Growing up in the Arab World Today* (2005) by Elsa Marston).

Although there will continue to be controversy concerning the ability of authors from ouside a given culture to characterize it authentically, we must make good choices from among the books that are currently available. Teachers must develop sensitivity and critical expertise when choosing Arabic YA books by learning about the culture themselves. In order for teachers to distinguish among texts that misrepresent and romanticize versus those that are more culturally authentic, it is helpful to read widely in both fiction and nonfiction genres and even consult Arab authors themselves. Indeed, the perspectives of Arab critics and theorists can enrich our appreciation of culturally reflective literature. Moreover, Woodson (1998) suggests a number of factors to think about when selecting multicultural books for students in general. Many of these apply to the selection of quality AYAL as well:

- The accurate portrayal of the culture or cultures depicted in the book includes not only physical characteristics such as clothing and food, but relationships among people within the culture and with people of different cultures.
- There is diversity within the culture; characters are unique individuals, not stereotypical representatives.
- Dialogue is culturally authentic, with characters using speech that accurately represents their oral traditions. Non-English words are spelled and used correctly.
- Realistic social issues and problems are depicted frankly and accurately without oversimplification.
- Minority characters are shown as leaders within their community able to solve their own problems. Cultural minorities do not play a supporting or subservient role while whites are seen as possessing all the power.

(Quoted in Landt, 2006, p. 695)

Paying attention to such characteristics of quality multicultural literature can facilitate the best selection of authentic Arabic young adult books for classroom reading.

Themes in Contemporary Arabic YA Literature

As a literacy researcher and a member of the Arabic culture, I developed a list of characteristics and themes that I have found to be specific to and typical of most of the available Arabic young adult texts that I have read and studied. These criteria emerged after I read, examined, and critiqued multiple Arabic young adult books written by Arab and non-Arab authors. Some of the major themes in classical Arabic literature include family togetherness, heroism, and supernatural elements. However, Western–Eastern conflicts and contemporary Middle Eastern struggles (e.g., the Palestinian cause and the Iraq wars) have become dominant themes in contemporary Arabic literature. Overall, I have found the following themes and characteristics to be common in AYAL texts that reflect cultural sensitivity and demonstrate at least a moderate level of cross-cultural awareness.

Religious Beliefs and Behaviors

In a large number of these stories, the hero is said to act according to Allah's will. For instance, a poor child accepts his poverty because it is his destiny determined by God. God may answer the wishes of good people, such as granting a good spouse or bestowing wealth. In addition, God punishes the evil characters that cause trouble for the main protagonists. Additionally, Islamic prayer is depicted in many of these narratives as a regular part of daily life. Several Arabic YA novels reflect this theme, including *Does My Head Look Big in This?* (2007) by Randa Abdel-Fattah; Taha Hussein's autobiography, *An Egyptian Childhood* (1992); *The Army of Lions* (1998) by Qasim Najar; and *Ahmed Deen and the Jinn at Shaolin* (1998) by Yahiya John Emerick.

Most of the children's and YA stories have moral themes, primarily taken from the Qur'an and Sunnah. Some of the common morals expressed through literature include "patience is the key for success," "satisfaction and contentment keep you out of trouble," "loyalty is always rewarded," and "stealing is usually discovered and punished." These lessons are meant to enhance and preserve the values of Arab culture. Examples of books with such morality themes include *The Fabulous Adventures of Nasruddin Hoja* (2001) edited by Abdassamad Clarke, *Tales of Juha: Classic Arab Folk Humor* (2007) by Salma Khadra Jayyusi, and *From the Land of Sheba: Yemeni Folk Tales* (2005) by Carolyn Han. Truth is one of the major themes in Nobel Prize-winner Naguib Mahfouz's *Fountain and Tomb* (1990).

Oppressive Rulers, Authority Figures, and Colonizers

Imprisonment, torture, and even political assassination are recurring topics in the Arab novel. The ruling authority possesses an army and has total power over anyone in his country. Naguib Mahfouz addresses the tragedy of the absence of freedom and the devastating effects that the deprivation of the Egyptian individual's basic rights had on the entire nation in his novel *Karnak Café* (2007). Many Syrian and Lebanese novels also address oppressive authorities, such as *A Hand Full of Stars* (1992) by Rafik Schami and *I'jaam: An Iraqi Rhapsody* (2007) by Sinan Antoon.

For many nations, the struggle for independence, revolution, social change, economic development, and confrontation with former colonizers and new world powers have all provided themes for literary works. Arabic literature is perhaps one of very few literary traditions with a distinct literary genre known as the prison novel (there is also such a tradition in Russian literature). A great majority of the writers have themselves experienced arrest, imprisonment, and even torture, and the history of the contemporary Arab intellectual is one of constant struggle with authorities. Many autobiographies were also subjected to censorship and confiscation, and this persecution forced some to leave their home countries. Thus, one of the most recurrent and haunting themes in Arabic literature is the authors' passionate cry for freedom from authoritarian rule. Many African (i.e., Moroccan, Algerian, Sudanese) novels address the colonizer's imposition of their French language rather than allowing native Arabic. Forcing the use of French was a means of spiritual subjugation. There are indeed many works by the best modern Arab adult authors that incorporate these recurrent themes, such as *Season of Migration to the North* (1970) by the Sudanese al-Tayeb Salih or, more recently, the five-volume *Cities of Salt* (1984–1989) by the Saudi Abdelrahman Munif. Two important Syrian novelists, Khayri al-Dhahabi and Nabil Suleiman, link these issues of freedom, prison, and political oppression with the social and political history of Syria and with the many cultural changes that took place over half a century through the fight for independence and the tribulations that followed.

Middle Eastern Conflicts and Wars

Middle Eastern conflicts and wars form the backdrop for the majority of the Arabic literature written since the 1950s. The war of 1948 in Palestine, which resulted in the state of Israel, created a sense of shock and consequent cultural unity that has ensured that the plight of the Palestinian people will remain a major topic for Arab authors. Even today, the Israeli–Palestinian conflict forms the backdrop for a number of children's and young adult novels—Shihab Nye's *Habibi* (1997) is one of the better-known books in this category. Meanwhile, the wars in Iraq became another major topic in such young adult novels as *Gulf* (1992) by Robert Westall and *Kiss the Dust* (1994) by Elizabeth Laird. These novels seem to be directed primarily toward an audience of American teens who have previously learned about such conflicts through television news and a few feature films.

Supernatural Elements That Shape Human Behavior

Supernatural elements are central in classical Arabic literature. Jinn, jinniyeh, ifreet, ghouls, ghouleh, giants, and angels are just some of the supernatural creatures that appear frequently. Two forces control human beings in many Arabic texts: good forces, including Allah/God and angels; and evil forces, such as jinn and ghouls. Good forces are thought to be more powerful than evil forces. In addition to supernatural elements, Arabic folk tales include magical elements that, most of the time, help the hero achieve his or her goals. Examples of such elements include a ring, the hairs of a horse, a crystal ball, slippers, and a flying carpet. Examples of books for children and young adults which contain such elements include *Kalilah and Dimnah: Stories for Young Adults* (2000) by an anonymous author, *Rumi Stories for Young Adults* (2000) by Jalal al-Din Rumi, *Attar Stories for Young Adults* (2000) by Farid al-Din Attar, and *Saadi Stories for Young Adults* (2000) by Muslih al-Din Saadi and Mehdi Azaryazdi. The tales of Aladdin, Ali Baba, and Sinbad in the *One Thousand and One Nights* are also good examples of Arabic fiction containing supernatural elements.

Heroism

Since the tribal structure was the nucleus of social and political life for a very long period in Arabic history, the values of such a culture continue to influence Arabic literature. Very often, hospitality to guests and strangers is essential. Values such as courage, honesty, honor, generosity, and loyalty are emphasized. Moreover, the hero is defined by characteristics such as pride, bravery in war, protecting the weak, and helping the poor. Even in contemporary young adult literature these cultural values are emphasized, for example in *Figs and Fate: Stories about Growing up in the Arab World Today* (2005) and *Santa Claus in Baghdad and Other Stories about Teens in the Arab World* (2008) by Elsa Marston and *In the Name of God* (2007) by Paula Jolin.

Culturally Appropriate Gender Roles

A woman is portrayed in traditional Arabic novels as a dependent person who needs the protection of a man, such as her father, brother, son, husband, or uncle. In contemporary young adult fiction, the female might be depicted as more independent and powerful, although certain gender hierarchies remain. Female adolescents, for example, are expected to prepare a variety of Arabic dishes and desserts to honor their relatives and guests. The female adolescent's honor is in her virginity before getting married and in her loyalty to her husband afterwards. A good example of the Islamic marital relationship occurs in the true story *Shah Jahan & the Story of Taj Mahal* (1996) by Julia Marshall and Joan Ullathorne. Such depictions of females might seem alien to US teens, but they realistically reflect gender roles and expectations in much of the Arab world.

Family and Community

Togetherness and brotherhood among family, friends, colleagues, and neighbors leading to mutual help, communal support, and collective wisdom are evident in such novels as *Seven Daughters and Seven Sons* (1994) by Barbara Cohen, *Habibi* by Naomi Shihab Nye, and *Figs and Fate* by Elsa Marston. Although reverence for parents and the elderly is highly encouraged, some modern novels depict conflict between traditional and contemporary culture which may result in rebellion against parental and/or cultural constraints, particularly for Arab teens living in the United States (e.g., *Habibi*, *Figs and Fate*, and *The Inheritance of Exile: Stories from South Philly* (2007) by Susan Muaddi Darraj). In these novels, the teen protagonists may find themselves torn between the expectations of their Arabic families and modern messages from the Western world.

Adjustment, Homesickness, and Assimilation

Contemporary AYAL includes stories of adjustment, homesickness, and assimilation to a new life, along with encountering feelings of isolation, loneliness, and poverty. In response to many stereotypes that describe all Arabs as "terrorists," a number of modern novels have emerged to address Arab/ Muslim adolescents who live outside their home countries: for example, *The*

Woman That I Left Behind: A Novel (2006) by Kim Jensen, *Muslim Teens in Pitfalls and Pranks* (2008) by Maryam Mahmoodian, *Road to Chlifa* (1995) by Michele Marineau, *The Bullet Collection* (2003) by Patricia Sarrafian Ward, and *Arab in America* (2007) by Toufic El Rassi. These books address the challenges of being Arab and Muslim when contemporary Arabs immigrate into the United States and other Western nations. Coming of age and discovering one's identity is a central theme, particularly when describing immigrant Arab teens struggling to fit into a new culture.

These challenges seem particularly acute for teen characters, who are also struggling with the normal biological and emotional difficulties of transitioning from childhood to adulthood. The attempt to define oneself in relation to the Westernized "other" covers a wide spectrum, ranging from a critical stance toward ridiculous blind imitation, to a deep involvement with foreign intellectual, spiritual, and aesthetic influences. Young adults struggle to modernize and retain their identity in books such as *A Mighty Collision of Two Worlds* (2002) by Safi Abdi, *Man from the East* (2001) by Mohsen El-Guindy, *The Bullet Collection* by Patricia Sarrafian Ward, and *The Inheritance of Exile* by Susan Muaddi Darraj.

An Examination of One Arabic Young Adult Text: *Habibi*—A Novel by Naomi Shihab Nye

In order for readers and teachers to encounter high-quality Arabic young adult literature with a range of perspectives, it must be made available to them in a way that matches their needs and interests. Additionally, it is important to demonstrate for secondary teachers methods of examining Arabic YA texts and determining their level of authenticity and appropriateness for classroom use. The following example illustrates the process I followed to examine and reflect upon the cultural authenticity of *Habibi* by Naomi Shihab Nye, a notable Arab American poet and novelist, using the list of criteria for authenticity outlined above.

What is it like to be young in Palestine today? That topic is the focus of this inspiring novel. Liyana Abboud, 15, moves with her family from St. Louis to Jerusalem. For her physician father, the move means going home to where he was born and educated. To Liyana, her younger brother, and her American mother, it brings about huge confusion. At first Liyana misses the United States, can't speak the languages, and feels uncertain at school, as she is trapped between two cultures. She is awkward with her bossy grandmother (Sitti) and overwhelmed by her huge extended family when she visits their village on the West Bank. The military occupation is always there, as is the simmering conflict between Jews and Arabs. In one horrifying scene, Israeli soldiers tear into Sitti's house and smash her bathroom. In a climactic episode after a Palestinian bomb has injured civilians, the Israelis shoot an innocent boy in the leg, and Liyana's father is held in prison overnight. Yet it doesn't have to be that way. Liyana meets and falls in love with a Jewish boy, and together they join the people from both communities who are trying to make peace.

I asked myself several questions as I considered the classroom value and cultural authenticity of *Habibi*. The first question was: does *Habibi* exhibit at least some of the characteristics of quality children's and YA literature? Liyana is an extremely likeable, well-rounded character, and I believe young readers will enjoy accompanying her on her journey to and through Jerusalem, as well as on her journey of self-discovery. The author introduces the reader to some Arabic words in an interesting self-dialogue:

> She [Liyana] walked the streets of old Jerusalem muttering her new words in Arabic . . . *Ana tayyib*—I'm fine. *Wa alaykum essalaam*—and upon you peace. *Shway*—a little bit. Watermelon was *hubhub*. It wasn't any harder to say *Ana Asif*—I'm sorry—than it was to say other things.
>
> (pp. 215–216)

The author is paying attention not only to Arabic words, but to Hebrew. Liyana had just learned one word in Hebrew, *shalom*/hello: "Liyana thought how both Hebrew and Arabic came from such a deep, related place in the throat. English felt skinny beside them" (p. 254).

Habibi portrays a mixture of cultures and beliefs similar to that experienced by its author, whose father is Muslim, Arab, and Palestinian, while her mother is Christian and American. Nye gradually moves the reader from one cultural scene into another. The reader gets a very accurate picture of how the Old City looks: "They [Liyana's family] entered a huge iron door that led into the Armenian sector of the Old City and wandered the curling streets as if they were in a maze. The streets were unevenly paved and Liyana kept tripping" (p. 76). A few miles later, Liyana's family reached the school. Her parents thought, "she might do best at an Armenian school called St. Tarkmanchatz deep in the Armenian district of the Old City. The students there were trilingual, speaking Arabic, Armenian, and English" (pp. 75–76).

Nye is also very successful in describing the daily social life and situation in Palestine. Arabs, for example, are famous for their hospitality and honoring their guests. In the novel, everybody came to greet and welcome Dr. Abboud's family, who had just returned from America: "The grocer showed up, and the postmaster, and the principal of the village school, and the neighbor, Abu Mahmoud, who grew famous green beans, and all of their wives and babies and teenagers and cats." This is just the greeting session but then "the whole gigantic family sat around forever, visiting, waiting for dinner to appear . . . everyone's favorite thing to do here—*sit in circle and talk talk talk*." Usually people eat in unison: "a huge tray of dinner appeared, hunks of baked lamb surrounded by rice and pine nuts . . . family members gathered around to dig into it with their forks" (p. 54). This is an accurate description of the Palestinian main dish called *mansaf*, but people usually eat it either with their hands or with a spoon, never with a fork (as the author describes it). While eating, the hosting family usually urges the guests to eat more: Sitti kept urging Liyana, through Poppy, "Eat the lamb." She said, "Liyana *needed it*" (p. 55). Even if someone goes to Arab restaurants, he or she might be served with more food than is needed. When Dr. Abboud's family had a meal at a restaurant,

> the owner . . . brought them steaming bowls of aromatic lentil soup . . . The table filled up with olives, purple marinated turnips, plates of *baba ghanouj* and *hummus,* and hot flat breads, even before the real lunch came . . . The handsome waiter slipped a plate of *baklava* onto their table for dessert. They hadn't even ordered it.
>
> (pp. 72–74)

Habibi displays the social values that Arabs have in common and discusses the positions and roles of men and women. Parents and society, especially in rural areas, encourage young Arab ladies to be good cooks:

> Sitti motioned Liyana and Poppy toward the mounded oven called the taboon, large enough to step into, beside her house. She showed Liyana how to slap bread dough into flat rounds and fling them onto a hot black stone to cook . . . Sitti's loaves were perfectly round, but Liyana's bread looked like Australia.
>
> (p. 82)

Girls' virginity is highly honored, and early marriage is sometimes encouraged: "Liyana wished Uncle Zaki, Poppy's elder brother, had not asked 'for her hand' for his son . . . Poppy got so furious . . . does she look ready to be married? She is fourteen years old" (p. 60). Although Liyana was very happy about her first kiss in America, she does not know what a kiss before marriage means in Palestine: "She wished she had not heard that an Arab boy who was found kissing a girl in the alley behind her house got beaten up by the girl's brothers" (p. 60).

The struggle between West and East becomes a critical issue in Arabic young adult literature when someone moves to a new place or culture, especially at an adolescent age, such as Liyana moving from St. Louis to Jerusalem/Palestine. Nye writes, "Maybe the hardest thing about moving overseas was being in a place where no one but your own family had any memory of you. It was like putting yourself back together with little pieces" (p. 84). Things are even worse if a person cannot speak the language of the mainstream culture. Liyana is split between two identities—between a new country and the country in which she was born. Like many young adults, she struggles with her identity, but like many Arabic teens this struggle is exaggerated by cultural and political realities that often disrupt their daily lives. Unfortunately, Liyana witnesses many aggressive acts in the novel. Israeli soldiers appear at Sitti's house and demand to see her grandson Mahmud, who is studying to be a pharmacist: "Poppy said the soldiers pushed past her into the house and searched it, dumping out drawers, ripping comforters from the cupboards . . . they went into Sitti's bathroom and smashed the bathtub with hard metal clubs they were carrying" (p. 185). To take revenge, the Palestinians would react with similar aggression. Liyana wonders at how the violence goes on like "a terrible wheel" (p. 235).

The Palestinian cause after the war of 1948 forms the backdrop of *Habibi* as well as many other Arabic novels written since the 1950s. Arabic children's literature stresses that the power of any authority looks thin if compared to Allah's power. An Arab's faith in Allah/God is passed down through the generations. Liyana's Muslim family challenges the Israeli soldiers by performing their prayers in public. While on their way to the Armenian school, they hear a muezzin give the last call to pray of the day over a loudspeaker from the nearby mosque. As a response to this call, Liyana's Muslim relatives "rose up in unison and turned their backs on Liyana's family. They unrolled small blue prayer rugs from a shelf, then knelt, stood, and knelt again, touching foreheads to the ground, saying their prayers in low voices" (p. 56).

In sum, I would say, yes, *Habibi* exemplifies many central characteristics of culturally authentic AYAL, including developmental appropriateness, relevance of issues to readers, general historical and cultural accuracy, and believability of characters. After this in-depth analysis of *Habibi*'s cultural themes and literary characteristics, I do not feel hesitant, as an Arab woman and researcher, to conclude that the book is a sound representation of the Arabic culture in general and of Arab children and young adults in particular. The most authentic characteristic of the book might just be its Arabic title, which means "my beloved."

Integrating AYAL into the English Language Arts Curriculum

Although it might seem valuable to integrate AYAL into the English language arts curriculum in both Arabic and non-Arabic secondary schools, the goals for and effects of integrating AYAL in Arabic-speaking countries might be different from those in non-Arabic-speaking countries. There are some important differences between the educational system in Arabic countries and those in Western nations that might influence the use of YA literature and how students receive it. First, the educational system in most Arabic countries is still more "traditional," more teacher-centered, than those in the United States and Western Europe. Second, English is taught and learned as a second language in Arabic-speaking countries; however, it is most likely a first language for American and many European students. Finally, the reading needs, general interests, and academic experiences of students who live in the Arab world might be different from those of Arab or non-Arab students who live outside the Arab world, such as in the United States.

Arabic young adult literature in non-Arabic-speaking countries such as the United States might be considered part of a "multicultural literature" curriculum. Through sharing AYAL in secondary schools, students and teachers celebrate students of Arab heritage and introduce the Arabic culture to non-Arab students. According to Landt (2006, p. 694), "Not seeing one's self, or representations of one's culture, in literature can activate feelings of marginalization and cause students to question their place within society." Moreover, teachers who incorporate multicultural YA literature into their curriculum expose students to viewpoints and experiences that can broaden adolescents' visions of self and the world. Thus, quality YA literature offers teens an avenue for self-reflection and personal development. As educators understand the importance of including AYAL in their curricula and become more confident in their ability to select appropriate high-quality writing, students will certainly enjoy the benefits. As Landt (2006, p. 697) writes,

> Imaginary barriers dissolve as students see themselves reflected in a diversity of cultures and recognize similarities across invented boundaries. What was strange becomes familiar when viewed through an age-mate's perspective. Doors open, eyes see, and minds grasp, as young adolescents encounter self within others.

When students read a story about another culture (e.g., Arabic culture), they may eagerly ask questions to try to make sense of the other world. They tend to analyze the characters' lives and create personal connections with them. They may make many inferences and logical conclusions to justify the characters' actions in the context of the Arabic cultural, social, or political system. Therefore, it is vital to select books that authentically reflect the diverse life experiences, traditions, histories, values, worldviews, and perspectives that make up Arab society.

If integrating Arabic young adult literature into the English language secondary school curriculum in non-Arabic-speaking countries is advantageous, then it may also be beneficial for Arab students who learn English as a second language in many Arabic-speaking countries. Although the English language is a secondary discipline in most Arabic schools, many teachers, educators, and parents emphasize the importance of mastering English in this global society where it is the language of politics and business. Some Arab parents send their children to private schools where they can learn all disciplines in English; others send them abroad for higher education. Research shows that many Arab university graduates tend to major in fields that require strong English, such as science and engineering. Reading literature written in English, literature that is particularly interesting to young readers and with which they readily engage, may positively affect adolescents' English-speaking ability.

Moreover, rapid globalization has increased the need for cross-cultural communication so that people have access to information all over the world. This growing need leads to greater demands on the foreign language teaching profession. Although Arab teachers, educators, and parents emphasize the importance of learning the English language, many research reports claim that the majority of Arab secondary students struggle with learning or enjoying English. Several studies have shown that a high percentage of Arab secondary school students drop out of school at this age level. According to Salwa Al-Darwish (2006), dropping out of school is often attributed to students' deficiencies in English before secondary school entry.

In most Arabic secondary schools, direct instruction by the teacher remains the primary method of teaching. As a result of this teacher-centered approach, most Arab secondary school students feel hesitant to ask questions or participate in the English classes; they seem to be passive recipients of the teacher's knowledge. Al-Darwish finds that Arab English language teachers are extremely reluctant to depart from the set lesson plans supplied in the teacher's manual by the Ministry of Education. While they would like to expand the official, irrelevant curriculum to meet their students' needs and areas of interest, teachers do not have the power or resources to make such a change. Their reliance on this official curriculum tends to remove innovation and creativity from their teaching and limits their opportunities to adapt the curriculum to the interests and abilities of their students. As a result of the teacher-centered curriculum, Arab secondary students can lack the motivation to learn and enjoy the English language, which is fostered through experiencing and responding to English texts such as novels, as well as authentic communicative experiences during which they use English in real-life situations.

Based on my teaching experience, as well as my experience as an Arabic student, I would say that integrating AYAL into the English language arts curriculum could have a positive effect in Arabic secondary schools, as YAL encourages students' personal response through written and oral language. As Virginia R. Monseau and Gary M. Salvner (2000, p. 101) write, "Students need to participate actively in their education—to read, write about, and talk about subjects of interest to them before they can really learn." Monseau and Salvner emphasize the importance of creating a comfortable learning–teaching atmosphere. They write that success in the classroom necessitates the establishment of an atmosphere of trust, where "readers can take chances without fear of being ridiculed for giving the 'wrong answer' and teacher attitude is crucial to the building of this trust" (p. 73). They also encourage the "response based approach" to literature teaching, arguing that reader-response theories have long suggested that what a reader brings to a work of literature is at least as important as the work itself. They believe that "teachers must realize the importance of engagement to the development of literary appreciation in students" (p. 73). Additionally, Roberta S. Trites (2000) suggests that during adolescence, teens must learn their place in the power structure. They must learn to negotiate the many institutions that shape them: school, government, religion, family, and so on. They must learn to balance their power with their parents' power and with the power of other authority figures in their lives. These struggles are perhaps especially acute for Arabic teens, as I noted earlier.

Arabic young adult literature could help create a generation of more flexible and active, rather than passive, reader-recipients. John N. Moore (1997) describes how a young adult novel may be interpreted from multiple perspectives. He assumes that "readers read differently and, consequently, construct different readings, even though they practice the same theory" (p. 187). He encourages teachers to be flexible with YA texts to allow themselves and their students to experience them from different angles. Moore quotes Henry Louis Gates, Jr. when he writes, "literary theory functioned in my education as a prism, which I could turn to refract different spectral patterns of language use in a text, as one does daylight. Turn the prism this way, and one pattern emerges; turn it that way, and another pattern configures" (p. 187). Such critical reading is certainly an active transaction with a text, necessitating both cognitive and emotional engagement.

In conclusion, I believe that the inclusion of culturally authentic Arabic young adult literature in the secondary classroom, whether that classroom be in the United States (or another Western nation) or in an Arab country, can have positive effects on teen readers, ranging from increasing their eagerness to read, to building critical thinking skills, to fostering mutual understanding and respect across countries and cultures. In a time when many movies and books stereotype Arab people as backward, violent fanatics, culturally authentic texts which portray the complete range of Arab life with all its beauty and human compassion, even during a time of warfare and aggressive political struggles, might just open the eyes and minds of contemporary teens.

References

Abdel-Fattah, R. (2007). *Does my head look big in this?* New York: Orchard Books.

Abdi, S. (2002). *A mighty collision of two worlds.* Bloomington, IN: Author House.

Al-Darwish, S. (2006). An investigation of teachers' perceptions of the English language curriculum in Kuwaiti elementary schools. Dissertations and Theses database (AAT 3218972).

Antoon, S. (2007). *I'Jaam: An Iraqi rhapsody.* New York: City Lights.

Attar, F. (2000). *Attar stories for young adults.* Cairo: ABC International.

Burton, R. (Trans.) (2001). *The Arabian nights: Tales from a thousand and one nights.* New York: Modern Library.

Clarke, A. (Ed.). (2001). *The fabulous adventures of Nasruddin Hoja.* London: Taha Taha.

Clinton, C. (2002). *A stone in my hand.* New York: Candlewick.

Cohen, B. (1994). *Seven daughters and seven sons.* New York: Harper Teen.

CTV. (2008). Boom in Arabic translation Post-Sept. 11. Online: http://www.ctv.ca/servlet/ArticleNews/story/CTVNews/1107635684436_24/?hub=Entertainment.

Darraj, M.S. (2007). *The inheritance of exile: Stories from south Philly*. South Bend, IN: University of Notre Dame Press.

El-Guindy, M. (2001). *Man from the East*. Ontario: Al-Attique Publications.

Emerick, Y.J. (1998). *Ahmed Deen and the jinn at Shaolin*. Columbia, MD: International Books and Tapes Supply.

Han, C. (2005). *From the land of Sheba: Yemeni folk tales*. Northampton, MA: Interlink Books.

Haykal, H. (1913). *Zaynab*. Cairo: Haykal.

Henderson, D. (2005). Authenticity and accuracy: The continuing debate. In D. Henderson & J. May (Eds.), *Exploring culturally diverse literature for children and young adults: Learning to listen in new ways* (pp. 266–276). Upper Saddle River, NJ: Pearson.

Hussein, T. (1992). *An Egyptian childhood*. Cairo: American University in Cairo.

Jayyusi, S.K. (2007). *Tales of Juha: Classic Arab folk humor*. Northampton, MA: Interlink Books.

Jensen, K. (2006). *The woman that I left behind: A novel*. Willimantic, CT: Curbstone Press.

Jolin, P. (2007). *In the name of God*. New York: Roaring Brook Press.

Kalilah and Dimnah: Stories for young adults. (2000). Cairo: ABC International.

Laird, E. (1994). *Kiss the dust*. New York: Puffin.

Landt, S. (2006). Multicultural literature and young adolescents: A kaleidoscope of opportunity. *Journal of Adolescent & Adult Literacy*, 49 (8), 690–697.

Mahfouz, N. (1957/2001). *The Cairo Trilogy: Palace Walk, Palace of Desire, Sugar Street*. New York: Everyman's Library.

Mahfouz, N. (1990). *Fountain and tomb*. Washington, DC: Three Continents Press.

Mahfouz, N. (2007). *Karnak café*. Cairo: American University in Cairo Press.

Mahmoodian, M. (2008). *Muslim teens in pitfalls and pranks*. Tempe, AZ: Muslim Writers Publishing.

Marineau, M. (1995). *Road to Chlifa*. Calgary: Red Deer Press.

Marshall, J. & Ullathorne, J. (1996). *Shah Jahan & the story of Taj Mahal*. London: Hood Hood Books.

Marston, E. (2005). *Figs and fate: Stories about growing up in the Arab world today*. New York: George Braziller.

Marston, E. (2008). *Santa Claus in Baghdad and other stories about teens in the Arab world*. Bloomington: Indiana University Press.

Monseau, V.R. & Salvner, G.M. (2000). *Reading their world: The young adult novel in the classroom*. (2nd edn). Portsmouth, NH: Boynton/Cook.

Moore, J.N. (1997) *Interpreting young adult literature: Literary theory in the secondary classroom*. Portsmouth, NH: Boynton/Cook.

Munif, A. (1984–1989). *Cities of salt*. New York: Vintage.

Najar, Q. (1998). *The army of lions*. New York: Amirah.

Nye, N.S. (1997). *Habibi: A novel*. New York: Simon Pulse.

Rassi, T.E. (2007). *Arab in America*. San Francisco: Last Gasp.

Rumi, J. (2000). *Rumi stories for young adults*. Chicago, IL: Kazi Publications.

Saadi, M. & Azaryazdi, M. (2000). *Saadi stories for young adults*. Cairo: ABC International.

Salih, Al-T. (1970). *Season of migration to the north*. Portsmouth, NH: Heinemann.

Schami, R. (1992). *A hand full of stars*. New York: Puffin.

Trites, R.S. (2000). *Disturbing the universe: Power and repression in adolescent literature.* Iowa City: University of Iowa Press.

Ward, P.S. (2003). *The bullet collection.* Minneapolis, MN: Graywolf Press.

Westall, R. (1992). *Gulf.* New York: Scholastic.

Culture and Language

The Two Tongues of Mexican American Young Adult Literature

Companion Chapters

These companion chapters will discuss Mexican American culture and language and advocate bringing them into classrooms through the agency of Mexican American young adult literature for the educational benefit of Mexican American students and their teachers.

The concept of "funds of knowledge" guides the discussion in the first chapter. Funds of knowledge, investigated by Luis Moll, Norma Gonzalez, and others (Gonzalez et al., 2005; Moll & Gonzalez, 1994), argues that Mexican American schoolchildren will perform better academically if schools as institutions and classroom teachers in particular make an effort to invite into the classroom the home culture and language from which the students come. Home culture and language can serve as an educational resource upon which to build a range of lessons and educational experiences. Part of the benefit of a funds of knowledge classroom falls to students as they are able to use their prior knowledge and language from home as a basis for educational experience in school. Teachers, who may not know about or understand the Mexican American culture and language of their students, also benefit from teaching in a funds of knowledge classroom by gaining a greater under-standing of their students and how to teach them. One way to bring home culture funds of knowledge into classrooms that serve Mexican Americans is to invite students to read culturally relevant young adult literature portraying Mexican American characters, values, situations, and language.

The following two chapters focus on the nature of Mexican American Mestizaje language, describing a hybridized amalgam of English and Spanish and articulating its importance in Mexican American culture and young adult literature.

These chapters are called "Two Tongues" not only because Spanish and English are literally two tongues, but because of the linked focuses, one on culture and one on language, and because the chapters have two voices. William's is the voice of a newcomer, a novice in the world of Mexican American YAL (MA YAL). The short period of two school years during which he read MA YAL along with his students at the University of Texas Pan American taught him volumes about Mexican American history, cultural values, and circumstances, making it easier for him as a "bolillo" (in the language of South Texas, literally white bread-roll) to understand and teach his students, 95 percent of whom were Mexican American.

René's is a voice of experience with an understanding of Mexican American YAL from the point of view of a Mexican American who grew up in deep South Texas, a stone's throw from the Rio Grande River. It is the bilingual voice of a professor of young adult literature who is also an author of MA YAL. René's novel *The Jumping Tree* (2001) was the first MA YAL title that William read as he was preparing to teach in the borderland.

References

Gonzalez, N., Moll, L., & Amanti, C. (Eds.). (2005). *Funds of knowledge: Theorizing practices in households, communities, and classrooms.* Mahwah, NJ: Lawrence Erlbaum.

Moll, L.C. & Gonzalez, N. (1994). Lessons from research with language-minority children. *Journal of Reading Behavior, 26* (4), 439–456.

Chapter 6

Funds of Knowledge and Mexican American Cultural Values in MA YAL

William J. Broz

"Funds of Knowledge [are] those historically accumulated and culturally developed bodies of knowledge and skills essential for household and individual functioning and well-being" (Moll and Gonzalez, 1994, p. 443). In proposing that teachers learn about their students' home culture and use that knowledge for teaching, Moll and Gonzalez offer the example of a teacher who learned that "many of her students' households had extensive knowledge of the medicinal value of plants and herbs" and created a thematic unit on the "curative properties of plants" (p. 445). These scholars refer to classrooms and teachers informed by their students' funds of knowledge as having been mediated or transformed. "Capitalizing on cultural resources for teaching allows both teachers and students to continually challenge the status quo, especially in terms of how the students are using literacy" (p. 451).

Moll and Gonzalez summarize their findings by positing as the basis for a transformed classroom a three-way relationship between a teacher (informed by funds of knowledge), students, and texts (also informed by funds of knowledge):

> The relationships between teacher and students always mediate the students' engagement with texts, as well as what literacy comes to mean for them within the classroom . . . So, in a sense, teacher–student relationships not only mediate but are mediated by the type of texts found in these classrooms.
>
> (p. 452)

Often in working-class schools the texts are standardized commercial products that have little or nothing to do with the students' lives. In literature classrooms, that can mean the canon of American literature, which is nearly devoid of Southwestern and Hispanic titles, or the informal canon of YAL including such ubiquitously assigned titles as *The Giver* (Lowry, 1993), *Where the Red Fern Grows* (Rawls, 1961), and *The Outsiders* (Hinton, 1967). Introducing MA YAL in classrooms with Mexican American students can be transformative. Further, related to the reader-response focus of other chapters of this volume, if the reader-response paradigm calls for students to use their own background knowledge and life experiences as a foundation for interpreting text, then teachers in funds of knowledge classrooms should use their understanding of students' funds of knowledge to select some of the texts for students to read and interpret for which students' cultural knowledge is a useful interpretive tool. For some Mexican American students, texts like *The Jumping Tree* by René Saldaña, Jr. (2001) and *The Tequila Worm* by Viola Canales (2005) will allow them to use their funds of knowledge as interpretive tools within the reader-response paradigm. According to Beatrice Mendez Newman (2009, p. 66), "Saldaña's and Canales's books are infused with the traditions and practices of the Hispanic culture of South Texas."

The Jumping Tree and The Tequila Worm

While the discussion below will examine *some*, though not all, of the Mexican American aspects of these two novels, it is important to note that these books are good "literature" (Newman, 2009, p. 71), with universal themes and characters with broad appeal. *The Jumping Tree* was listed as one of the "Top Ten First Novels for Youth" by the American Library Association *Booklist* in 2001, and was named among the "Best Children's Books of the Year" by the Bank Street College of Education in 2002—awards not exclusively for Hispanic books. It was also commended by the committee for the Americas Award for Children's and Young Adult Literature, given by the Consortium of Latin American Studies Programs in 2001. *The Tequila Worm* was named one of the "Top Ten First Novels for Youth" by the ALA *Booklist* in 2005, listed as a "Notable Children's Book" also by the ALA in 2005, recognized and recommended by both the National Council of Teachers of English and Social Studies in 2006, and won a Pen Center, USA Award in 2006. Additionally, the book received an honorable mention for the Americas Award in 2005, and was the 2006 Narrative Medal Winner of the Pura Belpré Award, given by the ALA "to a Latino/Latina writer and illustrator whose work best portrays, affirms, and celebrates the Latino cultural experience in an outstanding work of literature for children and youth."

An examination of the characters, content, and themes of these two young adult novels illustrates how MA YAL can bring Mexican American cultural values into classrooms. Through a series of vignettes, *The Jumping Tree* tells the story of Rey Castañeda from the sixth through the eighth grade growing up in a little Texas border town within sight of Mexico. Rey lives with his 'Apá (father), his 'Amá (mother), his big sister Lety, and his baby brother Javier. His father is a construction worker who emigrated from Mexico, crossing over illegally as a young man, but later becoming a US citizen. During these formative years, readers experience Rey's struggle to understand the kind of manhood his father is modeling for him, what it means to be a Mexican American with close ties to family in Mexico while living on the edge of a vast

Anglo-dominated country, and the loss of a best friend who leaves the path of school and education on which Rey remains.

The Tequila Worm is the story of Sofia Casas's academic and cultural education. While initial chapters portray Sofia as a child of seven or eight experiencing her first communion and enjoying traditional Mexican American holiday activities like making Easter *cascarones* and visiting the cemetery on the Day of the Dead, the central story of the book involves 14-year-old Sofia and her family deciding whether she should accept a scholarship to attend high school at a prestigious boarding school in Austin, 350 miles from her McAllen, Texas, home. This opportunity, which Sofia does accept, causes great concern among her family members, who fear that she will lose her close connection to them and to her Mexican American cultural roots. But with the help of her family and her new friends at school, Sofia survives and thrives, bridging white and Mexican American cultures while deepening her roots in family and tradition.

Mexican American Cultural Values

The purpose of connecting Mexican American cultural values to the content of these and other books is threefold. One benefit to teachers comes in the form of an enhanced, personal interpretive repertoire, which includes the names and brief definitions of traditional Mexican American cultural values that are useful as tools for understanding and interpreting the books themselves. Second, in the funds of knowledge/reader-response literature classroom, rather than regurgitate teacher-presented "right answers" to questions about books, students will be struggling to formulate their own interpretations. Teachers who are initially unfamiliar with MA YAL and the Mexican American cultural values that underpin themes and characters can use their newly acquired knowledge of traditional cultural values to understand student reactions to the texts and to help them articulate those reactions. Some students will feel a great deal of authority over these texts and offer high-quality culturally based interpretations that the teacher needs to be able to recognize, receive, and value. Third, exploring Mexican American cultural values by reading definitions and exploring how young adult titles contextualize those values is a way for teachers, in a general sense, to acquire funds of knowledge about Mexican Americans. However, these last two purposes must come with a caution.

Mexican American students will come into our classrooms representing a full range of personal and family closeness or distance from traditional Mexican American cultural values and a full range of closeness or distance from Spanish and Mexican American dialects. Avoiding stereotyping of books and students should be a constant concern.

Guidance from the Healthcare Professions

> Mexican Americans (Mexican heritage persons living in the United States)
> are the largest and fastest growing Latino subgroup representing 59.3%
> of the Latino population and 7.4% of the US population (US Census
> Bureau, 2001, 2004). Mexican-origin youth face the challenge of adapting
> to the mainstream culture while also maintaining ties with and adapting to
> the Mexican American culture; that is, they often experience socialization
> pressures to conform to ethnic standards at home while also experienc-
> ing socialization pressures to conform to mainstream standards in the
> broader community and at school (see Padilla, 2006). Several authors
> suggest that challenges created by this dual cultural adaptation process
> represent a substantial risk for Mexican American . . . youth.
>
> (Knight et al., 2009, p. 2)

The above quote comes from the June 2009 issue of the *Journal of Early
Adolescence*. The authors of the article acknowledge the support for their
research on Mexican American cultural values coming from the National
Institute of Mental Health and other health and science organizations. This
bears out what research for this chapter seems to suggest—that healthcare and
social service providers are increasingly aware that practitioners in their fields
need an understanding of Mexican American cultural values to serve their
patients and clients better. Many lists of Mexican American cultural values
(several used below) aimed at healthcare workers are available. The absence
of such lists aimed at preparing teachers to serve Mexican American students
seems to indicate a lack of awareness among school personnel of the value
for academic success of understanding and using the resource of individual
students' cultural backgrounds.

Familismo, machismo, respeto, collectivism, religion and spirituality, and
curanderismo (Chadwick Center for Children & Families, 2009; Taylor, 2004;
Padilla et al., 2001) are some of the Mexican American cultural values found in
The Jumping Tree, The Tequila Worm, and other MA YAL titles:

> *Familismo* is the preference for maintaining a close connection to the
> family. Latinos/Hispanics, in general, are socialized to value close relation-
> ships, cohesiveness, and cooperativeness with other family members.
> These close relationships are typically developed across immediate and
> extended family members, as well as close friends of the family.
>
> (Chadwick Center for Children & Families, 2009)

Familismo, often expressed as "*la familia*" (Bertrand, 1999, p. 115), is central to
both novels. Nearly every weekend, Rey's family in *The Jumping Tree* travels
to Mexico for a kind of family reunion that involves his father's parents, his
tios and tias (uncles and aunts), and his primos (cousins): "On 'Apá's side of

the family alone I had over 30 cousins, so when we all got together for one reason or another, it was a big, loud party" (p. 14). A major tension in the book is the threat to the closeness of his extended family occasioned by his father's recent conversion to the Baptist faith and consequent abstention from drinking. One of his brothers, Tio Santos, sees 'Apá's religious expression and sobriety as a diminution of 'Apá's manhood.

> *Machismo* refers to a man's responsibility to provide for, protect, and defend his family ... The service provider should be aware that there is currently some debate surrounding the negative connotations of *machismo*, including sexual aggressiveness, male domination, and arrogance.
>
> (Chadwick Center for Children & Families, 2009)

In every way, Rey's father displays the positive aspects of *machismo*, providing for and protecting his family:

> He'd get home from work laying cement all day, always long after the sun had already set, and he'd sit on the floor of his and 'Amá's room for close to an hour ... The smell of hard work, sweat upon layer of sweat, never seemed to wash off of him, though. I'd sit by his pile of work clothes ... trying to memorize that smell, 'Apá's smell, the bitter odor of work, and let it seep into my lungs, hungry for 'Apá's strength.
>
> (p. 23)

The uncle's aggressive display at a family gathering is where readers also see the negative side of *machismo*. "Are you too good for a shot with your brothers? Or, I know, this religion business has made you soft, like a woman" (p. 15).

Throughout the book, Rey struggles to understand his father's turn-the-other-cheek mentality in light of Rey's perceptions of family closeness and *machismo* as pillars of his world. But in the end Rey comes to understand the meaning of his father's internal strength: "Outside my door, I could hear him pacing. 'Apá, the man, was pacing back and forth like a lion might do to keep his cubs safe from all danger. I so wanted to be like him" (p. 181).

While *machismo* is largely absent from *The Tequila Worm*, all of the other values listed above spill from its pages. Sofia's conflict about pursuing her education at boarding school is rooted in *familismo*, displayed when everyone in her immediate (and, to some extent, extended) family must agree with the decision before she accepts the scholarship. Readers also see the value of *respeto* in play: "Deference to authority or a more hierarchical relationship orientation ... knowing one's place of respect in hierarchical relationships" (Chadwick Center for Children & Families, 2009). Sofia wants to accept the scholarship. Her father wants to let her take it. But an important and essential blessing for accepting this opportunity falls to Sofia's godmother, Tia Petra, who not only gives her approval but accepts family responsibility for Sofia's continued cultural education in Mexican American values. Tia Petra says, "Now *you* tell me all about this school and why you want to go there. As your godmother, I'll then see whether I think this is good for your education or not" (p. 56). To Sofia's parents, Tia Petra says, "Let her go, if that's her dream. And I promise you, as her godmother, that I'll help tutor her on everything she needs to know about her life here [in the Mexican American community in the Lower Rio Grande Valley]" (p. 58).

Perhaps because its underlying theme is the struggle to retain Mexican American identity and cultural values, *The Tequila Worm* also articulates Mexican American versions of collectivism, religion and spirituality, and *curanderismo*.

Though Sofia rejects the rite of passage into womanhood of the *quinceañera*, she accepts her family's view that becoming a Mexican American woman means becoming a "good *comadre*." Through many passages dedicated to the subject, the book defines a *comadre* as a lifelong member of a female circle of family and friends who consult and support each other through life's trials and joys. At the end of the book, Sofia says, "It had taken years, many years, for me to see the true meaning of becoming a good *comadre* . . . after Papa died so suddenly . . . Mama had kept her balance and serenity in this darkest of times, because of her *comadres*" (p. 198). This is an example of the value of collectivism. "Collectivism requires mutual empathy" (Taylor, 2004) among members of an extended family or community, such as a group of *comadres*. Readers also see the spirit of collectivism in the practice of family and friends sharing the expense of costly events like a *quinceañera* by accepting the request to become "sponsors." Sponsors who donate money are referred to as *padrinos* and *madrinas* (Canales, 2005, p. 95).

As a younger child, Sofia is preoccupied with standard aspects of Catholicism, such as nuns, and with its sacred rituals, such as communion and confession. As a teenager, she struggles to understand Mexican American Catholic beliefs about death characterized by the practice of constructing and maintaining "home altars" and Day of the Dead observances. She even has a home altar in her boarding school dorm room, a cause for some ridicule from a particular Anglo student. A rite of passage in Sofia's spiritual life is marked by her acceptance to be the *madrina*, responsible for cleaning and preparing the statue of the baby Jesus to be placed in the Christmas *nacimiento*, a three-dimensional diorama created each year by her *abuela* (grandmother). The importance of Sofia's religion and spirituality is also evident in her observance of the Mexican American post-burial ritual involving the family of the deceased, who gather to say the Catholic rosary on each of the nine days following the funeral. For traditional Mexican American students, a death in the immediate or extended family can mean absence from school for up to two weeks due to the importance of *la familia* and religious traditions, an important point of cultural awareness for teachers.

For non-Hispanic Americans, *curanderismo* is perhaps one of the most unique and unknown of all traditional Mexican American cultural values:

> A form of alternative therapy that tends to be used by Hispanic subjects is the ancient practice of *curanderismo*. *Curanderismo* is a diverse folk healing system of Latin America. It began with the Aztecan, Mayan, and Incan tribes and their religious beliefs of harmony with nature, spirit, and self. The Mexican Indians . . . believed that their gods punished sins with illness. Therefore, disease or illness was supernatural in nature. As a balance, some mortals, who were spiritually chosen, were given the power to heal the wounded spirit and cure the supernatural illness. This is the role of the *curanderos* and *curanderas*. . . [Consider that in 2001] Hispanics in Denver, Colorado make up 23.3% of the population . . . It is estimated that there are 150–200 *curanderos* in the Denver Metropolitan area.
>
> (Padilla et al., 2001)

While Rudolfo Anaya's *Bless Me, Ultima* (1972) contains a more extensive treatment of *curanderismo* in the person of the healer, Ultima, *The Tequila Worm* devotes several pages to this phenomenon as well. Sofia's sister Lucy has failed to recover psychologically from being hit by a car, even though doctors say nothing is physically wrong with her. As a result, Sofia witnesses a *curandera* cure Lucy of the *susto*, Mexican shock. In both *The Tequila Worm* and *Bless Me, Ultima*, *curanderas* are portrayed as religious, spiritual healers and herbalists whose powers are narrowly but importantly distinguished from those of *brujas*, or witches. When the young Sofia wants to dress as a *curandera* for Halloween, her mother explains, "A *curandera* . . . [is] someone special who heals others by praying to saints and using herbs. Dressing up as a *curandera* for Halloween . . . well, it just isn't right" (p. 26). In the Trino books by Diane Gonzales Bertrand (1999, 2001), Trino's more Anglicized Mexican American friends give him the finger when they get angry. Trino gives them *mal de ojo*, the "evil eye," the cure for which comes from a *curandera*.

It is important to recognize that naming cultural values and using them to interpret text is not the same as promoting or criticizing those values. And recognizing cultural values need not lead to negative stereotyping. *Curanderismo* can be seen as similar to the homeopathic medicine movement in larger American society. In 2009 the University of New Mexico offered a summer institute and for-credit college courses on *curanderismo*. Further, every cultural value can play out positively or negatively in fiction or in the real world. Readers admire Sofia's dedication to her family, but that dedication almost bars her from a tremendous and life-changing educational opportunity. Trino, in Bertrand's *Trino's Choice* (1999), is greatly supported by his immediate family relationships, but as the oldest son of a single mother, he nearly allows the pressures of *familismo* and *machismo* to lead him to criminal activity in order to get the money his family sorely needs. Similarly, the absence of a healthy *familismo* characterizes the situation of the protagonist in Gary Soto's *Buried Onions* (2006b); Eddie has no other family member to turn to as his tia pressures him, as a family responsibility, to murder the person who killed her son.

Socioeconomic Circumstances and Geopolitical Histories

Besides the illustration and articulation of Mexican American cultural values, MA YAL also portrays Mexican American socioeconomic circumstances and geopolitical histories. MA YAL often presents characters struggling with working-class financial problems. Sofia's father is a carpenter; her mother is described as a wife, mother, and homemaker. The issues of new dresses and expenses money for the boarding school are financial roadblocks to accepting the scholarship. In *The Jumping Tree*, Rey's father works at a tough construction job and his family has no money for luxuries like taking their dog to the veterinarian. In one poignant scene 'Apá takes Rey to view farm workers picking watermelons in a field beside the Rio Grande. Pointing out the workers, he tells Rey:

> I had to cross over illegally a few times to work, mi'jo . . . This was when I needed money to get married to your mom . . . So I crossed. I remember working in the fields right behind us . . . At school . . . they're going to teach you about being an American, mi'jo. That in this country, we speak English. That the only history that matters is American history . . . But no matter what they teach you . . . don't forget where you come from and don't ever be embarrassed about speaking Spanish. It's the language of our people.
>
> (pp. 49–51)

Another aspect of economic life for some Mexican Americans appears in the discussion about Rey's friend Chuy's family's annual trip north as migrant workers. Such trips have their own special name in the language of the borderlands—*los trabajos*, "the work":

> When money got tight, Chuy and his family—his mom and dad, brothers, sisters, grandparents, and cousins—would migrate up North to the trabajos, where they worked in the fields . . . Chuy would miss about a month of school, sometimes two, and he'd always come back a darker brown than he usually was. He also had new clothes and shoes . . . I liked his stories [of the social life in migrant camps] and that he got to miss school, but I didn't like seeing how tired his parents and grandparents looked when they got back. Their stooped shoulders, their weak smiles.
>
> (pp. 5–6)

As a point of reference, note that South Texas public schools and the University of Texas-Pan American (UTPA) in particular have enough students whose families have traveled north (or east) to work every year that the university has a special student support program called CAMP, the College Assistance Migrant Program, to meet the needs of students whose regular school year educations have been and still are disrupted by *los trabajos*. Cynthia DeFelice's *Under the Same Sky* (2003) is one MA young adult novel that addresses the northern end of *los trabajos*.

Urban poverty and the gangs and violence that come with it are also themes found in some MA YAL, such as *Trino's Choice* and *Trino's Time*, *Buried Onions*, and books by Matt de la Peña, *Ball Don't Lie* (2005) and *Mexican Whiteboy* (2008). However, inviting students to read a broad array of MA YAL titles will balance this picture.

MA YAL can show Mexican Americans in rising socioeconomic circumstances. In *The Tequila Worm*, Sofia's *comadre* and *prima*, Berta, comes from a family that is wealthy enough in the mid-1960s to buy her, a teenager, a new car with air-conditioning. And Sofia, like her creator Viola Canales, attends Harvard College and Harvard Law School to become a successful lawyer. Additionally, Saldaña's *A Whole Sky Full of Stars* (2007) pairs a clearly middle-class protagonist with a working-class protagonist. The same is true for Soto's *Accidental Love* (2006a). Both *My Father, the Angel of Death* (2006) and *Alamo Wars* (2008) by Ray Villarreal also feature middle-class characters.

In South Texas, where 85 percent of the population is Mexican American, billboards and the Yellow Pages are filled with listings for Mexican American physicians, lawyers, and professionals of every discipline. Mexican Americans are mayors, state and national congressional office holders, police officers, school superintendents, and hold most other public offices. Yet it is also true that since the 1950s, when such records were first kept, the three counties of the Lower Rio Grande Valley (Cameron, Hidalgo, and Starr) have been annually "among the poorest of all 5000 counties in the United States, according to the US Census and all other indicators" (Maril, 2009). Hidalgo County is the location of UTPA and the county in which Saldaña and Canales grew up and set their stories. Traditions of work and upwardly mobile economic struggle are part of the funds of knowledge of many Mexican Americans.

One of the most educational and enlightening features of both *The Tequila Worm* and *The Jumping Tree* is the way the books address Mexican American ethnic pride and shed light on Mexican American geopolitical history. "The history of Mexicans in the United States predates all other Latino groups. Upon the signing of the Treaty of Guadalupe-Hidalgo in 1848, Mexicans *became* Mexican-Americans" (Taylor, 2004; my emphasis). This treaty ended the US war with Mexico:

> The treaty was signed in Guadalupe Hidalgo, a city north of the capital where the Mexican government had fled as US troops advanced. Its

provisions called for Mexico to cede 55% of its territory (present-day Arizona, California, New Mexico, and parts of Colorado, Nevada and Utah) in exchange for fifteen million dollars in compensation for war-related damage to Mexican property.

(Hispanic Reading Room, Library of Congress)

Other provisions of the treaty called for the establishment of the Rio Grande as the Texas–Mexican border in Texas, instead of the Rio Nueces, hundreds of miles to the north.

This information is necessary background for understanding Sofia's response to Anglo student Terry's antagonistic statement, "Everything from Mexico—including tequila—has worms. So, why don't you . . . wiggle back across the border?" (p. 146). Sofia delivers a history lesson in her response: "My family didn't cross the border; it crossed us. We've been here for over three hundred years, before the US drew those lines" (p. 147).

Saldaña addresses these issues in Rey's school life in the chapter "Texas, Our Texas":

Our Texas [is] brown faces everywhere with the occasional white face peppering the throngs of Mexicans. Santa Anna, Pancho Villa, Gregorio Cortez: all these guys should be our heroes . . . Crockett, Austin, and so many other gringo names became nothing more to us than names in a book.

(p. 125)

Student Response to *The Tequila Worm* and *The Jumping Tree*

Mediating Texts: Creating the Desire to Write

Students in several English education courses and some first-year composition courses at UTPA read *The Tequila Worm* and *The Jumping Tree*, the latter group of students using these local texts as inspiration for writing about their own home cultures. In a 2009 *English Journal* article, Newman reports students saying that these books changed their lives and that they now want to become writers (p. 67). Rodrigo, a student of mine, says about reading *The Jumping Tree*, "It was like the book was not about Rey, but about me . . . I think every Mexican American boy or girl goes through these experiences in one way or another because that is the way our culture is . . . The fact that the book is about us makes me want to try and write."

Esmer, another of my students, explores a similar impact of having read *The Tequila Worm*: "After reading the book for the second time I realized I truly want to become a writer . . . *The Tequila Worm* has inspired me to be creative, assertive, and goal-oriented." In *Literature for Today's Young Adults*

(2005), Donelson and Nilsen cite an NCTE conference talk by Rudolfo Anaya, author of *Bless Me, Ultima*, who proposed that if members of minority groups cannot read books about their own cultures, it is hard for them to write about their own cultures: "[Anaya] couldn't use Hemingway or Milton as models. He could create plots like theirs, but then he was at a standstill because nowhere in the literary canon did he find people like the ones he knew" (pp. 296–267). Anaya and my students seem to be saying that the chance to read culturally relevant texts mediated the possible uses of literacy to include Mexican American students as writers.

Valuing and Validating Home Culture in the Classroom

Reflecting some of the pride and alienation Rey expressed in the "Texas, Our Texas" chapter of *The Jumping Tree*, my student Maria's comments upon reading *The Tequila Worm* demonstrate bitterness about having her culture excluded from the school curriculum, but also imply that the inclusion of Mexican American literature in my curriculum demonstrates a valuing of home culture:

> I find it disturbing that, at the age of twenty-five and living where Hispanics are the majority, this is the first book I have read that deals with my ethnicity. I enjoyed every page I read because I could relate to the character, as I am sure many other Hispanic readers would as well. Not only could I relate, but I learned a lot about my culture.

After reading *The Tequila Worm*, Zeta and Jennifer expand on the themes of cultural acceptance and understanding and remind me that my classroom is filled with individuals whose cultural backgrounds and attitudes vary. Zeta writes:

> To be honest, I have always had a hard time being proud of my heritage ... This book changed my view completely. I laughed aloud at most parts; people must have thought I was nuts. Memories came flooding back. I would definitely recommend this book to other Hispanic young adults who are struggling with the acceptance of their culture as well.

Jennifer states:

> My parents did not raise my brother and me in a dominant Spanish [language] household. I am bilingual enough to order food from a [Mexican] restaurant and ask my aunt if she has sugar ... *The Tequila Worm* was a funny and heartbreaking text that gave me a sense of order as to where I belong in society.

Using Mexican American Young Adult Literature in Classrooms

The pedagogical literature suggests that the best way to introduce any students to MA YAL, including Mexican American students, is in the context of thematic literature units that contain non-MA YAL titles as well (Newman, 2009, p. 70; Donelson & Nilsen, 2005, p. 301; Burke, 1999, p. 24). Teachers might introduce *The Tequila Worm* or *The Jumping Tree* in a unit of coming of age stories, for example, or in units with titles focused on family.

Further, the reactions of UTPA students to these books may be heightened by the fact that most of the students grew up within 50 miles of where Saldaña and Canales grew up and set their stories. For MA YAL to serve as a conduit for bringing funds of knowledge into any particular classroom, teachers, as they explore the funds of knowledge of their own students, should seek out local and regional MA YAL titles and authors. Teachers in California might turn to the books of Californians Gary Soto (*Buried Onions* and *Accidental Love*), Matt de la Peña (*Ball Don't Lie* and *Mexican Whiteboy*), and Malin Alegria (*Estrella's Quinceañera*, 2006). As Mexican Americans begin to live full time in new places across the country, books will appear that address the lives and cultures of Mexican Americans in those new contexts, such as *Under the Same Sky*, a story of contemporary migrant workers on *los trabajos* in upstate New York.

A caution comes from Dr. I. Moriah McCracken, who teaches Mexican American high school students from South Texas in dual enrollment college credit courses. She reports observing significant resistance in her students to being offered Mexican American literature—not just young adult titles, but literary works such as those by Richard Rodriguez and others. Those students say that they have read those books before and now they want the real, college literature. McCracken states, "They seem to believe that Anglo literature = college literature" (2009). I speculate that if those Mexican American students have read books like *The Tequila Worm* and *The Jumping Tree*, then it is possible they have already experienced their funds of knowledge being included in school curriculums and have benefited from classrooms mediated by culturally relevant texts. The students McCracken refers to are high school seniors in an academically accelerated program. I see Saldaña's and Canales's books as most important for sixth- to ninth-graders who may still be deciding whether engagement with school is worth their time: some public school districts in the McAllen area had a 50 percent high school dropout rate in 2007. The desire to invite Mexican American students to read culturally relevant literature should not be carried too far because culturally relevant literature represents only part of the literary offerings from which any student may benefit. Further, perhaps Mexican American titles were presented to these students apart from other literature, intentionally or unintentionally, as a novelty, rather than being integrated into the curriculum, as suggested above.

Home Language as a Key to Funds of Knowledge

Moll and Gonzalez (1994) place great importance on biliteracy, advocating biliterate elementary school programs in which all students graduate being able to read and write in both English and Spanish. The inclusion of Spanish and Mexican American words and idiomatic phases (in Spanish) in MA YAL runs the gamut from books like *Trino's Choice* and *Trino's Time*, in which Spanish/English code switching is discussed but rarely demonstrated, to *Accidental Love*, which uses 61 different Mexican American words or phrases and comes with a glossary notation for each, to *The Jumping Tree*, in which Mexican American words and phrases appear on almost every page, sometimes several times. The very least that teachers can learn from the inclusion of Spanish in these books is that many places exist in the US borderlands with Mexico where more Spanish than English is spoken every day by people who can speak English, who are not immigrants, many of whose parents were not immigrants, and some of whom may trace their generational roots back, on the spot where they still live today, to the late 1790s. Similarly, it would be a mistake for a teacher to assume that a student with limited proficiency in English is an immigrant or has immigrant parents. As Newman (2009, p. 67) reported, Viola Canales told a student audience at UTPA in 2008 about arriving to her first day of elementary school speaking only Spanish. In personal communication, Canales (2008) said this was because only Spanish was spoken in her home out of respect to her grandmother, who spoke no English, even though her parents, both US citizens, both US high school graduates, were bilingual. Many UTPA students today affirm that this practice of Spanish-only home language is still very much alive.

In *The Jumping Tree*, when seventh-grader and budding history scholar Rey Castañeda addresses the issue of living in a culture that speaks a unique language, he is really referring to his linguistic funds of knowledge. As noted above, Rey is impressed and incensed by the Texas history unit in his textbook. His teacher, Mrs. Sauceda, seems to follow Moll and Gonzalez's advice and invites in from the community a resource to help inspire these particular students' inquiry and intellectual growth. When the guest, Amado, a Chicano activist, arrives wearing a Che Guevara T-shirt and urges Rey and his class-mates to "Stay brown," Rey is most impressed by the language that Amado speaks: "Amado talked to us using our language. Not Spanish, definitely not English, but 'Mestizaje' he called it. 'It's a third language; for many of us, our first language, ¿que no?'" (pp. 131–132).

In the following companion chapter, Professor René Saldaña, Jr. offers a scholarly elucidation of the point that so impressed Rey.

References

Alegria, M. (2006). *Estrella's quinceañera*. New York: Simon Pulse.

Anaya, R. (1972). *Bless me, Ultima*. New York: Grand Central Publishing.

Bertrand, D.G. (1999). *Trino's choice*. Houston, TX: Piñata Books.

Bertrand, D.G. (2001). *Trino's time*. Houston, TX: Piñata Books.

Burke, J. (1999). *The English teacher's companion: A complete guide to classroom, curriculum, and the profession*. Portsmouth, NH: Boynton Cook.

Canales, V. (2005). *The tequila worm*. New York: Wendy Lamb Books.

Canales, V. (2008). Comment made to author during visit to UTPA.

Chadwick Center for Children & Families. (2009). San Diego, CA. Online: http://www.chadwickcenter.org/WALS.htm.

DeFelice, C. (2003). *Under the same sky*. New York: Farrar, Straus and Giroux.

de la Peña, M. (2005). *Ball don't lie*. New York: Delacorte Press.

de la Peña, M. (2008). *Mexican whiteboy*. New York: Delacorte Press.

Donelson, K. & Nilsen, A. (2005). *Literature for today's young adults* (7th edn). Boston, MA: Allyn and Bacon.

Hinton, S.E. (1967). *The outsiders*. New York: Viking Press.

Hispanic Reading Room. (2009). The treaty of Guadalupe Hidalgo. Online: http://www.loc.gov/rr/hispanic/ghtreaty/.

Knight, G.P., Gonzales, N.A., Saenz, D., Bonds, D., German, M., Deardorff, J., Roosa, M., & Updegraff, K. (2009). The Mexican American cultural values scale for adolescents and adults. *Journal of Early Adolescence*, 20 (10), 1–38.

Lowry, L. (1993). *The giver*. New York: Bantam.

Maril, L. (2009). Personal communication via email. [Maril, the former chair of the Sociology Department at UTPA, is the author of several books on the borderlands and South Texas, including *The poorest of Americans: The Mexican Americans of the Lower Rio Grande Valley of Texas*, 1990.]

McCracken, I.M. (2009). Personal communication via email. [McCracken teaches composition and literacy in the English Department at UTPA.]

Moll, L.C. & Gonzalez, N. (1994). Lessons from research with language-minority children. *Journal of Reading Behavior*, 26 (4), 439–456.

Newman, B.M. (2009). "Living authors, living stories: Integrating local authors into our curriculum." *English Journal*, 98 (3), 66–72.

Padilla, A.M. (2006). Bicultural social development. *Hispanic Journal of Behavioral Sciences*, 28, 467–497.

Padilla, P., Gomez, V., Biggerstaff, S., & Mehler, P. (2001). Use of curanderismo in a public health care system. American Medical Association. Online: http://archinte.ama-assn.org/cgi/reprint/161/10/1336.pdf.

Rawls, W. (1961). *Where the red fern grows*. New York: Doubleday.

Saldaña, R., Jr. (2001). *The jumping tree*. New York: Dell Laurel-Leaf.

Saldaña, R., Jr. (2007). *A whole sky full of stars*. New York: Dell Laurel-Leaf.

Soto, G. (2006a). *Accidental love*. Orlando, FL: Harcourt.

Soto, G. (2006b). *Buried onions*. Orlando, FL: Harcourt.

Taylor, A. (2004). A cultural exploration of the Latino community. *NASP Communique*, 33 (1). Online: http://www.nasponline.org/publications/cq/cq331latino.aspx.

US Census Bureau (2001). *Projections of resident population by race, Hispanic origin and nativity: Middle series, 2050-2070*. Online: http://census.gov/population/projections/nation/summary/np-t5-g.txt.

US Census Bureau (2004). *We the people: Hispanics in the United States* [Census Special Reports]. Washington, D.C.: US Department of Commerce, Economics and Statistics Administration.

Villarreal, R. (2006). *My father, the angel of death.* Houston, TX: Piñata Books.

Villarreal, R. (2008). *Alamo wars.* Houston, TX: Piñata Books.

Chapter 7

Mestizaje

Forging Identity through Hybridity

René Saldaña, Jr.

Mestizaje, for the purpose of this chapter, is defined as a hybrid language composed of Spanish and English that is particular to the Mexican American. Mestizaje is not to be confused with bilingualism (that is, the ability to speak two languages). Nor is it a bastardization of either or both of its parent languages. It is, instead, a carefully constructed third language that borrows from each of its parent tongues such components as sentence structures, parts of speech, and words. One example would be the phrase "parquear el carro," to park the car. The pronunciation is Spanish, and the suffix -ar is also borrowed from that parent tongue, as in "estacionar," the actual Spanish word for parking one's car. The root word, "parq," comes from the English "to park." Blend the two and the result is something vaguely recognizable and at once completely foreign to speakers of either Spanish or English. Mestizaje is not a language of exclusivity, though. Quite the contrary, it is a tongue necessitated out of a desire to be counted where a people had previously gone uncounted. The above is a prime example of the language spoken in the "alternative space, the third country between the United States and Mexico," the Mexican American space in the United States mentioned in *Chicano Poetics: Heterotexts and Hybridities* by the late Alfred Arteaga (1997, p. 34), poet and University of California, Berkeley Professor of Chicano and Ethnic Studies.

As a border people whose physical features more resemble those of Mexicans, Mexican Americans do not gain full entry into the Anglo American mainstream. However, because Mexican Americans are born north of the Rio Grande, they are also not regarded as Mexican by their Mexican counterparts. This linguistic hybridization on the part of Mexican Americans, then, is an attempt to identify themselves, on their own terms, with Mestizaje being the principal means for accomplishing this undertaking. Mexican Americans want to show their ties to both parent languages, countries, and heritages, but at once they choose to separate themselves by speaking a language considerably different from both tongues of origin, thus fashioning a separate and distinct identity.

Before moving forward, a brief explanation of the Mexican American genesis is in order. The Mestizo Indian, as a people, was the product of a mixing of two different races, the Spanish conquistador and the Mexican Indian. Exerting their power as the conquerors, the Spanish took advantage sexually of the Mexican Indian women. From this violent union, a new breed of people was born. It found itself in a bad predicament because this new race was neither Spanish nor Indian. When the Mestizo offspring attempted to identify with either parent, they were shunned, ostracized, rebuffed, left to fend for themselves. Considered a bastard nation, they not only learned to fend for themselves, they survived, strengthened themselves, multiplied, and constructed their own identity out of a necessity to exist.

Similarly, Mestizaje, the language of the Mexican American, what others have called Spanglish, caló, or code switching, was born out of a need to validate its speakers in a society which was quick to disown them. When the Treaty of Guadalupe Hidalgo was signed on February 2, 1848, thus ending the war between the United States and Mexico, land was exchanged for a relatively small sum of money ($15 million for the whole of the present-day Southwest) and for the assurance that the United States would not invade Mexico. But no concern on the part of either government was shown for the people who for generations had lived on and worked the very land being haggled over. Their land, in essence, was sold off, and the people along with it. They had been Mexican citizens all of their lives, and with the stroke of a pen they had become American citizens. These people, like the Mestizo Indians, found themselves displaced and having to re-identify themselves. Arteaga writes, "People were acquired with the lands, and the 'Americanization' of natives" commenced (1997, p. 82). But how did previously non-Americans transform themselves into "Americans"?

Simply put, they were forced to learn the way of the colonizer/conqueror, which, in this case, preached "an English-only ethos . . . [a] single-language and single-voiced monologue" (Arteaga, 1997, p. 73), or they succumbed to the new powers-that-be, and, in so doing, lost everything that they and their forefathers had worked to own. There was no space available for a separate and different tongue because "to begin to conceive Chicano [Mexican American] space is to begin to erase the nation" (Arteaga, 1997, p. 92). Like their forebears, the sons and daughters of Cortés and Marina (conqueror and conquered), the newly stamped Mexican Americans also found themselves in a state of limbo. Because they no longer lived in Mexico, they were not Mexicans; because they were not born in the United States, nor did they look or speak American, they were not American.

So, what were Mexican Americans to do? Should they allow themselves, their people, and their culture to be trampled upon by assimilating into the status quo, or should they do whatever was in their power to create for themselves a distinct place in America? And if they chose the latter, how would they go about it? The answer was simple: they would create a new space for themselves where there had been none, which included language as their most obvious tool and work of art. They defined (in some cases even redefined) what it was to be American. As Burciaga (1993, p. 63) describes it, "We were caught on a razor sharp edge of two vastly different cultures, and in trying to identify with each side, while condemned by both sides, we denounced both and identified as a third alternative with a little and a lot from each side." It has been long in the making, but today's Mexican Americans have inherited a rich and genuinely American language.

For the present-day Mexican American, "the language of the people is a reflection of Spanish and English in confrontation with each other, and the music and rhythms . . . thereby produced give imaginative writers a material that is new and vital," writes John S. Christie in *Latino Fiction and the Modernist Imagination: Literature of the Borderlands* (1998, p. 71). This material that Christie discusses appears in most Mexican American writing in the form of a coexistence within the whole of seemingly dichotomous emotions: a hatred and love for parent countries, cultures and histories; a desire to attain the "American Dream" and an absolute loathing of it; a working for a better future via a connection to the past; and a need for acceptance by the status quo along with a self-imposed isolationism resulting from a sense of disconnectedness.

Mexican American poets Carmen Tafolla, Josephine Cásarez, and Trinidad Sánchez, and Mexican American YA writers Diane Gonzales Bertrand, David Rice, and Matt de la Peña, express in their works the language and consequently the politic of the Mexican American, the tongue of the barrio, which at times involves speaking in what Cordelia Candelaria, in her article "Code-Switching as Metaphor in Chicano Poetry" (1998, p. 91), describes as the "six different language systems" of the Mestizo:

- standard edited American English;
- English slang (regional dialects and vernaculars including varieties of black English);
- standard Spanish;
- dialectical Spanish (regional vernaculars including caló);
- English/Spanish or Spanish/English blends of bilingualism;
- an amalgam of pre-American indigenous languages, mostly noun forms of Nahuatl and Mayan.

According to Carl R. Shirley and Paula W. Shirley (1988, pp. xv–xvi), "This occurs in the speech of the bilingual people because a word or phrase in one language most readily occurs to a speaker at the moment of utterance, not because of a lack of knowledge of the other language." In other words, Mestizaje happens naturally. Arteaga believes that "[t]his alternative is not so much racial, as in the synthesis of the mestizo, as it is cultural . . . [It is] an alternative language for the making of alternative space, the third country between the United States and Mexico" (1997, p. 34). The ramifications of such a vision can be interpreted as both negative and positive; and both consequences are encapsulated in the following statement by Arteaga: it is a discourse that "opposes standard English and opposes the canonical literary telos. It conflicts with the authoritative discourse" (1997, p. 74). On the negative side, this overt opposition can be misconstrued as an attempt to subvert the traditional discourse, in this case English. Put another way, this seemingly reactionary act of speaking an alternative language other than the dominant tongue can be seen as separatist in nature. Nothing could be further from the truth, though. This open challenge to the linguistic status quo is a sincere effort to add to America's language portfolio, not to supplant or subjugate. Said another way: Mestizaje is an attempt to demonstrate the multiple linguistic components that make up the great nation of America.

Carmen Tafolla (2004) says as much in her collection of poetry *Sonnets and Salsa*. Tafolla, considered one of the madrinas of Chicano/a poetry, fiercely advocates on behalf of young Mexican American students and their hybrid language in much of her writing. Though *Sonnets and Salsa* is not specifically marketed at Mexican American young adult readers, it is a text that should be made available to them because in it they will find poems that speak directly to them and about them. Many of the poems deal rather candidly with the issues young Mexican Americans face on a daily basis, more than a few of the pieces addressing the language question. In her poetry, Tafolla contends that America is not a monocultural, monolinguistic nation, but one that makes room for all, and key to America's greatness is not merely a recognition of the many differences of its citizens but a genuine appreciation of and love for said differences, language included. In the funds of knowledge-based classroom, and through the use of culturally authentic literature, these differences can be addressed and discussions on stereotypes can unfold, resulting in a better understanding of diversity.

Easier said than done, though. In her poem titled "In Memory of Richi," Tafolla describes an all too common scene for children whose first language is not the dominant English. It is Richi's first day of school. The boy, whose name is pronounced in Spanish beginning with a hard 'r', meets a teacher in the hallway, for whom this is also the first day. The teacher introduces himself to the boy, and Richi tells him his name, at which point the teacher attempts to repeat it, except that he Anglicizes it, calling the boy Ritchie. Proud of his name, the boy corrects the teacher, repeating the correct pronunciation, rolling the "r" "like a round of wealth/and, deep in Spanish tones." At the end of the school day, the teacher calls out to the boy from down the hallway: "Richi," he says. But the boy corrects him a second time:

> the light and wealth all gone
> from his new eyes,
> "No.
> Ritchie."

(p. 67)

The poem's title indicates a passing away, a death. In this instance, it is not the literal death of the boy, but rather the unfortunate demise of a culture due to a relentless assault on his language. More often than not the attack is sub-conscious on the part of the member of the dominant culture, but it is a very real attack, nevertheless. Mexican American students' language and culture are daily invalidated by English-only policies and sentiments in school and without. Richi and others like him understand fully that school is for learning, and they know that ultimately the goal is to earn that education in order to continue successfully in the largely English-speaking worlds of academia and employment. When the linguistic assault is constant, though, children will understand well that theirs is considered a lesser language, and, as Gloria Anzaldúa (1987, p. 80) says in her now-classic work *Borderlands/La Frontera: The New Mestiza*, "Repeated attacks on our native tongue diminish our sense of self."

In a similar vein, David Rice takes up the issue of one language rendering the other ineffective. In the story "Her Other Son," Tommy believes his is one of the more fortunate families in town. "We were rich," he says, because they paid their maid, Catalina, $35 a week rather than the standard $25 (Rice, 2003, p. 14). Catalina lives with Tommy's family during the week, and on the weekends she travels back to the border town of Las Flores to care for her grandsons. At times, the family accompanies Catalina to do some shopping. When Tommy was eight, on a return trip from Las Flores, as they neared the checkpoint at the bridge, Tommy's mother coached her boys on how to answer the border patrolman, who would certainly ask if they were American citizens. When the officer asked the all-important question in a "stern" voice, Tommy panicked and couldn't answer. When his father ordered the boy to answer in the affirmative, Tommy "looked at the chain-link fences with razor wire on top and then at [his] reflection in the border patrol agent's sunglasses, and [he] shook his head." The father decided to answer in his son's stead, saying, "He is my son, and we have been here a lot longer than you have." At which the agent furrowed his brow and asked, "I'm sorry, sir, what was that?" (pp. 18–19). Tommy's father recognized that there is great power in language, and he'd just overstepped with this officer of the law. He'd spoken freely, without the border patrolman's permission. If Tommy's father had continued down this path, he would have surely been pulled aside for a more thorough questioning and the standard search for contraband. With this in mind, the man "clenched the steering wheel and looked toward the sign saying WELCOME TO TEXAS . . . 'He's my son and you're scaring him'" (p. 19). From then onward, on similar return trips, Tommy is practically incapacitated by fear, recalling clearly the officer's abusive tone that put his father in his place. Later in the story, Tommy visits Las Flores one final time, to mourn with Catalina, who has lost one of her grandsons. At the bridge, a border agent asks the now-familiar question, and once more Tommy remains silent (pp. 27–28). He is not the fearful boy of years past, though. He chooses to remain voiceless not because he, too, knows his place in this little linguistic power skirmish but because he is only now beginning to realize his place in the greater world that involves life and death, great joy and great sadness. His silence, this go-round, is the silence of authority.

Unlike Richi/Ritchie, Tommy finds within him the wherewithal to endure the linguistic onslaught that they both confront. So too will young Mexican American readers, who are given every opportunity to see for themselves their lives being presented on the page in the classroom, literature carefully chosen by their teachers, which carries weight with readers. After all, in the classroom power dynamic, teachers are the authority figures, and if they put their stamp of approval on this literature in the same way as they do every other literature, then it must be right and great work.

Another writer who tackles language issues for Mexican Americans is Josephine Cásarez, a San Antonio poet and playwright who writes about her own childhood experiences. In one poem, "Up Against the Wall" (1993), she recalls an almost daily punishment in Mrs. Kelley's elementary classroom, where the child Josephine is ordered by the teacher to stand against the wall as the penalty for one thing or another. It gets to the point when the child "know[s] how many bricks / it took to build this side already" (p. 14). In another of her poems, "Me, Pepa Makes It Big" (1995), Cásarez explains the reason for her daily chastisement: Mrs. Kelley, who expects her students to know how to spell her name correctly, changes the poet's name without the child's permission. "She called me Josephine," in spite of the girl's name being Josefina, but "La Gringa Kelley / Couldn't pronounce it in her Texas drawl" (p. 11). Unlike Richi in Tafolla's poem, Josephine *no se déja*; that is to say, she does not let herself be taken in or taken advantage of. She "lead[s] the rebellion in the fifth grade," by changing her teacher-given name to Pepa, "like my tía, the one with the big feet." Later in the poem, she explains that she will not allow anyone to "keep [her] down, / Keep [her] quiet." She takes back the power of language: "Yolanda became 'Yoli' / Diana became 'Pudgy' / David became 'El Ratón,'" and so on (p. 12). By taking ownership of their language, Mexican American students give themselves permission to put to full use their funds of knowledge in the classroom. They give themselves permission to consider their home and ethnic cultures valid and to draw on them in the school setting. In such cases, language and culture are the means to a better opportunity for academic success.

In Diane Gonzales Bertrand's *Trino's Choice* (1999), readers meet Trino, a middle schooler who is trying, among other things, to reconcile for himself his languages. One day, hiding in a bookstore from Rosca and his fellow thugs, he bumps into Lisana, a school type, who introduces herself. In so doing, she smiles at his use of the word "abuela," Spanish for grandmother. He is glad at her reaction because he "wasn't sure if her type even knew Spanish. In his neighborhood, Spanish and English words mixed together like mud and water. Pieces of two languages often got him in trouble with schoolwork, especially with the *gringo* teachers" (p. 11). The two become friends and decide to come back to the bookstore later for a reading by the poet Emilce Montoya. The first piece the man reads stuns Trino because it "was a blend of Spanish and English, words of the *barrio* people" (p. 38). The boy is bewildered because, as he says to Lisana in reaction to hearing these barrio words being uttered proudly, publicly, "It's different from stuff in school," to which she responds with the question, "Isn't that the best part?" (p. 39). But how could he know the answer? Throughout his education, this boy has been told that his language, that of barrio people, is substandard, second class, and useless in an academic setting. Now aware that his barrio tongue is one of the many languages of poetry, he gains an appreciation for it, and for himself. Mexican American students who are given such an opportunity in the classroom to use their Mestizaje to complete their assignments (reading and writing both) will flourish because they then will understand that they do not exist on the periphery but are an integral part of the whole.

The late Trinidad Sánchez, Jr. did not write specifically for young adults, either, but when he was living, the majority of the people attending his readings were the younger set. In his book of poems *Why Am I So Brown?* (1991), Sánchez asks simple yet elemental questions that arise because of the disconnectedness expressed by the community he is so much a part of. In one of his performances, Sánchez explained the origin of his title poem, "Why Am I So Brown?" Raquel Guerrero, the daughter of one of his friends, came home crying after school one day. During recess, the other children had teased her because of her skin color, and she demanded of her father an answer to that question: why *was* she so brown? Sánchez's poem attempts to answer the innocent's question. In his response, instead of condemning the white children who pointed out her difference and ridiculed her for it, he puts a positive spin on the situation. He tells Raquel that "God made you brown, mi'ja, / color bronce—color of your raza, your people / connecting you to your raíces, your roots" (p. 4). Brown, as a voice, he writes,

> is not a color . . . it is:
> a state of being, a very human texture
> alive and full of song, celebrating—
> dancing to the new world
> which is for everyone.
> (p. 4)

A person's color does not stop at the skin level; it reaches well below the surface, into the person's core. Sánchez believes it to exist in the mind, at the edge of a fingertip's reach, in the sound of celebration, in the act of dancing. And so can be every other color and culture if and when the figurative borders are erased. Sánchez dreams of a new world where questions such as the one posed by young Raquel Guerrero are moot.

In de la Peña's novel *Mexican Whiteboy* (2008), the main character, Danny Lopez, struggles, in part, with his ethnicity. He is a modern-day Mestizo, except that he is Mexican on his father's side and Anglo on his mother's, rather than European Spanish and Mexican Indian:

> Danny's brown. Half-Mexican brown. A shade darker than all the white kids at his private high school, Leucadia Prep . . . Only people [there] who share his shade are the lunch-line ladies, the gardeners, the custodians. But whenever Danny comes down here, to National City—where his dad grew up, where all his aunts and uncles and cousins still live—he feels pale. A full shade lighter. Albino almost.
> Less than.
>
> (p. 2)

During the summer, he and Uno, a black teen he befriends in the neighborhood, hatch a plan to make money. Danny has a great pitching arm, though he doesn't look the part of a solid pitcher, and so they will hustle ball players across town. If Danny can strike them out, then he and Uno win the cash pot; if the batter can get the bat on the ball, the boys lose. They eventually go up against Kyle, a baseball phenom, and it is not to be. Danny cannot strike out Kyle. Even when Uno calls double or nothing, Kyle takes a cut at a curveball and connects for a home run. The boys lose big, and when Barker, one of Kyle's buddies, has collected their winnings, he tells Uno, "Now get your black ass outta here" (p. 238). A fight ensues, and Danny beats Barker to a pulp. The two eventually make their way off the diamond, and Danny revisits what had just taken place:

> The pitches he threw. The swing of Kyle's bat. The money in Barker's hand. The punches he landed. When he stepped off the mound a second ago something died inside of him, because he lost, but now he feels something brand-new taking its place.
>
> (p. 239)

And what is this "brand-new" thing unfurling inside of him? It is the realization that life has nothing to do with him being white or Mexican, or whether he can strike out a batter; it has to do with knowing that he can only be who he is. He tells his cousin Sofia toward the end of the novel, "I'm like me . . . I'm just myself" (p. 241). That is the answer, in essence, that Sánchez offers Rachel Guerrero in his poem: you are brown because you are; own it, plain and simple.

When a Mexican American student does not take ownership of his or her Mexican Americanness, of his or her language and culture, then "[t]he colonial self is present, here and central," writes Arteaga, "the other, there and marginal, absent. The self differs in essence from the other. They are not like us: they are not our color; their god is not God; their beliefs are not true, not science, and so on" (1997, p. 79). There fails to be cohesion within the self, much less among the diverse communities of which Mexican American students are a part.

The greater point that Sánchez makes over and over in his poetry, similar to Arteaga's, Tafolla's, Cásarez's, Bertrand's, Rice's, and de la Peña's, is that there has to be a place in America for multiple discourses, for different tongues. One language might seem at odds with the other, but in order for there ever to be a truly American community, there have to be spaces available for the multitudes of languages that comprise America.

Anzaldúa writes, "I am my language. Until I can take pride in my language, I cannot take pride in myself. Until I can accept as legitimate Chicano Texas Spanish, Tex-Mex and all the other languages I speak, I cannot accept the legitimacy of myself" (1987, p. 59).

In so writing, these Mexican American poets and YA novelists have helped to document the construction and the ongoing development of the Mexican American identity. As Professor Ernesto Padilla (1992, p. xiii) says in his preface to Tafolla's poetry in *Sonnets to Human Beings*, these authors give us the "feeling that we are walking around in the barrio, and we are delighted to meet such interesting people, who talk to us as if we were old friends. They are old friends by the power of magic, the magic of great literature." This magic has everything to do with a new language created by the common man and woman of the barrios; the language is neither strictly Spanish nor strictly English, but a third language, a mix or blending of the two that then becomes the Mexican American's natural language, Mestizaje. In other words, it is a new language come about because Mexican Americans, like the original Mestizos, are an ostracized people that has to forge its own way, force its own space. Mexican Americans are not Mexican, no matter how sincerely they attempt to connect with the mother culture; nor are they American, no matter how hard they work at attaining the status quo. They are forced into hyphenation: Mexican-American, a citizenry of secondary worth, one whose Mexican heritage keeps them from "being" wholly American, and whose Americanness keeps them from being accepted by Mexicans as one of their own. As a result, this bastard race gives birth to its own culture, its own history, and its own language in the form of the Mexican American, which expresses disenchantment, frustration, and ultimately speaks of revolution and victory. There is no need whatsoever, though, for a legitimate citizenry of America to be excluded simply because it is different. The worst that could ever happen to Mexican American students is for their funds of knowledge to be discounted or disqualified simply because the funds, like the students and their language, fall outside of the main. These students bring a wealth of knowledge to the reading table. What a shame indeed, then, when educators ask them to care about literature and their own literacy yet fail to validate their worth by not providing them with culturally relevant texts. When these students neither see nor hear themselves in the texts educators do present to them, when their funds of knowledge are barred from the discussion, their approach to the house of literacy will be a hesitant one, a reluctant one, and they will "turn the key and walk into the empty house, / Alone, like the rest of la raza, / . . . stranger[s] in [their] own home" (Tafolla, 1992, p. 54).

References

Anzaldúa, G. (1987). *Borderlands/la frontera: The new mestiza.* San Francisco, CA: Spinsters/Aunt Lute.

Arteaga, A. (1997). *Chicano poetics: Heterotexts and hybridities.* Cambridge: Cambridge University Press.

Bertrand, D.G. (1999). *Trino's choice.* Houston: Piñata Books.

Burciaga, J.A. (1993). *Drink cultura: Chicanismo.* Santa Barbara, CA: Joshua Odell Editions.

Candelaria, C. (1988). Code-switching as metaphor in Chicano poetry. In G. Fabre (Ed.), *European perspectives on Hispanic literature of the United States* (pp. 91–97). Houston, TX: Arte Público P.

Cásarez, J. (1993). Up against the wall. In A. de Hoyos (Ed.), *Mujeres grandes: Anthology: Número uno* (pp. 14–15). San Antonio, TX: M&A Editions.

Cásarez, J. (1995). Me, Pepa makes it big. In A. de Hoyos (Ed.), *Mujeres grandes: Anthology 2: Número 2* (pp. 11–12). San Antonio, TX: M&A Editions.

Christie, J.S. (1998). *Latino fiction and the modernist imagination: Literature of the borderlands.* New York: Garland.

de la Peña, M. (2008). *Mexican whiteboy.* New York: Delacorte.

Padilla, E. (1992). Preface. In C. Tafolla, *Sonnets to human beings and other selected works* (pp. x–xiii). New York: McGraw-Hill.

Rice, D. (2003). *Crazy loco: Stories.* New York: Speak.

Sanchez, T., Jr. (1991). *Why am I so brown?* Chicago: MARCH/Abrazo Press.

Shirley, C.R. & Shirley, P.W. (Eds.). (1988). *Understanding Chicano literature.* Columbia: University of South Carolina Press.

Tafolla, C. (1992). *Sonnets to human beings and other selected works* (E. Padilla, Ed.). New York: McGraw-Hill.

Tafolla, C. (2004). *Sonnets and salsa.* San Antonio, TX: Wings Press.

Part II

Why Should Teachers Teach YAL?

In the section that follows, our focus shifts from the teen readers of YAL to the motives and responsibilities of the teachers who teach it. While most teachers who select YAL do so primarily to motivate recalcitrant teen readers, it is valid to ask if this reason is sufficient. Should we select student readings based on what we think they will *like* the best? On the one hand, a teacher might reasonably argue that if a student isn't compelled to read the book, it doesn't matter what is assigned. Simple student engagement with the text is a prerequisite to critical thought or a complex emotional response. On the other hand, should canonical texts be abandoned in favor of more contemporary, linguistically accessible YA books that encourage teens to "relate" to characters and plot? How important is personal and emotional growth when contrasted (perhaps unfairly) with intellectual development?

In addition to motives behind simply selecting literature to be read, the literature teacher must also make decisions about how to direct classroom instruction about these books. What is the range of acceptable response to literature? How should a teacher assess student response to YAL? What kinds of classroom activities are appropriate when asking students to interact with YA literature? These questions are among those explored in the section that follows.

Chapter 8

Engaging and Enchanting the Heart

Developing Moral Identity through Young Adult Fantasy Literature

Aliel Cunningham

In an age of standardized testing and critical analysis, logical reasoning and efferent understanding of texts have understandably come to the forefront of all education spheres—whether scientific, literary, historical—and have even crept into our conception of character education. Rosenblatt (2005) and others have pointed out this out-of-balance proportionate emphasis given to strengthening and developing the logical and efferent side of a child's mind, often at the expense of developing the heart and soul. Our Western bias, inherited from the Enlightenment, prefers knowledge that can be proven—a rational and coherent system of observable, countable facts. Any knowledge that does not come from a logical formula or reasoned analysis is generally regarded with suspicion. We see the same bias in Dickens's *Hard Times* (1854) character, Mr. Gradgrind, who was obsessed with eliminating nonsensical "fancy" from the minds of his students in favor of practical rules and facts.

We would like to think we have come a long way since Dickens's *Hard Times*, written 150 years ago, and in many respects we have. Rosenblatt (and others) brought to our awareness the need for students to play with language as well as dissect it, and appreciate certain texts from an aesthetic perspective rather than a purely analytical one (2005, pp. 101–103). As Rosenblatt goes on to say, "Some (and not only those Gradgrinds who consider literature a dispensable 'frill') fear that primary focus on aesthetic experience means a wallowing in feelings alone. Literature, we can reply, deals with all that is basic in human life, from the most humble to the most ideal" (2005, p. 105). In the course of time, what was begun in the literature classrooms spilled over into the science and math classrooms. Although still harried by standardized testing, educators have learned to value and encourage the creative expressions of the imagination. Parents too have become more interested in their children reading widely, not just reading textbooks and finishing homework assignments.

Over the past few decades, parents and educators alike have begun anew to address yet another aspect of education that is lacking in a purely rationalistic mode of education—that of developing the character or moral identity of the child. Morals are hard to argue from a logical standpoint. They are hard to deduce from a mathematical formula. They are slippery things, changing their form from culture to culture. But there they remain, from Aristotle's time until now, essential to the well-rounded education of future generations in every culture around the world. In the Western tradition, this heavy educational burden has often fallen to the domain of the literature classroom—everything from character development to cultural appreciation to societal injustice has been within the purview of the literature teacher. According to reading expert David Russell (1970, p. 241), the literature class should provide the reader "with such opportunities [as] enable him [sic] to better understand himself as a person, as a member of a human community not circumscribed by a narrow extent of time and space, and as the possessor of a continually developed heritage of literature that can help give direction to his aesthetic and moral life."

Even outside the literature class, lifelong learning goals that parents and educators have set for children include recognizing life options, assuming responsibility for actions, demonstrating consideration for individual differences, using a wide variety of strategies for managing complex issues, reflecting on their roles as community contributors, monitoring and evaluating their progress, and creating a positive vision for themselves (Gaddy et al., 1996, p. 95). Considering these goals, it has always been an enigma to me why some of the best (and undeniably most captivating) literature for developing such "moral identity" has been largely overlooked by parents and educators alike. I speak, of course, of young adult fantasy literature.

This is not to say that a plethora of articles and essays has not been generated on the topics of Harry Potter, *The Lord of the Rings*, *The Golden Compass*, *The Spiderwick Chronicles*, Earthsea, and Narnia—many of them written by scholars in a tone of bemused curiosity as to what psychological phenomenon could be the source of their universal popularity with kids and adults alike. However, few articles have dealt seriously with evaluating fantasy's educational value in terms of developing character and moral identity, both in the classroom and out of it. This chapter attempts to give a brief overview of young adult fantasy literature, define what it is (and more importantly what it is *not*), and explore the concept of moral or character development that I argue fantasy, more than many other young adult genres, can encourage.

Defining Fantasy

Before we can discuss the potential hazards or benefits of fantasy, it would be helpful to have a working definition. However, if you asked 30 different fantasy authors to list the basic components of fantasy, you would likely get 30 different responses. Likewise if you asked readers of fantasy what makes the stories so compelling. Like all genres, fantasy literature has its epics and its duds. This is important to keep in mind because, as Peter Kreeft points out, before a story can affect us it must engage us: "Before a movie or a book can please, inform, challenge, satisfy, educate, edify, or relax us, it must fascinate us enough to persuade us to give it some of our time, that is, our life, our lifetime" (quoted in Baehr & Baehr, 2005, p. 139).

For my purposes, the definition of fantasy will center more on what it accomplishes, rather than on the specific details of which it consists. However, there are some specific components that are fairly common, if not ubiquitous. Some of these have been explored in detail in other articles, but in brief here are some surface generalizations that are used to set fantasy stories apart from other genres:

1   Fantasy stories are usually set in a separate or parallel world.
2   In this parallel world, there is usually the presence of non-human creatures that can talk, reason and interact with humans as autonomous characters.
3   Fantasy stories almost always utilize some aspect of the magical, miraculous, or supernatural.
4   Many fantasy plots are centered on a meaningful quest or journey during which the main character matures, gains wisdom/insight, or comes of age.
5   Virtually all fantasy stories have moral language woven throughout them from beginning to end—whether implicitly or explicitly—identifying and revealing that which is good and evil, brave and cowardly, just and unjust, noble and treacherous.

Many have overlooked fantasy literature with the mistaken notion that the genre tends to be simplistic and escapist in nature or is "mere" entertainment. Others have failed to see any practical value in fantasy's unwieldy plots and fantastical characters. In this chapter, these objections and others are reviewed and discussed. I will then look at six different ways fantasy literature can be used to reveal, explore, and shape the moral identity of teen readers.

Fantasy as First Things

> I am concerned with a certain way of looking at life, which was created in me by the fairy tales, but has since been merely ratified by the mere facts.
> (Chesterton, 1908/1995, p. 50)

In almost every culture, there is a canon of "first" stories in the form of nursery rhymes, lullabies, or fairy tales. These stories tell children about the nature of the world and who they are in that world. Why do we start our children cutting their teeth on such fantastical stories as *The Three Little Pigs, Goldilocks, Snow White, Cinderella, Little Red Riding Hood, Aesop's Fables,* and *The Frog Prince?* My contention is that these first stories are fantastical in nature because, whatever else fantasy stories have in common, it is this: they speak in the language of "first things," of that which is foundational, essential, or central to our perspective and worldview. In every logical deduction about the world, you must start with your set of premises. Without those "first" stated premises, all the logical reasoning and facts in the world remain as useless as a recipe without ingredients. These first things are the building blocks by which we construct our framework of identity and reality.

Fantasy is the genre of first things, and we discover that we do not abandon our need of them when we leave the nursery. As fantasy author Ursula K. Le Guin points out,

> The great fantasies, myths and tales . . . speak *from* the unconscious *to* the unconscious, in the *language* of the unconscious. Though they use words, they work the way music does: they short-circuit verbal reasoning, and go straight to the thoughts that lie too deep to utter. They cannot be translated fully into the language of reason, but only a Logical Positivist, who also finds Beethoven's Ninth Symphony meaningless, would claim that they are therefore meaningless. They are profoundly meaningful, and usable—practical—in terms of ethics; of insight; of growth.
>
> (Quoted in Dickerson & O'Hara, 2006, p. 174)

Le Guin illustrates that there are some essential qualities of humanity and identity for which reason, deduction, and analysis alone prove to be inadequate in uncovering or fashioning. Much as we would like to in the Western tradition, it is very hard to reason your way to a moral identity without first having an internalized concept of the world as it *should* be. It is precisely at this point where fantasy excels. In its ability to portray a picture of how the world should be, how it has fallen from that ideal, and what it will take to right what has been wronged, fantasy has few rivals. You cannot teach morals or character like you teach geometry or physics. Understanding of moral issues—justice, patience, bravery, forgiveness—is not something you can assess with a multiple-choice test. However, what you cannot accomplish through didactic teaching and testing you can engage and explore through the lens of the heart—that is, the imagination and imaginative literature. Terry Pratchett, another well-known sci-fi author, echoed this sentiment about fantasy while speaking at the annual Booksellers Association Conference:

> This is part of the dangerous process of growing up . . . So, let's not get frightened when the children read fantasy. It is the compost for the healthy mind. It stimulates the inquisitive nodes. It may not appear as "relevant" as books set more firmly in the child's environment, but there is some evidence that a rich internal fantasy life is as good and necessary for a child as healthy soil is for a plant, for much the same reasons.
>
> (Quoted in Pierce, 2001, p. 66)

Defining Bad Fantasy

Before we get too far in our discussion, I would like to state a broad caveat. I am not arguing that any book that falls into the fantasy genre automatically has the best qualities of fantasy, or contains the best tools for developing a child's moral identity. Anything in the literary world that becomes popular will have its sincere imitators. There is a lot of literature published under the fantasy label that misses the mark in either engaging the imagination or challenging the mind. These stories are often very forgettable, falling into the trap of stereotyping characters and placing them in a flat world that feels like a thinly disguised copy of something we have read before. In these stories, the magic of enchantment has no ring of truth to it. When judging what is "good" fantasy and "bad" fantasy, you get to the heart of one of its hallmarks—the ability to cause us to stand in awe and marvel, the ability to enchant our hearts.

Fantasy author Philip Pullman demonstrates his deftness in invoking such wonder in the award-winning novel *The Golden Compass* (1996, p. 300):

> Above and ahead of them the Aurora was blazing, with more brilliance and grandeur than she had ever seen. It was all around, or nearly, and they were nearly a part of it. Great swathes of incandescence trembled and parted like angels' wings beating; cascades of luminescent glory tumbled down invisible crags to lie in swirling pools or hang like vast waterfalls.

All fantasy authors know how crucial evoking wonder is, but, ironically, the stories that make little impact are those that focus on developing that aspect almost to the exclusion of all else, including plot and characters: "In such cases, overreaching brings down all, for the attempt to make everything wonder-filled cannot be sustained. To emphasize everything, of course, is ultimately to emphasize nothing" (Senior, 2001, p. 87). The obvious point that follows this realization of the incredible power enchantment can hold over the reader, especially the young adult reader, is to realize that it can be used to glorify both good and evil. Just because a given author is a talented writer with this capacity to evoke wonder, that does not automatically mean that the moral vision he or she is portraying is a sound one. However, the fantasy genre has been shaped in such a way that it would be a difficult task to write an effective amoral fantasy that was not self-contradictory. I do not presume to say which fantasy authors are always the "right" ones, but rather aim to encourage educators, scholars, and parents to do some of their own exploring of the moral visions in fantasy literature.

Isn't Fantasy Escapism?

Another charge that has often been leveled against the fantasy genre (particularly by educators) is that fantasy does not encourage students to face up to the real world with its real-life scenarios, moral dilemmas, and social and cultural dynamics. The argument can be paraphrased: how do you expect children to grow up and deal with the harsh realities of life when their heads are filled with fluff and nonsense like unicorns, magic wands, and moving castles? As far as I can tell, those who would make this argument have nothing against fantasy *per se*. It is a harmless enough diversion, they would agree, like watching cartoons or visiting the circus. But it has little to say when it comes to the business of growing up, or of understanding the world around us, or of solving the mystery of who we are. Hence, fantasy is viewed as a tempting place to run and hide when you need an escape from the trials, hardships, and disappointments encountered at every phase of life.

To those who hold this view, I would give a two-pronged rebuttal. First, I would concede the point that fantasy can be a tempting escape from your own problems, but I would counter the assumption that this is inherently a bad thing. Fantasy has the ability to bring you into a mythical universe fraught with problems of its own. It engages your imagination and takes you on a journey with tough moral choices and battles around every corner, and ends up returning you to your own troubles with a fresh set of tools to deal with them. As Mass and Levine (2001, pp. 19–20) reflect in their introduction to fantasy,

> Fantasy literature has no more element of "escapism" than any other work of fiction. In fact, good fantasy literature is often based around the notions of exploring social, political, personal, and even spiritual issues. Exploring this new world allows readers to re-formulate their opinion on any number of things. Rather than escaping, the journey through this other world is often a vehicle for the exploration of questions that have a direct bearing on the real world.

The second point to be addressed is the question of whether fantasy really has so little resemblance to our own world. From its label, it is understandable why so many have a misunderstanding as to what good fantasy emulates. It does not experiment with how far it can distance itself from the "real" world. Instead, quality fantasy literature makes deliberate connections to what would be familiar and true of readers' world experiences. In fact, Dickerson and O'Hara (2006, p. 203) in their review of fantasy literature have said, "we have contended that all stories must contain some grains of truth, or they cannot stand as a story." Fantasy allows us to see what is true and familiar in a way that forces us see it anew—and maybe really for the first time. As William Senior, a professor at Broward College, notes in his essay "An Integral Sense of Wonder," "Fantasy invokes wonder by making the impossible seem familiar and the familiar new and strange" (2001, p. 80).

C.S. Lewis, renowned author of the Narnia series, once remarked on the need for fantasy by making the argument that "spells are used for breaking enchantments as well as for inducing them. And you and I have need of the strongest spell that can be found to wake us from the evil enchantment of worldliness which has been laid upon us for nearly a hundred years" (quoted in Baehr & Baehr, 2005, p. 116). By "worldliness," I take Lewis to mean familiarity with the world in a cynical sense. As the old saying goes, familiarity tends to breed contempt. I have noticed this curious facet of human nature in my own reading habits. Give me a story that is close to my own experience (a teacher who moves to a small, Midwestern town to pursue graduate studies), and I will immediately start looking for ways in which my story differs from that of the teacher in the story. I will start evaluating whether the author's style and description are true to life or lack authenticity. However, by the same token, give me a story about a princess who lives in another world and is imprisoned against her will because she teaches birds to talk and become spies for her kingdom, and I will immediately start looking for ways to connect my understanding of the world with hers. Fantasy creates that space between us and the world that allows us to rediscover ancient truths and see old things for the first time.

Pullman addresses this notion when he discusses the *His Dark Materials* trilogy:

> Lyra and Will and the other characters are meant to be human beings like us, and the story is about a universal human experience, namely growing up. The "fantasy" parts of the story were there as a picture of aspects of human nature, not as something alien and strange. For example, readers have told me that the daemons, which at first seem so utterly fantastic, soon become so familiar and essential a part of each character that they, the readers, feel as if they've got a daemon themselves. And my point is that they have, that we all have. It's an aspect of our personality that we often overlook, but it's there. That's what I mean by realism: I was using the fantastical elements to say something that I thought was true about us and about our lives.
>
> (Quoted in Dickerson & O'Hara, 2006, p. 202)

Fantasy literature is an interesting paradox in that it has the ability to transport you to another world and engage and fascinate your senses in that other world, all the while drawing upon the real world for its meaning and depth, and ultimately its very shape. Jules Zanger (2001, p. 36), a professor of English at Southern Illinois University, commented on this facet of the genre: "Fantasy . . . always exists in a symbiotic relationship with reality and its conventionalized representations, depending on it for its existence and at the same time commenting upon it, criticizing it, and illuminating it."

The structure of the fantastic world comes from the same bricks and mortar that make up our everyday world. If it is a good fantasy story, it has an internal order and logic, and an inner consistency. So the reader soon discovers that he or she has not really escaped the bonds of logic and rationality by slipping into a fantasy; it is simply disguised under a new face and name.

If that's the case, some may wonder, why bother with fantasy at all? Ah! Because there is often a transcendent magic discovered in that other world that can be brought back with the reader-traveler and gives him or her new insights into the everyday world. This magic is what C.S. Lewis alluded to when he said, "[the fairy tale] . . . far from dulling or emptying the actual world, gives it a new dimension of depth. [The reader] does not despise real woods because he has read of enchanted woods: the reading makes all real woods a little enchanted" (Lewis, 1966, pp. 29–30).

You may wonder why I am separating the fantasy genre from the rest of young adult literature. Does not most young adult fiction literature have many of these same merits? This chapter is not trying to argue that fantasy is the only or the best young adult literature; I only argue that it deserves a place in young adult education because of its hallmark qualities which uniquely qualify it to work alongside other genres within young adult literature to complete and balance the explorations of the world and the self. In the balance of this chapter, I examine five potential effects that fantasy stories can have on the shaping of readers' understanding of themselves in relationship to other selves and the world—in essence their defined "moral identity." These five effects can be viewed as steps toward developing moral identity: awakening, inspiring, empowering, guiding, and evaluating. These steps are not sequential, but work simultaneously and recursively. They are by no means exclusively the domains of fantasy literature, but each is an example of the potential benefits fantasy literature can bring to the education of the mind and heart of teen readers.

Fantasy Awakens: The Power of Wonder

> In the evanescent delicacy she felt something as profound as she'd felt close to the bear. She was moved by it; it was so beautiful it was almost holy; she felt tears prick her eyes, and the tears splintered the light even further into prismatic rainbows.
>
> (Pullman, 1996, p. 184)

As I've already noted, one of the hallmarks of fantasy literature is the ability to awaken a sense of wonder or enchantment with passages such as the one above from *The Golden Compass*. Many fantasy authors employ depictions of what can almost be called a holy beauty that has been lost or is just beyond the reader's grasp. This simultaneous nearness and elusiveness creates a yearning within the hearts of those who catch a glimpse of its glory—like those watching the final shimmering of a falling star or the last rays of a fiery sunset fading into a darkening horizon. These moments captured in fantasy awaken the soul and call out to the wider world in a longing to discover the wonders of life in all its complexity. We see such moments embodied in Tolkien's characters, the high elves, who are both beautiful and sad. Through them we are made conscious of a lost noble age and a passing beauty.

Once the reader has awakened to wonder and been enchanted with marvels in other worlds, that sense of wonder can become a fresh lens by which to see the actual world and become sensible to the beauty of life, with a renewed sense of its precious and fragile nature. As Tolkien says in his essay on fairy stories,

> Faerie contains many things besides elves and fays, and besides dwarfs, witches, trolls, giants, or dragons: it holds the seas, the sun, the moon, the sky; and the earth and all things that are in it: tree and bird, water and stone, wine and bread, and ourselves, mortal men, when we are enchanted.
> (Tolkien, 1966, p. 9)

Fantasy also awakens our curiosity and our desire to explore. Many schools today include the fostering of "intellectual curiosity" as one of their stated goals in the healthy development of young adults. Fantasy literature fosters this curiosity better than any other genre I know when it invites you to step into unknown realms and explore. Peter Kreeft sums it up this way:

> Why are we fascinated with passages into other worlds? Surely because they are *other*. All otherness is fascinating. Birth, death, God and sex are probably the four most fascinating things in life, for they are all other worlds to us. We seem to be *designed* for otherness, for wonder and surprise, for exploration of new worlds, not just new data.
> (Quoted in Baehr & Baehr, 2005, p. 142)

For those young adults who have become cynical and hardened through their life experiences, fantasy offers what Pullman calls a "'reenchanting' [of] the imagination . . . in a world where many have lost the traditional comforts of religion and the safe haven of a loving family" (Lenz, 2003, p. 54). This idea of reenchanting the imagination reminds me of a story I heard concerning the etymology of the Hebrew word *chanak*. (It is translated in English as "train up.") One of the meanings of this word is influenced by a ritual used by many ancient midwives to entice babies to suck. They would dip a finger in a dish of crushed figs and massage the babies' gums to give them a thirst for their mothers' milk—literally a thirst for life. Fantasy is well suited to serve this same purpose in those who have lost their passion for discovery in life or curiosity in its mysteries. It satisfies a desire for a world that transcends the realm of logic, reason, and the five senses; it satisfies the hunger for mystery and exploration of worlds unknown.

Fantasy Inspires: The Triumph of the Improbable

Fantasy, along with Science Fiction, is a literature of possibilities. It opens the door to the realm of "What If", challenging readers to see beyond the concrete universe and to envision other ways of living and alternative mindsets. Everything in speculative universes, and by association the real world, is mutable.

(Pierce, 2001, p. 65)

Some of my favorite lines in Tolkien's fantasy depict the ringing voice of inspiration and possibility. They read, "Still round the corner there may wait / A new road or a secret gate / And though I oft have passed them by / A day will come at last when I / Shall take the hidden paths that run / West of the Moon, East of the Sun" (Tolkien, c. 1965/1993, p. 308). Do you get the sense of what those lines convey? Any given day, an unlooked-for adventure or possibility may come my way. Fantasy is the literature of hope and optimism in the sense that it opens a window overlooking a horizon of novel possibilities (even impossibilities) perhaps never considered before by the reader. In this atmosphere of astonishing potential, readers are challenged to redraw the lines of what they had considered within the realm of possibility.

Of course, every story has boundaries and every character limitations, but the one aspect of fantasy that inspires its readers to expect the unexpected, count on the improbable, and dare to act beyond the bounds of common sense is the presence of its defining feature—that is to say, magic. When discussing the magical element of the fantasy genre, Mass and Levine (2001, p. 18) describe it this way:

> The focus on the supernatural introduced to readers one of the most ubiquitous elements of fantasy: the invoking of magic . . . [Through magic] the reader can delve into another level of exploration that pushes the very boundaries of what he or she has come to understand about the way the natural world operates.

In the world of fantasy, magic is a deadly serious thing and is never laughed at or explained away (Little, 2001, p. 52). In fact, those who dismiss or ignore it are usually portrayed as being either ignorant or foolish: "no Muggle would admit their key keeps shrinking—they'll insist they just keep losing it. Bless them, they'll go to any lengths to ignore magic, even if it's staring them in the face" (Rowling, 1999a, p. 38). With magic being such a crucial element of fantasy, it may be surprising that its nature is often left vague or unexplained, and descriptions of how it works are rare or completely absent. However, as Chesterton points out, this holds for the actual world as well as the fantasy one: "We can say why we take liberty from a man who takes liberties. But we cannot say why an egg can turn into a chicken any more than we can say why a bear could turn into a fairy prince" (1908/1995, p. 52). It is this mystery behind the magical power that enhances its application of possibility in the real world. The more science reveals about the nature and scope of the universe, the more we marvel at its magic and possibilities.

One way in which fantasy encourages young adults to consider new horizons in their own thinking is the common device of talking animals or magical creatures, often portrayed as comprising other cultures and races. This convention is found in fantasy stories as wide-ranging as the Harry Potter series, *The Chronicles of Narnia*, *The Lord of the Rings*, *His Dark Materials*, *The Spiderwick Chronicles*, *The Goose Girl*, *Eragon*, and *Howl's Moving Castle*. Tolkien once said, "Fairy tales satisfy the desire of men to hold communion with other living things" (1966, p. 13). These stories open the mind and heart to the possibility of embracing those we find very different from ourselves. Fantasy teaches its readers not to be fooled by outward appearance. Instead they are encouraged to discern the heart and discover what possibilities might reside just beneath the surface.

This philosophy of championing the power of possibility comes out in other deeply influential ways. Fantasy accentuates the power of optimism in the face of looming defeat. This is epitomized in Tolkien's *The Return of the King* (c. 1965/1993). His heroic characters repeatedly champion the power of possibility and the rallying of hope in dark situations where others are filled with fear and despair:

> The reason of my waking mind tells me that great evil has befallen and we stand at the end of days. But my heart says nay; and all my limbs are light, and a hope and joy are come to me that no reason can deny. Eowyn, Eowyn, White Lady of Rohan, in this hour I do not believe that any darkness will endure.
>
> (1965/1993, p. 241)

Fantasy heroes usually refuse to accept the status quo or inevitable defeat. They are constantly challenged to come up with creative solutions to escape their present predicaments. For example, in Shannon Hale's *The Goose Girl* (2005), Isi uses her ability to listen and direct the wind to escape from raiders and enemies. Another example can be found in Diana Wynne Jones's *Howl's Moving Castle* (2001). In this story, Sophie (a young girl who has been bewitched to look like an old woman) must use her wits to solve the riddle of Calcifer—the fire demon—and gain her true form again. Mass and Levine echo this observation in a chapter entitled "What is Fantasy?":

> Proponents of the genre argue that not only isn't Fantasy literature dangerous, but it is essential to the stimulation of a person's imagination and creativity. Children often learn the roots of how to think "outside the box" by being exposed to literature that has no boundaries. It is the nurturing of this creative spirit that has led to most of the scientific, medical and even social advancements of modern society. In all of its many guises—fairy tales, mythology, folklore, and modern fiction—fantasy

literature can have a powerful influence on the way people, young or old, look at the world in which they live.

(2001, p. 24)

Fantasy Empowers: Issues of Destiny and Consequences

Harry gripped the edges of the stool and thought. Not Slytherin, not Slytherin. "Not Slytherin, eh?" said the small voice. "Are you sure? . . . Well, if you're sure—better be GRYFFINDOR!"

(Rowling, 1997, p. 121)

The next step is linked closely with the former goal of inspiration—but it takes this idea of possibility out of the realm of magic and puts it into the hands of the hero. Fantasy rarely portrays characters as victims. The characters are often given tasks to accomplish and endowed with certain gifts and friends to accomplish their mission:

Fantasy, more than any other genre, is a literature of empowerment . . . The catch—there is always a catch—is that empowerment brings trials. Good novels in this genre never revolve around heroes who, once they receive the "Spatula of Power," call the rains to fill the dry well, end the war and clear up all acne.

(Pierce, 2001, p. 66)

Here, Tamora Pierce, a fantasy author herself, highlights the point that magic in fantasy rarely solves all your problems; in fact, it usually works to the hero's disadvantage because the villain's magic powers are almost always more potent than the main character's. So, empowerment in fantasy does not relate nearly as much to magic as to plots in which the characters are put in control of their destiny in a way that holds them accountable for their choices.

Some critics of fantasy may criticize this aspect of empowerment because they could argue that some readers don't really have control over what happens in their lives. However, some experts, like Pierce (2001, p. 63), believe that young adults respond "to the idealism and imagination in fantasy, and that genre inspires and empowers them with hope and optimism." The underdog heroes in fantasy literature are much like the main characters in other genres: the odds are stacked against them. What set fantasy heroes apart, however, are the explicit powers, weapons, gifts, tools, or guides they are often given to see them through their journey. These gifts can be seen as representing tools of empowerment, tools that give the characters (and the readers) a choice in how they will face their enemies.

Complicating this picture of empowerment in fantasy is the prevalence of prophecy, character destiny, and the influence of fate. These characteristics are more explicit in some stories than others, but there are numerous examples of heroes who have a destiny to fulfill: Lyra in *The Golden Compass* (1996), Frodo in *The Lord of the Rings*, Arren in *Earthsea*, the four children in *The Chronicles of Narnia*, and, of course, Harry Potter. In the final book of the Harry Potter series, *Harry Potter and the Deathly Hallows*, this destiny and expectation are made crystal clear when Scrimgeour, the Minister of Magic, asks, "Did [Dumbledore] wish to give you that sword, Potter, because he believed, as do many, that you are the one destined to destroy He-Who-Must-Not-Be Named?" (Rowling, 2007, p. 129). In fantasy stories, the presence of prophecy seems to speak more to the purpose and impact of a life than it does of mere future knowledge. Through the prophecies or destinies, the characters are endowed with a sense of purpose and heightened realization that their actions and choices have consequences that will have a dramatic impact on the universe.

The way these characters interact with these foretold prophecies or inherited destinies sets up an intricate and elusive web of cause and effect. Whether the characters hear of the prophecies spoken about them or not, and how such knowledge affects their decisions and understanding of who they are in relation to others in the story, is a complex trail to follow. In some cases, as in *Voyage of the Dawn Treader* (Lewis, 1952), a prophecy serves as an encouragement: "Knowing the prophecy, and sensing he was destined for this great end, gave him the courage to keep sailing to the utter East" (Neal, 2007, p. 207). In *The Lion, the Witch, and the Wardrobe* (Lewis, 1950/1978), a prophecy makes Lucy a kidnap target for Tumnus, and later it protects Edmund. Likewise, Lyra in *The Golden Compass* is affected by a prophecy because those who know about it are either her instant friends or her enemies. Prophecy has a similar effect in the Harry Potter series, where knowledge about Potter's potential destiny makes him a target for Voldemort and his Death Eaters and simultaneously earns him powerful friends among the Order of the Phoenix.

Whatever their eventual role in the story, the presence of prophecies in each case counters the idea that these central characters have fallen into their present role by accident or coincidence. Fantasy stories are interwoven with the idea that our lives are purposeful and our actions have consequences that have an impact not only on our own future but on the futures of others.

This idea of choice and consequence is seen best in those characters who betray innocent people. We see it in Edmund's decision to go to the White Witch and the chain of consequences set in motion because of that decision (Lewis, 1950/1978). Similarly, we see the consequences for Peter Pettigrew when he betrays Harry Potter's parents and therefore Harry grows up an orphan. Harry's godfather, Sirius, takes Peter to task, saying, "You sold Lily and James to Voldemort . . . YOU SHOULD HAVE DIED RATHER THAN BETRAY YOUR FRIENDS, AS WE WOULD HAVE DONE FOR YOU!" (Rowling, 1999b, p. 375).

These instances of betrayal serve to accentuate the potential that we have for changing the future—for good or for evil. The reader gets a sense of his or her own power to affect circumstances and surroundings. Within fantasy stories (not to mention the real world) there are battles to be fought against injustice, cruelty, cowardice, and apathy. The reader sees that the main character is given both the tools and a mission in which they must succeed, or die trying. Without a sense of purpose, there is little basis on which to construct a moral conception of the world:

> [Young adults'] minds are flexible, recognizing few limits. Here the seeds are sown for the great vision, those that will change the future for us all. We give our charges goals, heroes whose feats they can emulate, knowledge of the past, but they also need fuel to spark and refine ideas, the same kind of fuel that fires idealism. That fuel can be found—according to Jung, Bettelheim, Harding, and Joseph Campbell—in the mighty symbols of myth, fairy tales, dreams, legends—and fantasy. Haven't we felt their power? . . . Arthur and Dr. King.
>
> (Pierce, 2001, p. 64)

Fantasy Guides: Navigating a Moral Universe

> "All I can say is that all of us, humans, witches, bears, are engaged in a war already, although not all of us know it. Whether you find danger on Svalbard or whether you fly off unharmed, you are a recruit, under arms, a soldier."
>
> (The Witch in Pullman, 1996, p. 270)

Once the reader of fantasy has been awakened to the wonder of living life, inspired by its possibilities, empowered by its sense of power and purpose, then this next aspect of fantasy answers the culminating question—what is all of it for? The moral compass (no pun intended) of the fantasy universe is set by what the author points to as "true north." This may vary widely depending on the author (Lewis versus Pullman would be the clichéd case in point), but one thing they all have in common is that there is a "right" side and a "wrong" side. Many have criticized fantasy for being too simplistic, too black and white. To a degree, I would say that criticism is fair. Most fantasy stories are not postmodern in the sense of portraying a relative morality within its thematic material. Within the moral universe of the fantasy realm you can usually find characters who possess a wholesome goodness and others who have an unhealthy meanness; as well as characters who embody the greatest good or, on the flip side, the darkest evil. Dickerson and O'Hara (2006, p. 203) make this point when discussing *The Golden Compass*: "Pullman's story also suggests that the battle involves moral choices, and that this morality is not defined subjectively, but exists in the fabric of the universe."

One excerpt from *Harry Potter and the Order of the Phoenix* illustrates the pervasiveness of morality throughout the story to the extent that even the "dark" characters make moral judgements: "'You do not seek to kill me, Dumbledore?' called Voldemort, his scarlet eyes narrowed over the top of the shield. 'Above such brutality, are you?'" (Rowling, 2003, p. 814). And later, when the servant of Voldemort is talking: "'A foolish young man I was then, full of ridiculous ideas about good and evil . . . Lord Voldemort showed me how wrong I was. There is no good and evil, there is only power, and those too weak to seek it'" (quoted in Dickerson and O'Hara, 2006, p. 246). In this extract we see the view that there is no such thing as good and evil satirized in the mouth of a villain. Without clear delineations between good and evil actions, the world of fantasy crumbles, losing its power and allure.

The pervasiveness of a moral order in the fantasy universe is its essential organizing element. When the movie version of *The Lord of the Rings* was first released, several articles addressed the question of why it was attracting such a large and enthusiastic following. One of the reasons given was this tendency of fantasy literature to portray the universe as having an ordered structure. This does not mean that there is no danger or chaos, or that there are no ambiguous characters whose true nature is not revealed or whose actions have both positive and negative consequences. It means that there is an implicit belief in a good that must be preserved at all costs and an evil that has to be fought at every turn. As Dumbledore tells his students after the death of Cedric in *Harry Potter and the Goblet of Fire* (quoted in Dickerson and O'Hara, 2006, p. 247): "'if the time should come when you have to make a choice between what is right and what is easy . . . remember Cedric Diggory.' Moral right is not defined by personal convenience. It is a choice that must be made."

In the fantasy genre, moral categorization is inescapable. Not only is one side portrayed as having the moral high ground and the other as the evil aggressor, but they are almost always at war. In fantasy literature the battle-ground, in all its forms, is the place where the moral character of each hero is tested and revealed. Another benefit of the structure of morality in fantasy stories is in satisfying the universal need for justice. This cry for justice is one that is heard on every news channel, and in every home; it is heard in the highest and the lowest court. It is the cry of all who battle racism, poverty, oppression, and terrorizing violence the world over. Whose claim to justice is valid? Whose rights are more important? What is fair? These questions raise issues that shape the moral identity perhaps more than any other. Fantasy literature often grapples with them, and rarely concludes with moral ambi-guity. Such endings satisfy our sense of justice: "stories help bridge the gap until such a time when our own world will be set right, evil defeated, wrongdoers punished and rewards given" (Neal, 2007, p. 210). This kind of conclusion is typical in fantasy literature. As Aragorn tells Eowyn in Tolkien's *The Return of the King*, "Awake! The shadow is gone and all darkness is washed clean!" (c. 1965/1993, p. 144).

Fantasy becomes an effective genre for exploring moral themes because it strips away the veneer of the familiar and the ordinary, and gives the reader distance to view the world iconically. We see ideals lived out in (albeit flawed) heroic characters, fears embodied in dragons, and evil personified in villains. This exploration of ultimate themes in a strange world is key to the magic of fantasy literature. As Mass and Levine (2001, p. 22) point out,

> By creating new worlds and weaving a brand new canvas on which to paint the battle between these forces, fantasy authors free the readers of preconceptions and prejudices. Long standing biases may fall away, and new perspectives can be achieved, helping readers to judge moral standards in a new and objective way. This freedom to think and grow outside of "normalcy," especially when dealing with issues as complex as morality, is one of the primary attractions of fantasy literature.

In the imaginative world of fantasy, magic is often seen through the lens of morality—almost as if you can see the nature of the characters' hearts through their use (or misuse) of magical powers. The reader participates in this struggle as he or she follows the heroic characters trying to navigate their way through obstacles and decide who to trust and which side to join.

However, it is never easy to discern which side is "right" and who is trustworthy. There is a cautionary note in every adventure to be wary of the "dark side," because it is so easy to fall under its charms. As Voldemort tells Harry, "'See what I have become?' the face said. 'Mere shadow and vapor . . . I have form only when I can share another's body . . . but there have always been those willing to let me into their hearts and minds'" (Rowling, 1997, p. 293). In several instances there are clear repercussions for failing to be discerning when it comes to allowing the dark side to influence judgement or manipulate words and actions: Ginny Weasley telling her secrets to Tom Riddle's diary, Edmund trusting the White Witch, Enna falling in love with her captor in *Enna Burning* (Hale, 2004), Lyra trying to save Roger in *The Golden Compass*.

One of the hallmarks of fantasy literature is characters in disguise—Strider as a weather-beaten wanderer, Lyra as a daemon, Sophie as an old woman, the White Witch as a kind queen, and in the Harry Potter series there are innumerable instances of "transmogrification" where one character takes on the likeness of another. Many times these disguises serve to cloak their true identity at first, but those who are discerning can start to see that the true nature of the character eventually will be revealed—no matter how clever his or her disguise.

These examples appeal to a wide audience in that the stories are some of the most publicized and widely known in the genre, but it doesn't take long to get a sense of the pervasiveness of this strong sense of right and wrong throughout the genre. Two main thrusts of the fantasy plot are to characterize and clarify which side is right and help the hero navigate his or her journey around possible pitfalls or side paths that could lead into the heart of a moral "mirkwood," so to speak, where there is no regard for that which is right and true.

Fantasy Evaluates: There and Back Again

One of the most apt titles for a fantasy story is found in Tolkien when he has Bilbo write a book entitled "There and Back Again: A Hobbit's Adventure." This title is fitting because this is precisely what fantasy literature aims to do— take the reader on an adventure only to return home with hard-earned insight and a clarified sense of purpose and moral identity. In an essay that looks at the major conventions of fantasy literature, William Senior (2001, p. 87) writes, "One popular and pervasive fantasy paradigm centers on a naïve and inexperienced hero who takes a voyage to grow into his or her potential."

Young adult literature specializes in the "coming of age" theme—going through a rite of passage or on a journey, with the characters (and often the readers) growing in the process. In Narnia, the four children grow through their adventures and battles to take their places on thrones as kings and queens. In *The Goose Girl*, a princess must go on a journey where she learns to defend herself and discovers her powers of perception and language before she is ready to take her place as queen. Every year at Hogwarts, Harry has to face ever more dangerous situations and journeys as he matures in his magical expertise and understanding of his purpose.

In the ultimate example, Sam and Frodo leave the Shire to journey toward Mt. Doom and the adventures and dangers that will change and mature them. Finally they return to the Shire, not as humble hobbits, but as wise mentors who have kept company with elves and lords. This theme of "there and back again" comes up repeatedly in fantasy literature, with the idea that you must leave your comfort zone to discover your potential, your purpose, your very identity. Then, when you return home with the battles fought, the adventures survived, and the wisdom gained, you have fresh insight into who you are and the true nature of the world, and a new understanding of your place within it.

The irony is that fantasy is usually considered a children's genre or, at the very least, childish, when the most pervasive theme running through all fantasy stories, like a broad golden streak, is the journey toward adulthood. Jeanne Walker (2001, p. 73) explores this idea:

> As we have seen, fantasy instructs its readers in the norms and truths of an identifiable social community. It portrays these truths as the standard by which adulthood is measured. And adulthood is the valued goal; unlike some kinds of fiction, fantasy does not pretend to present a snapshot of the world that is value-neutral. Far from it. To read fantasy is to be confronted by the fact that if we, the readers of the book, cannot be shaped into adults with the hero, in some sense we will die. In fantasy, death or assent are the two choices.

Why is this so crucial when discussing the shaping of moral identity? This theme of coming of age is coupled with the need for mentors. How do the characters know who they are to become or how they should be changing? Which traits should be shed and which encouraged and developed? As Connie Neal (2007, p. 69) points out, "Mentors help heroes figure out the meaning of what they're going through and keep them moving in the right direction while developing their skills." This hero's journey often personifies the struggles of both mind and soul to navigate the muddy waters of self-knowledge and one's place in a dangerous universe filled with pitfalls and possibilities. As Chesterton (1908/1995, p. 54) comments, "Every man has forgotten who he is. One may understand the cosmos, but never the ego; the self is more distant than any star." Fantasy, at its core, understands perhaps better than any other genre that unless you know the problems and potential buried within yourself, you will never have anything to offer the world around you.

Often there is a mistaken notion that fantasy merely makes for good storytelling, but because of its unrealistic setting or supernatural powers, it has nothing to offer the readers by way of instruction or wisdom that could be applied to the real world. However, not only has fantasy something to offer its readers in the way of character instruction and wise decision-making, but this instruction is often one of its primary motivations. Ursula K. Le Guin made this statement about the genre: "A Fantasy is a journey. It is a journey into the subconscious mind, just as psychoanalysis is. Like psychoanalysis, it can be dangerous, and *it will change you*" (quoted in Mass & Levine, 2001, p. 24; emphasis in original). In one of her stories, one of her characters reflects on the direct implications stories have on the listener. Arren says:

> "The old stories told to children, the myths, began 'As long ago as forever and as far away as Selidor, there lived a prince . . .' And then a moment later it dawns on him that he, himself, was the prince. But in the old stories, that was the beginning; and this seemed to be the end."
>
> (Quoted in Dickerson & O'Hara, 2006, p. 174)

So, as you can see, fantasy does not aim to be harmless in the sense that it has no lasting effect on its reader. The authors want to take the heroic characters *and the readers* on a journey. If they are successful, they will eventually bring their readers home again with an informed psyche that has the ability, as Tolkien says, to "see much of our own world reflected and diffracted, cast in a clear new light" (quoted in Gough, 1999, p. 8).

Conclusion: Speaking the Language of the Invisible Realm

> Fantasy, through the medium of wonder, not only allows us to see things as they aren't; it lets us realize things as they are—from the inside-out.
>
> (Senior, 2001, p. 88)

In the interest of fair play, I want to take a moment to make explicit one of the assumptions upon which this chapter has been built: most parents and teachers have a vested interest in shaping and strengthening a certain kind of moral orientation and discouraging or weakening another. This premise assumes that we want our children to gravitate toward an orientation that will help them distinguish between honesty and lies, bravery and cowardice, kindness and cruelty, wisdom and foolishness, sacrifice and self-centeredness, genuine friendship and its forgery. This assumption presupposes that the moral universe is a real one, albeit an invisible and abstract one. I say this because it brings us back to the question: what "good" can reading fantasy stories do us? If we assume that the moral realm is a real one where real battles are taking place every day for how our young people's characters and hearts will be shaped, then it must also follow that one of the best ways to influence that which is invisible to the eye is to speak the language of the invisible—through the eye of the imagination.

This idea of a real world that is invisible to the naked eye (or to the uninitiated) is deeply embedded in fantasy literature. In fact, there are several examples in the fantasy stories I have mentioned in this chapter that include this concept of an invisible realm that is real, but often ignored. In *Harry Potter and the Sorcerer's Stone* we read:

> The people who hurried by didn't glance at it. Their eyes slid from the big bookshop on one side to the record shop on the other as if they couldn't see the Leaky Cauldron at all. In fact, Harry had the most peculiar feeling that only he and Hagrid could see it.
>
> (Rowling, 1997, p. 68)

The magical world of Harry Potter is invisible to the Muggles (non-magical people)—not because they can't see it, but more often because they don't want to see. In Narnia, the same idea is illustrated in *The Last Battle*, where Aslan says of the dwarves who think they have been trapped in a stable and refuse to see the sky and fields around them: "They will not let me help them. They have chosen cunning instead of belief. Their prison is only in their own minds, yet they are in that prison; and so afraid of being taken in that they cannot be taken out" (Lewis, 1956/1994, p. 148). Lastly, we read on the jacket of *The Spiderwick Chronicles*, "There's much you need to know, so read carefully. There is an invisible world around us and we hope that you, dear reader, will open your eyes to it" (DiTerlizzi & Black, 2004).

In this modern era of political correctness, there is a real fear of even mentioning the topic of educating for moral character or moral identity, let alone discussing the underlying philosophies and complex issues that are necessarily bound up in such notions. Understandably, there is some hesitation to take character education seriously, as it is often conflated with indoctrination or religious education. So, this chapter has been addressed to those brave souls who have decided that educating the heart is worthwhile. For once you start looking at fantasy with more than a patronizing glance that expects no more than a cute, inventive story, once you dig deeply into its paradigms and prevalent themes, a surprising concept begins to emerge. Far from being merely a cute story with witches and wizards, fantasy literature is interested in ultimate things: mortality, eternity, beauty, love, belonging, wonder, sacrifice, and community. Anything that does not pass this test of endurance is cast aside in fantasy as unworthy. Le Guin echoes this sentiment when she argues:

> For fantasy is true, of course. It isn't factual, but it is true. Children know that. Adults know it too, and that is precisely why many of them are afraid of fantasy. They know that its truth challenges, even threatens, all that is false, all that is phony, unnecessary, and trivial in the life they have let themselves be forced into living. They are afraid of dragons because they are afraid of freedom.
>
> (Quoted in Dickerson & O'Hara, 2006, p. 258)

Whether it is "the grey havens" of *The Lord of the Rings*, or "the last battle" in *The Chronicles of Narnia*, or "the republic of heaven" in *The Golden Compass*, most fantasies end on this reverent note for that which is ultimately most important in life. At the conclusion of this chapter, I would like to invite readers to enter the invisible landscape that encompasses the dense jungles and rocky terrain of growing up and growing into one's full potential. Imagine what tools and experiences you would want your child to be equipped with in order for him or her to come home safely on the other side. I suggest that one of the essential tools—along with logical deduction, critical analysis, scientific experimentation, historical knowledge, and plain common sense—is a reflective and inspired imagination. The contention of this chapter is that one of the best diets that the reader's imagination can feast upon to promote healthy, well-rounded character traits and moral insights includes a large dose of fantasy—because it speaks in the language of the invisible. In the words of Dickerson and O'Hara (2006, p. 258), "The myth-maker, the teller of fairy tales, and the writer of fantasy all may speak profoundly to the human soul. They do so through art, and imagery, including the magic in many of its forms, and as such they speak directly to the soul through the imagination."

In my own experience, fantasy literature, more than any other, has taught me to look at all of life as an unfolding story and a meaningful drama. Through my research on this topic, I have discovered that I am not the only one to respond to fantasy in this way. Again in the words of Dickerson and O'Hara (2006, p. 253), "That's why stories engage us, because the space between 'Once Upon a Time' and 'The End' is where we live our lives." I invite you to explore fantasy young adult literature and consider how it might help adolescents in your life live more fully.

References

Baehr, J. & Baehr, T. (2005). *Narnia beckons*. Nashville, TN: Broadman & Holman.

Chesterton, G.K. (1908/1995). *Orthodoxy*. San Francisco, CA: Ignatius Press.

Dickens, C. (1854). *Hard times*. London: Bradbury & Evans.

Dickerson, M. & O'Hara, D. (2006). *From Homer to Harry Potter: A handbook on myth and fantasy*. Grand Rapids, MI: Brazos Press.

DiTerlizzi, T. & Black, H. (2004). *The Spiderwick chronicles*. New York: Simon and Schuster Children's Publishing.

Gaddy, B., Hall, W., & Marzano, R.J. (1996). *School wars: Resolving our conflicts over religion and values*. San Francisco, CA: Jossey-Bass.

Gough, J. (1999). Tolkien's creation myth in the *Silmarillion*—northern or not? *Children's Literature in Education*, 30 (1), 8.

Hale, S. (2004). *Enna burning*. New York: Bloombury USA Children's Books.

Hale, S. (2005). *The goose girl*. New York: Bloomsbury USA Children's Books.

Jones, D. W. (2001). *Howl's moving castle*. New York: Green Willow Books.

Lenz, M. (2003). Story as a bridge to transformation: The way beyond death in Philip Pullman's *The Amber Spyglass*. *Children's Literature in Education*, 34 (1), 47–55.

Lewis, C.S. (1950/1978). *The lion, the witch, and the wardrobe*. New York: HarperCollins.

Lewis, C.S. (1952). *Voyage of the Dawn Treader*. London: Geoffrey Bles.

Lewis, C.S. (1956/1994). *The last battle*. New York: HarperCollins.

Lewis, C.S. (1966). On three ways of writing for children. In *Of other worlds: Essays and stories*. New York: Harcourt, Brace, and World.

Little, E. (2001). Re-evaluating some definitions of fantasy. In W. Mass & S.P. Levine (Eds.), *Literary movements and genres: Fantasy* (pp. 52–62). San Diego, CA: Greenhaven Press.

Mass, W. & Levine, S.P. (Eds). (2001). *Literary movements and genres: Fantasy*. San Diego, CA: Greenhaven Press.

Neal, C. (2007). *Wizards, wardrobes, and wookies*. Downers Grove, IL: Intervarsity Press.

Pierce, T. (2001). Fantasy books for adolescents inspire and empower. In W. Mass & S.P. Levine (Eds.), *Literary movements and genres: Fantasy* (pp. 63–68). San Diego, CA: Greenhaven Press.

Pullman, P. (1996). *The golden compass*. New York: Alfred A. Knopf.

Rosenblatt, L. (2005). *Making meaning with texts*. Portsmouth, NH: Heinemann.

Rowling, J.K. (1997) *Harry Potter and the sorcerer's stone*. New York: Scholastic Press.

Rowling, J.K. (1999a) *Harry Potter and the chamber of secrets*. New York: Scholastic Press.

Rowling, J.K. (1999b) *Harry Potter and the prisoner of Azkaban*. New York: Scholastic Press.

Rowling, J.K. (2003) *Harry Potter and the Order of the Phoenix*. New York: Scholastic Press.

Rowling, J.K. (2007). *Harry Potter and the deathly hallows*. New York: Scholastic Press.

Russell, D.H. (1970). *The dynamics of reading*. Toronto: Ginn-Blaisdell.

Senior, W. (2001). An integral sense of wonder. In W. Mass & S.P. Levine (Eds.), *Literary movements and genres: Fantasy* (pp. 79–97). San Diego, CA: Greenhaven Press.

Tolkien, J.R.R. (c. 1965/1993). *The return of the king.* Boston, MA: Houghton Mifflin.

Tolkien, J.R.R. (1966). On fairy-stories. In *The Tolkien reader.* New York: Random House.

Walker, J.M. (2001). Fantasy allows children to question the status quo. In W. Mass & S.P. Levine (Eds.), *Literary movements and genres: Fantasy* (pp. 69–77). San Diego: Greenhaven Press.

Zanger, J. (2001). Fantasy literature both reflects and denies reality. In W. Mass & S.P. Levine (Eds.), *Literary movements and genres: Fantasy* (pp. 35–45). San Diego, CA: Greenhaven Press.

Chapter 9

Beyond the Comics Page

Pedagogical Opportunities and Challenges in Teaching Graphic Novels

Lisa Schade Eckert

This chapter examines the ways in which teachers are, and are not, using young adult graphic novels in literacy instruction. I analyze the results of a survey I distributed in the spring, summer, and fall of 2008 to secondary school English teachers in which I asked, "Do you teach graphic novels?" and "Please explain why or why not." I added these questions to a larger survey about literacy teaching practices almost as an afterthought; they seemed very straightforward, and I naïvely felt the results would be somewhat predictable. With the publication of many research and pedagogical journal articles in recent years touting the viability, flexibility, and credibility of including graphic novels in English language arts instruction, I was certain the results would indicate that a large percentage of teachers were at least experimenting with these texts. What I found when the results came in, however, was quite the opposite.

The surprising and troubling finding from this survey is that few teachers reported using graphic novels in their classrooms, and a large percentage of teachers who responded supported canonical and traditional pedagogies, even in light of decades of research indicating that students can, and should, engage in a much wider variety of literate behaviors in an intentional, critical way. As a teacher-educator at a state land grant institution, it is my responsibility to inspire pre-service teachers to develop and expand their pedagogical repertoires and professional identities, but it is also my responsibility to portray the "state of education" they will be entering as student teachers accurately. I discovered that practicing teachers are reluctant to implement significant change in literacy instruction. Teachers reported that the standardization of literacy curricula enforced by high-stakes assessments makes it difficult, even professionally dangerous, to experiment with different forms of text; the fact that professional development is entirely driven by these standardizations and assessments only exacerbates the problem. While many studies of the efficacy of including graphic novels in the secondary classroom as well as articles written to share teacher experiences with inclusion of such works exist, the results indicate that such research might be slower to influence literacy instructional practice and, consequently, effect the systematic change in literacy pedagogies that research reported in journal articles might lead us to expect.

How can there continue to be such a wide gulf between research, theory, and practice? In this article, I raise concerns about larger issues of pedagogy, ideology, and policy as I discuss the survey results and weigh the challenges and opportunities of teaching graphic novels in the secondary English classroom.

Multimodal and New Literacies

New literacy studies re-examines the notion of "text," broadening it to include multimodal texts which can consist of words, images, hyperlinks, and/or video, attempting to "catch up with these staggering changes in media choices that have occurred over the last 25 years and with what they mean for how to define *literacy*" (Kist, 2005, p. 3; emphasis in original). Students encounter and engage with this vast barrage of texts every day both in and out of school; consider the illustrated science textbooks, images included in history textbooks, the deeply embedded and ubiquitous visual landscape of the Internet in which one can produce and consume multimodal texts instantaneously, and other media available to adolescents. Yet the "traditional" literacies which emphasize a neutral and universal set of reading and writing skills for decoding and encoding written text still dominate classroom instruction, largely because state and national assessments continue to measure student achievement in traditional ways. Graphic novels can serve as a bridge over the chasm between a multimodal text-rich culture and traditional assessments. They are hard-copy, hold-in-your-hand books, retaining some of the traditional notion of "text," but their visual and iconic language offers teachers the opportunity to engage students in critically examining how they manipulate and are manipulated by different textual modalities.

Research Methodology

This project was a mixed method study involving quantitative and qualitative responses to an online survey emailed to a random group of secondary English teachers in Indiana and Montana. Mixed methodology provides more opportunities to identify and analyze teacher impressions of, and pedagogical interest in, various instructional methods, including the use of graphic novels. It was important to combine a quantitative "snapshot" of teacher impressions with a fuller picture of qualitative data indicating teacher degree of pedagogical interest in multiple texts. The overall purpose of the survey was to investigate how teachers in rural, suburban, and urban areas use and contribute to teacher research, but, as I indicated above, the responses to the questions concerning graphic novels were particularly surprising. We received 160 valid survey responses from teachers with a wide array of teaching experience and degree levels.

Interestingly, at first glance, 20 percent of teachers indicated that they teach graphic novels, while 80 percent indicated that they do not. This correlated with years of teaching: a significantly higher percentage of early career teachers indicated that they teach graphic novels, which, also at first glance, did not seem surprising. The quantitative results seemed to yield a straightforward and overwhelming response against the use of graphic novels in the classroom. Yet a qualitative analysis of the reasons cited for both answers somewhat complicates the results. When respondents' explanations are taken into consideration, the picture is much bleaker in that it shows how difficult it is for teachers to enact progressive pedagogies, even in light of research indicating that such pedagogies are beneficial to student achievement. These difficulties raise questions about professional development, theoretical and pedagogical approaches to teaching literature, continued emphasis on the traditional canon, and lack of support for implementing new instructional methods. And, upon further reflection, it makes sense that such innovative methods as including graphic novels would flounder if it is primarily early career teachers, who have the most to lose in terms of tenure and job security, are most enthusiastic. Experienced, mentor teachers should be leading the way in developing progressive pedagogies. But this did not seem to be the case at all with the respondents to this survey.

In the following close analysis of the data, I include specific themes and responses that are representative of those I received, then I use those responses to frame discussion of larger theoretical issues. To analyze the qualitative responses both for and against using graphic novels in the classroom, I developed thematic codes, correlated these codes with the quantitative "yes" and "no" responses, and confirmed this analysis with an outside auditor who also coded the responses; our coding correlated 96 percent of the time. This makes it sound as though the responses were easily categorized and clearly indicated both an understanding of the graphic novel genre and what it meant to include these texts in class curricula. Actually, it was much more complicated than that. When the data was thematically coded and analyzed, two important points became clear: I had not included a definition of "graphic novel" and, consequently, the term was not at all clear to some respondents; and, in reality, fewer than 20 percent of respondents are intentionally including graphic novels in their literacy instruction. I admit it simply did not occur to me that I would need to offer a definition and, as I have indicated, this meant I had to infer how individual respondents defined the genre from what they said.

Just What Is a "Graphic Novel"?

Demonstrating a clear understanding of "graphic novel" as a genre was a central consideration in both the "yes" and the "no" responses. Nine respondents from each side of the issue clearly were not familiar with the genre of graphic novels: they interpreted "graphic" to mean "illicit" or "violent" in the context of more traditionally canonical texts. This was interesting, as Will

Eisner, author of several graphic novels, coined the term "graphic novel" in 1978 to describe the genre of his book *Contract with God* (McCloud, 2000, p. 28). The term stuck and 30 years later most cultural theorists and literary scholars have accepted this identifier for the genre, as well as sub-genres, of the graphic novel and agree that simply to refer to such texts as "comics" is a disservice to the creators, audience, and critics of the genre. James Bucky Carter (2007, p. 1) defines the graphic novel as a "book length sequential art narrative . . . comprising a single story line (or arc), or an original, stand-alone graphic narrative." Scott McCloud, in *Understanding Comics: The Invisible Art* (1993, p. 9), also defines the genre of comics and graphic novels as "sequential art."

However, research into pedagogical applications for graphic texts was being conducted even before Eisner's seminal text. Studies as early as the 1940s indicated students were engaged and learning with what were then called "comics" (Yang, 2003). In addition,

> Pilot studies in the early 1990's [designed] to compare the amount of information retained from comic books and standard history books indicated greater retention of information from the comic book as well as more vigorous discussion and debate that expanded concepts of the comic book presentation.
>
> (Heath & Bhagat, 2005, p. 589)

Recent publications cite multimodal literacy instruction, industry/marketing innovation, improving public perception and institutional scrutiny, improving gender and multicultural representation, and a diversification of genre as reasons for inclusion of graphic novels in the classroom (Versaci, 2001; Yang, 2003; Schwarz, 2006; Carter, 2007).

This scholarly attention emphasizes that the genre of graphic novels has garnered much popular, scholarly, and pedagogical attention in recent years, and multiple research articles have appeared in well-respected journals. So why did the unfamiliarity with the definition of "graphic novels" become a salient theme and crucial point of tension in this cross-section of secondary English teachers?

This unfamiliarity was true for both "yes" and "no" responses, but the reasons cited by respondents sometimes provided information necessary to clarify whether the respondent was referring specifically to graphic novels. For example, this respondent indicated that she/he did teach graphic novels. But the explanation revealed uncertainty in his/her concept of the genre:

> I don't know if graphic describes the *Absolutely True Diary of a Part-Time Indian* by Sherman Alexie, but I do teach that one as well as other graphic short stories. I teach them because they're fun. Kids dig it. And like it or not, that's the point. With graphic materials, they want to read more; they enjoy the shock value and it works as a wonderful hook to get their

interest. That whole make a picture in your head is much more effective with graphic novels, and it's a great place to start. I teach 9th grade struggling readers for part of the year, and not to profile, but they tend to be boys. They are enthralled with the possible danger and scandalousness of graphic material. Not that I do it solely for shock value! It just sets the scene for an active, engaged audience. When they're least expecting it, you can slip in lessons about higher-level material.

(May 23, 2008)

This teacher is obviously engaged and student-centered, willing to risk introducing new material to engage students in literate behaviors. And the question about Alexie's novel is relevant; the images enhance the text but are not central to the narrative, as they are in a graphic novel. But his/her reference to the "possible danger and scandalousness of graphic material" raises the question of whether he/she is referring specifically to the "graphic novel" because both descriptors could also refer to an "illicit" or "violent" text. There is no reference to the value of teaching image and art as a means to encourage critical literacy, or even literacy, in his/her classroom. Consequently, even though I would love to visit this teacher's classroom and am confident that it would be a lively and student-centered space, I question whether she/he is really teaching graphic novels.

Further examples of "yes, I teach graphic novels" answers apparently attributable to a misunderstanding of the term "graphic novel" include the following:

• Some of the novels approved by our corporation are graphic in parts. Some of the situations present in the novels parallel incidents in real life that students will face. These novels are also valuable in teaching theme and conflict resolution. (August 12, 2008)
• How do you define "graphic"? Adult situations = yes. (May 27, 2008)

Clearly, these respondents are not teaching the genre of graphic novel, as I defined it previously.

Defining graphic novels as a genre factored in the "no, I do not teach graphic novels" category for the same reasons, as evinced by the following responses. However, I feel more confident about qualitatively (as opposed to quantitatively) labeling these as "no" responses because it is likely each respondent is not teaching graphic novels based on the reasoning behind the responses, even though they often do not explicitly say they are not using graphic novels:

• Do you mean graphic description of sex, violence, etc.?? If so, the only one I've attempted was *The Color Purple*, and I did have some parent complaints. Now I make those books optional reading. (May 27, 2008)

- If by "graphic" you mean literature with sexual innuendos and such—no. It's not classroom appropriate. (August 19, 2008)
- Graphic novels as in extremely violent? Again, I teach 8th grade. I teach *1984* with my single class of seniors, but I don't know if I would classify that as a graphic novel. (August 13, 2008)
- Is *All Quiet on the Western Front* considered graphic? (June 6, 2008)
- Define graphic?? Mice and Men [*sic*]? (May 30, 2008)

When the rationales for the "yes/no" question take into consideration this confusion over what constitutes a "graphic novel," the percentage of teachers clearly teaching graphic novels falls to just 14 percent (23 out of 160).

The 14 percent Who Do Teach Graphic Novels

Respondents who do teach graphic novels cited several reasons for using them in the classroom. Even though the number of enthusiastic "yes" respondents was small, their rationales were enlightening and inspiring:

- Graphic novels can be very powerful. I specifically teach *Maus I* and *Maus II* [by Art Spiegelman]. Both of these graphic novels help students become stronger readers of all types of literature because they have to read between the lines and pay special attention to explicit symbols. (August 4, 2008)
- Graphic novels have a great appeal to many readers, especially reluctant readers. (June 1, 2008)
- I sometimes use graphic novels to have all the students understand schema[ta] in more difficult books. I also use graphic novels for differentiation. (July 18, 2008)
- Graphics are an additional way to provide connections between the reader and the text. (August 24, 2008)
- Reinforces reading strategies; offers opportunities to teach values and the truth behind historical events; reinforces short story elements in depth; provides opportunities for cooperative learning re sensitive issues. (June 16, 2008)
- The visual aspect of graphic novels helps to make imaginative literature accessible and enjoyable for this generation of students. It makes it easier to bridge the students' world with the world of the text. The graphics can prompt interesting discussions about interpretation, and many students love the opportunity to create their own graphic interpretations. (August 5, 2008)

"Paying attention to explicit symbols," as the first respondent above pointed out, corresponds with the field of semiotics, a theoretical approach uniquely appropriate for analysis and teaching of graphic novels. Semiotics is the study of signifying systems that "rely on conventions to sustain relationships between the sign and the signifier and signified" (Kress, 1998, p. 73). For example, a word in a given text is a *signifier*, and the thing (whether a concrete item or an abstract emotion) the word represents is the *signified*; images and other iconic signs function within a text in the same way. Signifying systems in standardized curricula often privilege traditional analytical skills of decoding and encoding written textual signs; yet new literacy studies proponents argue these should be broadened to include varied communication media, such as visual signifying systems, as well. James Gee (2003, p. 18) calls these systems "semiotic domains" and defines them as "any set of practices that recruits one or more modalities to communicate distinctive types of meanings." These meanings are communicated by

> [w]ords, symbols, images, and artifacts [which] have meanings that are specific to particular semiotic domains and particular situations . . . [Learners] must be able to situate the meaning of that word, symbol, image, or artifact within embodied experiences of action, interaction, or dialogue in or about the domain.
>
> (p. 24)

Michelle Zoss (2009, p. 185) concurs, pointing out that "valuable thinking and learning also occur in sign systems that are nonlinguistic." Engaging in critical examination of how the visual elements of a graphic novel interact with text is a complex cognitive exercise that spans content area and grade level. Literacy instruction should include

> multiple and varied opportunities for students to encounter texts based in language and image, and to think and respond [within a] semiotics-based curriculum that seeks to expand the sign systems available for adolescents to use to perceive, think about, respond to, and compose within schools.
>
> (p. 189)

Gunther Kress (1998, p. 76) identifies this as "synaesthesia, the transduction of meaning from one semiotic mode in meaning to another . . . an activity constantly performed by the brain." In other words, reading graphic novels is not as straightforward as looking at pictures to illustrate a written text and is more complex than code switching; graphics add layers of signifiers to a semiotic system, and layers of complexity for the reader. In essence, rather than simply adding another decoding task to enhance a text, the sequential art of a graphic novel *multiplies* the interpretive challenges and opportunities for analysis and interpretation. In fact,

> close study of eye movements in reading comics indicates that the eye moves between words and pictures rapidly, so that neither the word

nor the picture text remains linear in a left-to-right pattern . . . [Graphic novels] promote multiple layers of attention and habituate readers to relating such layers to one another.

(Heath & Bhagat, 2005, p. 590)

In light of this research, Lemke (1998, p. 285) argues that educators

simply cannot get by anymore thinking that there is just one thing called literacy or that it is simply what individual minds do when confronted with symbols one at a time . . . [Many texts] combine visual images and printed text in ways that make cross-reference between them essential to understanding them.

Unfortunately, the difficulty in expanding literacy instruction to include multimodal texts is the partial result of the relatively naïve notions of visualization as decoding practice which dominate current educational practice. Visualization is seen as an unproblematic kind of translation from one semiotic mode into another, rather than as a complex, interrelated semiotic system—as a simplistic kind of translation from one language to another rather than emphasizing the layered interaction of multiple semiotic systems within a text (Kress, 1998, pp. 55–76). Consequently, graphic novels are often considered "easier" reading and are therefore incorporated into remedial instruction, which may partially explain the remaining responses indicating that they are not yet considered appropriate for classroom instruction.

Unqualified or Uninterested?

Of teachers who do not include graphic novels in their instructional plans, 20 percent reported feeling unqualified and/or said they didn't have the time to investigate or develop new instructional plans to include them. Often they cited unfamiliarity with graphic novels or lack of "expertise" to teach them effectively in the classroom. I make a distinction between those responses that misidentified the genre and those that cited "lack of time/unqualified" as reasons for not teaching graphic novels because there was not a clear indication from the second set of responses that respondents were referring to anything other than the genre of graphic novels as I define it, although in-depth knowledge of the genre remains a sticking point.

The "no" answers to the question "Do you teach graphic novels?" followed a predictable pattern within these two themes:

- I do not have the time to add anything else, do not have appropriate knowledge base of the genre, and so have not found relevance for this inclusion.
- I have not had enough experience with graphic novels.

The underlying issue in this theme is the lack of time and professional development offered to teachers in support of developing progressive pedagogies. Some respondents indicated that while they do not teach graphic novels currently, they were enthusiastic about the concept and would be interested in doing so if provided with appropriate opportunities for professional development:

- I would REALLY like to at some point just to be able to introduce a new genre that is here to stay, but a) they're Greek to me (how cliché!) and I would have to have the time to do the research/prep; and b) they appeal to such a small group of my honors students that I can't justify finding the time to do the prep. (October 13, 2008)
- I'd love to start doing this, because I know there is real value in these types of books. I haven't, honestly, because there are little resources at my school to help me with this. I'd have to take lots of time out to develop a unit on that, and I just don't have the time with all other Indiana State Academic Standards that have to be taught in the 7th grade. (May 27, 2008)

Too often, "professional development" initiatives in schools provide little time for deep pedagogical reflection, discourage open-ended discussion of crucial issues in literacy instruction between teachers, and rarely address systemic change. Instead, professional development is based on a "curricular learning paradigm [in which] someone else will decide what you need to know and will arrange for you to learn it all in a fixed order and on a fixed schedule" (Lemke, 1998, p. 293) and driven by standardization. Teachers often report that professional development workshops amount to nothing more than learning the latest assessment trend (e.g., 6 Traits of Writing, Step Up to Writing), are scheduled for the afternoon following an already busy school day, involve hired "facilitators" or "experts" with little follow-up, and/or focus on the basic application of a new technology (grading programs, lesson plan uploading to web pages, etc.). The demands made upon teachers by standardization, regimentation, and record keeping conveniently tax the time they can devote simply to maintaining the status quo; finding the additional time and energy to investigate and implement new instructional methods becomes a seemingly overwhelming task. As a result, as Donna Alvermann (2009, p. 19) observes, "classroom teachers have been reluctant to incorporate various aspects of the new literacies into their instruction, even on a trial basis."

But there is a clear distinction between the responses coded to "unqualified/lack of time" and those coded to "lack of interest/disapproval," and another 20 percent of respondents indicated they were uninterested or even hostile to the idea of using graphic novels in their classroom instruction. Also embedded in these responses is a conservative adherence to canonical text and "high" art. One respondent referred to graphic novels as "worthless junk" and another as "idiotic." The following examples indicate a deep suspicion of using graphic novels in the classroom, essentially dismissing them as an effective means to engage students in complex literate behaviors. It is also noteworthy that these responses do not reflect student-centered pedagogies but seem to follow more prescribed instructional approaches:

- I have no experience with these materials. Also, the students who like these will pick them up on their own. I'd rather expand their horizons. (May 30, 2008)
- I see them as little more than comic books, and at the upper level of instruction, I feel that students' time would be better spent actually reading rather than looking at pictures. I say that having compared, for example, the "graphic novel" version of Beowulf to the text format, finding the comic book version sadly lacking in detail and in richness of description. Furthermore, I think that they blur the line between academia and mindless entertainment, and there is no reason to incorporate them into a setting that needs to promote the business of learning, when so much is at stake. (May 22, 2008)
- Simply not enough time to include these selections. Personally, I am not a fan, but the kids read them—a lot. In fact, on their own many kids want to read these because "they have cool pictures." I find it a bit disturbing. (May 25, 2008)
- I don't particularly like the format of graphic novels—I am a linguistically intelligent person, so the pictures detract more from the text for my learning style. However, I encourage my picture smart students and my struggling readers to pursue these texts during reading workshop. (October 14, 2008)

The comment "I'd rather expand their horizons" is particularly ironic in this context. Continually to present the same kind of literacy activity and textual analysis, the traditional in school or academic literate behaviors, does not expand students' horizons but limits them, often alienating students who identify more strongly with out-of-school literacies. James Gee (2003, pp. 60–61) refers to these identity markers as "real-world identities" and argues that students whose real-world identities conflict with a "damaged" identity as a learner in school require "repair work" on the part of educators. These students have learned throughout schooling that their identification with "non-literary" texts (e.g. graphic novels, popular fiction, magazines, online texts) does not transfer to in-school, traditional literacies; they would benefit from the "extend[ed] . . . range of literacies" (Hull & Schultz, 2006, p. 290) graphic novels help to provide as part of comprehensive literacy curricula. Teachers must have the flexibility to overcome preconceived notions of student literacy success and develop pedagogies that nurture students who may not be predisposed to demonstrate the literacy competencies they already possess (p. 291) because they fall outside the realm of "academic." The respondent above who described some students as "picture smart" seems to be supporting a dichotomous learner identity that privileges students who are also "linguistically intelligent." Educators would do well to "value the ways in which young people express their ideas and learning" (Zoss, 2009, p. 185) by engaging them in a broad array of literate activities which include analysis of text and visual media.

Because adolescence is a time of deep emotional, physical, and intellectual change, students benefit from a wide variety of artistic expression which offers alternative worldviews, challenging and expanding the subjectivities they bring to the task of making sense of written and visual discourse. It is also important that educators consider that adolescents are naturally multitaskers, and research indicates those who engage in multiliteracies such as surfing the Web at the same time as engaging in the more traditional literate behaviors inherent in "doing school" are as successful as their "on-task" peers (Alvermann, 2009, p. 22). This "following of several narratives at a time parallels the mental activities of youngsters [who are multitasking]" (Heath & Bhagat, 2005, p. 590). Experimenting with a broad array of text through this kind of multitasking serves to stretch the adolescent worldview; teaching graphic novels requires students to transfer these skills and critically interrogate how they interpret the narrative at hand using everything they know.

The field of study known as "cultural studies," which refers to cross-disciplinary scholarly analysis of cultural signifiers and phenomena, including institutions, practices, and products, is particularly appropriate for a discussion of expanding the canon of secondary English study and engaging students in analysis of multimodal texts. Cultural studies theorists often concentrate on how a particular phenomenon relates to matters of ideology, race, social class, and/or gender. For example, a cultural analysis of literature is concerned with the identification of what constitutes text (written text, images, paintings, etc.), how texts are endowed with social meanings or "truth," and how they come to be valued by particular populations within the cultural milieu. Of chief concern are the ideological boundaries drawn between "high art" and "low art." Often these boundaries reproduce hegemonic stratification in cultural and social institutions, such as school. The question of what is "literature" as opposed to "popular fiction" or which texts are worthy of academic analysis and which should be relegated to "pleasure reading" fall under this category. Often those texts that reproduce society's hierarchies and support the ideological views of the dominant group (traditionally this group is white, conservative, and male) are often privileged, supporting a view of literacy that discourages discussions of the very power relations that sustain its hold on literacy instruction.

Graphic novels often include text, images, visuals, and narrative themes that fall outside the dominant realm of cultural aesthetics and, consequently, do not reproduce societal class/cultural stratification, but instead interrogate and complicate existing sociocultural injustices. For example, *American Born*

Figure 9.1 Moment Within Moment

Source: Image from page 214 of *American Born Chinese* by Gene Luen Yang, copyright © 2006 Gene Luen Yang. Reprinted by arrangement with Henry Holt and Company, LLC.

Chinese (Yang, 2006) includes the character of Chin-Kee, an intentionally offensive caricature of Asian Americans, providing a foil for the teenage protagonist, Jin Wang, who tries desperately to fit into the social milieu of his suburban American high school. Yang brilliantly layers the separate narratives of Jin Wang, Chin-Kee, and the Chinese mythological character of the Monkey King to confront issues of adolescent outsider identity and the struggle to fit in. The art of the narrative captures the moment when Jin Wang clearly begins to develop a sense of authentic identity and embrace his cultural ethnicity more vividly and succinctly than mere words ever could (see Figure 9.1). This "moment within moment" is peculiar to graphic novels and not found in other art forms.

Art Spiegelman's *Maus I* (1986) depicts Jewish characters as mice and Nazi characters as cats, a blatant reference to the victimization of Jews during World War Two. But things are complicated by depictions of Americans as dogs, the French as frogs, Poles as pigs, etc. What does it mean that each culture is so clearly delineated? Is it so easy to draw cultural borders? Inherent in the debate about including graphic novels in the English classroom is tension between progressive pedagogies and a hegemonic system that imposes the canon, defines acceptable understandings of what constitutes knowledge, and creates power differentials to maintain existing school order. Yet, as John Frow (1997) eloquently puts it, this

> tight-lipped refusal of new or different ways of dealing with texts is death to the spirit (and death, in the long run, to the discipline) . . . Cultural studies supposes a pedagogy in which students are at least as fully in control of much of the subject matter as are the teachers . . . literary studies will not survive if it is taught as a form of religion.

Lack of Community, Curricular, and Administrative Support

Cultural studies also offers opportunities for teachers who chafe at the restrictions imposed by the institutions of schooling. Few teachers who responded to the survey seemed to feel they have the authority or power in the face of standardized curricula or community or parental involvement in determining curricular foci, and they had little faith in administrative support for progressive instructional methods to change literacy curricula dramatically. Fifteen percent of respondents indicated they had no access to classroom sets or sufficient materials for teaching graphic novels in their classrooms. When curricular requirements limiting their teaching and spending options are taken into consideration, that number grows to 28 percent of respondents, and becomes the most powerful theme influencing teachers who would consider teaching graphic novels if they could. As budgets shrink in a time of recession, and student performance on standardized tests looms as the single largest determiner of academic achievement, many teachers reported they simply did not have access to the funds necessary for purchasing classroom sets of graphic novels to include in their pedagogical repertoire. However, many teachers did indicate they use graphic novels as supplementary materials, often with the support of the school librarian. Here are some of the reasons teachers cited for not including graphic novels:

- Because the curriculum requires "classics." (May 27, 2008)
- Haven't seriously considered teaching them. Would love to teach, say, *Maus* or *Persepolis*. Don't know if my department/school/community would consider this proper material for instruction. Also: I think the conservative community I teach in might find some of the material objectionable. (October 6, 2008).
- No money (May 27, 2008)
- I don't have any classroom sets, and the anthology I have does not contain any [graphic novels]. (May 27, 2008)
- Our school does not have copies. (May 27, 2008)
- I have read about teaching graphic novels, but none are available in our school. (May 27, 2008)
- Not an available resource in my school. I have shown them examples of personal graphic novels. They are allowed to read graphic novels for silent reading. (May 21, 2008)

This lack of external support poses the most daunting challenge for teachers who are interested in including graphic novels in their classrooms. Hopefully, providing examples of curricula and research supporting the use of graphic novels in English language arts classrooms, such as those provided here, will help teachers construct an argument for their inclusion.

Throughout this chapter, I have touched on research and themes which link teaching graphic novels to adolescent identity development. One particularly salient metaphor which recurrently appeared throughout my research and in my own writing is that of the bridge. As adolescents transition from childhood to adulthood, their experience of "text," in all possible cultural, personal, ideological, technological, and educational modalities, is transformative— many of these experiences are not directed by a teacher in school. Including multiple textual modalities in a pedagogically sound, learner-centered class-room encourages students to bridge the many gaps that loom in their journey to adulthood: gaps between in-school and out-of-school literacies, gaps between their authentic identification with text and standardized assessments of their engagement with text in school, gaps between their sense of agency in choosing and interpreting text and their surrender to curricular requirements stripping away such choice, gaps between valuing and identifying with texts available via the Internet and technology and valuing and identifying with traditional written texts, and gaps in their understanding of the world as a child and the realities of the adult world they are entering.

"'Reading the world,' [Paulo Freire] famously wrote, 'always precedes reading the word, and reading the word implies continually reading the world'" (Freire & Macedo, 1987, p. 35, cited in Hull & Schultz, 2006, p. 286). I would argue for expanding this idea to a broader concept of text than written words, but the overall importance of the role of reading multiple texts in establishing and expanding subjectivities is well taken. By tapping into the long tradition of sequential art and narrative familiar to most teens, graphic novels provide teachers with a particularly rich genre for engaging students in high-level, high-interest critical analysis of the world around them and bridging these gaps in conceptions of literacy and value judgements defining what constitutes literature. Graphic novels also offer a clearer connection between reader and author:

> the forging of an emotional connection between creator and reader . . . [is] far different from the [one] forged in cinema and prose. The partnership between creator and reader in comics is far more intimate and active . . . comics' symbolic static images may cut straight to the heart without the continual mediation of prose's authorial voice.
>
> (McCloud, 2000, p. 39)

Rather than privileging the new critical approaches still emphasized in the hegemonic literary canon (whether or not this is acknowledged, the ideology of exegesis is still prevalent in most literature textbooks), graphic novels intentionally link the creator with the reader, giving students a behind-the-scenes glimpse of the creative process, allowing a unique reciprocity between reader and creator subjectivities. Adolescents particularly identify with the rare sense of agency this provides, presenting opportunities to interrogate the status quo and voice their developing sense of how they position themselves within that world. As one teacher (cited previously in this chapter) eloquently put it, teaching graphic novels "makes it easier to bridge the students' world with the world of the text."

Conclusion

With such a wide array of pedagogical invitations available, it is surprising that graphic novels have not more quickly assumed a central place in English language arts curricula, especially in conjunction with young adult novels. It is more than inclusion of visual text as code switching, but rather emphasizes interactive interpretation of text. Simply including graphic novels in secondary schooling as another vehicle to teach the same literacy lessons does not go far enough; we should ensure our conception of literacy is one that does not merely add "kinds" of literacy but engages students in intentionally recognizing and examining the multiplying literacies that are central to modern culture. It is up to practicing teachers and researchers to "question the adequacy of present theories of semiosis and their effects. If we do not, we deny ourselves the possibility of actively participating in the shaping of this 'age'" (Kress, 1998, p. 75).

I would like to end this essay with the words of one teacher-respondent, which offer as succinct a summary as I could manage:

> I think the notion of what exactly makes up a text is ever expanding. We have to give students real-world situations in their reading lives, so I think it's important to allow students to choose what they read. To answer your original question then, I teach/coach students strategies to respond to literature they choose and help students make connections that lead to expanding their reading selections—some of these books chosen are young adult literature and graphic novels. I think we make a grave mistake as educators though when we teach books rather than students.
>
> (May 27, 2008)

References

Alvermann, D. (2009). Sociocultural constructions of adolescence and young people's literacies. In L. Christenbury, R. Bomer, & P. Smagorinsky (Eds.), *Handbook of adolescent literacy research* (pp. 14–28). New York: Guilford Press.

Carter, J.B. (2007). *Building literacy connections with graphic novels: Page by page, panel by panel.* Urbana, IL: NCTE.

Freire, P. & Macedo, D. (1987). *Literacy: Reading the word and the world.* Westport, CT: Bergin & Garvey.

Frow, J. (1997). Literature, culture, mirrors: John Frow responds to Simon During. *Australian Humanities Review.* Online: http://www.australianhumanitiesreview.org/emuse/culture/frow.html.

Gee, J.P. (2003). *What video games have to teach us about learning and literacy.* New York: Palgrave Macmillan.

Heath, S.B. & Bhagat, V. (2005). Reading comics, the invisible art. In J. Flood, S.B. Heath, & D. Lapp (Eds.), *Handbook of research on teaching literacy through the communicative and visual arts* (pp. 586–591). Mahwah, NJ: Lawrence Erlbaum.

Hull, G. & Schultz, K. (2006). Literacy and learning out of school: A review of theory and research. In H. Luria, D.M. Seymore, & T. Smoke (Eds.), *Language and linguistics in context* (pp. 275–305). Mahwah, NJ: Lawrence Erlbaum.

Kist, W. (2005). *New literacies in action: Teaching and learning in multiple media.* New York: Teachers College Press.

Kress, G. (1998). Visual and verbal modes of representation in electronically mediated communication: The potentials of new forms of text. In I. Snyder (Ed.), *Page to screen: Taking literacy into the electronic era* (pp. 53–79). New York: Routledge.

Lemke, J.L. (1998). Metamedia literacy: Transforming meanings and media. In D. Reinking, M.C. McKenna, L.D. Labbo, & R.D. Kieffer (Eds.), *Handbook of literacy and technology* (pp. 283–301). Mahwah, NJ: Lawrence Erlbaum.

McCloud, S. (1993). *Understanding comics: The invisible art.* New York: HarperCollins.

McCloud, S. (2000). *Reinventing comics: How imagination and technology are revolutionizing an art form.* New York: HarperCollins.

Schwarz, G. (2006). Expanding literacies through graphic novels. *English Journal,* 95 (6), 58–64.

Spiegelman, A. (1986). *Maus, a survivor's tale.* Volume 1: *My father bleeds history.* New York: Pantheon Books.

Versaci, R. (2001). How comic books can change the way our students see literature: One teacher's perspective. *English Journal,* 91 (2), 61–67.

Yang, G. (2003) *Comics in Education.* Online: http://www.geneyang.com/comicsedu/.

Yang, G. (2006). *American born Chinese.* New York: Square Fish.

Zoss, M. (2009). Visual arts and literacy. In L. Christenbury, R. Bomer, & P. Smagorinsky (Eds.), *Handbook of adolescent literacy research* (pp. 183–196). New York: Guilford Press.

Chapter 10

Pedagogues and Demigods
Captivity, Pedagogy, and Young Adult Literature in an Age of Diminished Expectations

Jeff Spanke

> I don't believe any of you have ever read *Paradise Lost*, and you don't want to. That's something that you just want to take on trust. It's a classic . . . something that everybody wants to have read and nobody wants to read.
>
> (Mark Twain)

> Education is an admirable thing, but it is well to remember from time to time that nothing that is worth knowing can be taught.
>
> (Oscar Wilde)

When Mary Rowlandson emerged from the clutches of a tribe of Algonquian Indians in May 1676 after nearly 12 weeks of captivity, she had no way of knowing that the narrative which spawned from her saga would in turn spawn arguably the first uniquely American literary genre: the Indian captivity narrative. Written with earnest, bland prose and penned as a genuine first-person account of her captivity, Rowlandson's narrative recounts 20 "removes" or journeys in which she suffered—among other things—starvation, depression, spiritual corruption, and the death of her youngest daughter, Sarah. Still, through the "sovereignty and goodness of God," the civilized white Puritan woman was able to withstand the horrific conditions of the uncultivated Indian savages. Historian Richard Slotkin (1996) notes that Rowlandson's narrative provided America with its first coherent mythical literature—a literature that, though originally relaying factual accounts, later would become manipulated by others for their own motives. Influential Puritan minister Increase Mather, most scholars agree, likely had a hand in crafting Rowlandson's narrative so that it functioned as a warning to his Puritan settlers about what might happen should their faith in God falter. More than simply an isolated account of the tribulations of 17th-century American life, Rowlandson's written account blazed the trail for later forms of the captivity narrative—a genre predicated upon the relocation of the protagonist into unknown and oftentimes violent surroundings where survival results solely from moral redemption and spiritual fortitude in spite of threats or temptations to an otherwise savage form of life.

Though in the mid-19th century American literature began to shy away from the spiritually based, ritualistic, episodic stories seen in Rowlandson's tale of Indian savagery, this chapter argues that, as a distinguishable literary genre, captivity narratives exist just as prominently today as they did in late 17th-century Massachusetts. The narrative structure, social resonances, circumstances of production, and psychological ramifications of contemporary young adult literature, I contend, bear striking similarities to canonical captivity narratives. Not only do both genres contain protagonists plagued with the brutal savagery of the "wilderness" but, in separate but equally effective ways, they meticulously dichotomize the relationship between the hero and the corrosive Other. In other words, Rowlandson's homogeneous Indian savage—the antithesis of Puritan social cohesiveness—evolves, in YAL, into the nemesis of contemporary adolescents: control, certainty, morality, and family.

For the purposes of this chapter, I shall not engage in a discussion over whether YAL is, in fact, a literary genre. While I am aware that such a debate certainly exists, I feel engaging in it is inappropriate, given the parameters of my argument. Therefore, for this chapter, I shall define YAL as any literature which contains:

1   the presence of characters to whom adolescents can relate;
2   plotlines similar to the experiences of teenagers; and
3   more "accessible" language than one may find in texts not traditionally classified as YAL.

In many respects, tales of Indian captivity and those found in contemporary YAL evoke similar images and narrative patterns.

It is interesting, however, how character roles become inverted as they translate from captivity narratives to YAL. Historically, captivity narratives functioned along the premise of placing the moral protagonist in savage surroundings. However, I argue that the savagery of adolescence becomes the new protagonist, with adulthood/mainstream society assuming the role of Other. What confounds this framework, as I'll discuss later, is that, logically, the only way to overcome adolescence is essentially to grow up, thus succumbing to the realities of adulthood. YAL resists this inevitable process of aging by sensationalizing adolescence not as a moment in a logical progression of human development, but rather as a sort of social construct: a mode of cognition and behavior the likes of which YAL, by its very nature, offers little incentive to overcome.

In addition to being sensational and melodramatic by nature, both YAL and Indian captivity narratives inevitably attract a mass readership (Sturma, 2002). The commercial success of captivity narratives throughout most of the 17th to 19th centuries mirrors the burgeoning rise in popularity of YAL in the last 40 years. When once horrific tales of captivity fueled the plots of dime novels written in the 17th and 18th centuries, the issues blanketing today's YAL resonate with the subject matter found in television shows, Internet blogs, and teen movies. In fact, one subtitle for Rowlandson's narrative—"The Cruel and Inhumane Usage she underwent amongst the Heathens"—seems to indicate to the reader that her story would resonate with such critically acclaimed YA novels as *The Breadwinner* (Ellis, 2001) and *The Other Side of Truth* (Naidoo, 2002) (Kestler, 1990, p. 69). Thus, I first wish to examine the analogous manner by which one may juxtapose the genre of YAL with the seemingly lost genre of captivity narratives and, in doing so, hope to cast YAL as a genre that, like captivity narratives, came to fruition during a time of uncertainty and change.

Much as Rowlandson's narrative emerged when such a testament of spiritual perseverance was necessary (for reasons I'll discuss later), I argue that the rise of YAL coincides with a shifting in the national consciousness beginning in the 1960s and 1970s. The remainder of this chapter will address the pedagogical concerns I have with introducing YAL into the secondary English classroom and the dualistic captivity I fear may ultimately result. By "dualistic captivity," I mean that the intertextual captivity of the text's characters manifests itself externally in the students. Therefore, I argue that teaching YAL creates a form of captivity wherein, in addition to the literal captivity narrative of the texts themselves, the classroom becomes the new text with the students/characters being held captive by the teacher/author/Other.

Introduction of Main Characters: YAL versus Captivity Narratives

In a 2002 article, Michael Sturma makes a compelling argument suggesting that Indian captivity narratives and the testimonies of alien abduction follow nearly an identical narrative framework and overarching thematic metaphor. One may view Sturma's "transculturalization"—the process by which the author of the captivity narrative or the abductee crosses a frontier and is immersed into another culture—as one of the most fundamental components of YAL. Whether the main character moves to a new school, new town, prison, or foreign country, or undergoes a change in political regime, a pervasive tenet of YAL is that the stories tend to begin with some sort of watershed moment—a moment that, as in captivity narratives, usually involves the physical relocation of the protagonist(s).

Once the frontiers have been crossed, the captives/adolescents are often plagued with feelings of helplessness and isolation. In the case of captivity narratives, this feeling of despair almost always results from physical isolation in the woods or mountains, whereas in YAL the isolation can be both literal *and* psychological. As I'll demonstrate later, however, oftentimes, even in captivity narratives, the protagonist continues to experience feelings of psychological isolation after being rescued. A common motif in both YAL and captivity narratives is the feeling of helplessness that develops once the character is situated in the new environment. Rowlandson writes, "I must turn my back upon the town and travel with them into the vast and desolate wilderness, I know not whither" (quoted in Kestler, 1990, p. 33). Captives/adolescents are often symbolically divested of the external confines of their own culture as they traverse their new surroundings.

In keeping with this framework, YAL inverts one of the basic attributes of the traditional captivity narrative in that when once the couth protagonist must prevail in uncouth circumstances, now the teenage savage *is* the protagonist, with civilization becoming the dreaded Other. Just as Puritanism was for Mary Rowlandson, adolescence in YAL serves as some sort of contrived, yet inescapable, *concept*—as opposed to merely a stage in one's life—with which the characters constantly struggle as they attempt to reconcile their place in the wilderness of society. Only through constant prayer and incessant faith, so preached Increase Mather, did Rowlandson escape from the confines of the wilderness unscathed. Similarly, YAL insists that characters must rely on their adolescence, however difficult, in order not to be corrupted by the dangers of "the greater world." Thus, the reversal of character roles which renders the vulnerable yet savage adolescent captive under society's thin veneer of stability results in YA characters no longer seeking to achieve moral redemption (as was the case in traditional captivity stories), but rather a sense of moral ambiguity.

In traditional captivity sagas, it is the white woman (often of Puritan heritage) who most often finds herself at the mercy of the Other. As Sturma argues, it is her sexual vulnerability at one level that "reflects the anxieties about the limits of European male power on the frontier and the fear that white women might be seduced to the Indian side" (2002, p. 325). Interesting here is the idea that adolescence evolves into a sort of "passing" phenomenon wherein, like race or gender, age contains a performative component. The adolescents in YAL cannot actually *become* adults, but in order to survive in their new environment, they must play a role different from their culture of adolescence. As I will discuss in the latter sections of this chapter, the perpetuation of infantilization by YAL has its roots in a greater social shift beginning in the 1960s and 1970s—an era Tom Wolfe (1976) termed the "me decade."

In addition to frontier crossing and the mortification and helplessness that result, another thematic element shared by YA and captivity narratives rests in the notion of capitalizing on, as Sturma puts it, "the popular fascination with cross-cultural romantic relationships and forbidden intimacies" (2002, p. 326). In fact, opponents of YAL despise the genre precisely because of its perceived advocation of sexual experimentation and endorsing of immoral behavior. As Don Gallo (2008, pp. 113–114) argues, however, ironically, many of these opponents hold up the Bible as the best (or only) example of "literature they want their children to read, ignoring the fact that the Bible overflows with sex, violence, treachery, betrayal, theft, adultery, incest, bigamy, illegitimacy, and mayhem." Yet despite the Bible's lurid subject matter, the spirituality of Scripture remains perhaps the primary cause of captives' survival.

If Puritanism is to Mary Rowlandson as adolescence is to the main characters of YAL, then what role does the Bible serve to teenagers? For Puritans like Rowlandson and the hundreds of captives whose stories came later, the Bible serves as the voice for their culture—the culture that was stripped from them once they were taken captive. More than simply a reminder of the cultural circumstance whence they came, the Bible offered these Puritan captives a means by which they might seek spiritual guidance and assurance that their time in the wilderness bore no permanence. As a type of refuge, the Bible's role manifests itself in entirely new ways when translated into the YAL genre. Technology, the Internet, and pop culture offer adolescents the same mode of escape from their adult captors—an arena where only teens can communicate and any attempt by outsiders to infiltrate this sacred terrain will be met with harsh denial. I liken this parallel between the Bible and technology to Andrew Newman's (2003) conceptualization of early American captivity narratives as the "literacy frontier."

Newman's literacy frontier "stands as an abstract cultural boundary that existed in the imagination of some Anglo-Americans who, in crossing it, felt compelled to invoke literacy as a primary symbol of their identity" (2003, pp. 31–32). Thus, Mary Rowlandson's use of scripture served a dual purpose in that it both offered a means of cognitive escape and acted as a cultural boundary, defining her status as a Puritan woman in terms of what she was not: a savage. For this reason, Rowlandson's narrative, like virtually all other stories depicting captivity, was written in the first person. This allows the writers better to reconcile their anxieties and desires about being in an entirely alien environment. Because of this cultural literacy marker, Rowlandson does not welcome attempts by her English-speaking captors to communicate with her. In one such instance, she reports,

> [t]here was another Praying Indian, who told, that he had a brother, that would not eat Horse; his conscience was so tender and scrupulous (though as large as hell, for the destruction of poor Christians). Then he said, he read that Scripture to him, 2 Kings 6.25. There was a famine in Samaria, and behold they besieged it, until an Asses head was sold for four-score pieces of silver, and the fourth part of Kab of Dove's dung, for five pieces of silver. He expounded this place to his brother, and shewed him that it was lawful to eat that in a famine which is not at another time. And now, says he, he will eat horse with any Indian of them all.
>
> (Quoted in Newman, 2003, p. 38)

According to David Sewell, "Rowlandson is apparently scandalized that the praying Indian should quote Scripture with such levity. Literacy, she seems to feel, is a dangerous thing for Indians . . . Literacy, like guns, gives the Indians more firepower than they can be trusted with" (quoted in Newman, 2003, p. 38).

So what role, then, does technology play in the link between Puritan scripture and adolescent cultural identity? The concept of e-mail, YAL author and editor David Levithan believes, has revolutionized the role of the author, especially in teen literature (cited in Beaman, 2006). Now that YAL authors are establishing websites of their own on which they place commentaries about their latest books and engage in instant chats with fans and readers all across the world, the relationship between author and adolescent reader is becoming much more intimate. Through this technical medium, teen readers have the opportunity to formulate a voice which reflects their unique culture. In other words, cyberspace has become the scripture for the readers of YAL. Like captivity narratives, the majority of YAL is written in the first person, and several books are now even being written using the discursive format of online chats (e.g., *ttyl* (2004) by Lauren Myracle). The adolescent literacy frontier, therefore, exists just as pervasively in YAL as in Newman's perception of captivity narratives.

It is indeed an ironic element of civilized societies that their people have historically recognized the value of tempering their joys with tales that chronicle the misfortunes and tragedies of others (Vanderbeets, 1972, p. 5548). Captivity narratives and YAL are no exceptions. Richard Vanderbeets traces the journey of captivity narratives' "archetypal initiate" from the initial Separation, to the spiritual/physical Transformation, and finally to the Return, usually in the form of escape, release, or redemption. Described by Vanderbeets as ritualistic passages that "touch on fundamental truths of experience," captivity narratives do more than simply attract readers through their "sectarian religious feeling, narrow chauvinism, or morbidity" (p. 5562). They also accentuate—albeit critically—the culture which produced them. An interesting component of Vanderbeets's ritualistic captivity narratives rests in the idea that, as he puts it, "those who were literally torn from their homes and carried into Indian captivity were for the most part dead to their families and friends" (p. 5554). One notices an eerily similar phenomenon in YAL, wherein the task of locating a solid familiar network—or the sheer presence of any parents/guardians at all—within the adolescent's life often proves quite arduous.

Obviously, in captivity narratives the heroine cannot write intelligently on the whereabouts of her friends and family, for her status as a captive combined with her remote and uncharted location render her unable to do so. Yet since often in YAL the isolation experienced by the adolescent is a psychological one deriving from his/her status as an adolescent and not *necessarily* a physical relocation, authors must make a more concerted effort to conceal the presence of parents and/or guardians. First-person narratives, in this case, allow for the narrative voice to negate the parents because of their perceived inability to aid in the coping with the new situation: the psychological corrosion that accompanies adolescence. In other words, through first-person narratives, YAL can function well without parental or other authority figures because these people haven't the capacity to engage in the literacy moment of adolescence: they just don't speak the language. Whereas, in captivity narratives, the savages who spoke English were often considered "less savage" (though, as previously discussed, potentially more dangerous) than their native counterparts, adults who have captured the vernacular of adolescents are often more accepted in YAL. A common trope is to present these figures in the form of teachers.

However, with this acceptance comes marginalization within the academic arena. Robin Williams, Richard Dreyfuss, Julia Roberts, and Kevin Klein have all played fictional teachers on screen who, though loved by their students, were ultimately fired because of their unconventional pedagogical methods. Real-life teachers such as LouAnne Johnson and Ron Clark (about whom fictional movies have also been made) demonstrate that even iconic educators quickly flee teaching to work as authors or tour the lecture circuit. This salient myth of the rogue (white, Christian), saintly pedagogue exemplifies the pervasive assumption that teachers and students, in their purest forms, should remain in separate spheres, and, in doing so, renders students once again in the confines of the Other in front of the classroom. Sometimes, this assumption regarding the separation of teachers and students can lead to skepticism about bringing YAL into the classroom, especially when taught by a teacher who falls into the more mainstream model that these texts appear to detest so adamantly. In the case of YAL and children's media, though, teachers aren't the only people typically absent from the characters' life. Parents seldom serve as anything other than financial support to, or the source of mortification for, the children in contemporary YAL. With each passing generation, the presence of parents has exponentially decreased to where, currently, few readers would even wonder why the savage teen seems to be alone in his/her cruel world.

Still, despite the congruency in narrative structure and thematic elements between YAL and captivity narratives, for me the single most defining characteristic shared by the genres is the trauma and mortification that result from the crossing of the frontier. For I contend the depiction of adolescence/captivity as traumatic and mortifying reflects the excess of a uniquely crafted cultural shift that contributed to the popularity of captivity tales in Rowlandson's era just as YAL is now gaining a more salient readership in 21st-century America. When once, as Annette Kolodny (1993) argues, captivity narratives provided moral or religious instruction, offered political justification for British expansionists' intentions, or presented utopian alternatives to European civilization, contemporary YAL functions very much as a textual manifestation of what Christopher Lasch (1979) terms the "culture of narcissism."

In the next section of this chapter, I will examine how captivity narratives and YAL reflect the anxieties of the respective cultures in which they are produced. It is my contention that both modes of writing not only dichotomize the relationship between self and Other but retard the development of their intended readership. In other words, if captivity narratives endorsed a fear and loathing of American Indians (or any non-Christians), YAL perpetuates adolescents' anxieties over adulthood and their place in a society that has become more focused than ever on consumption rather than production. Teaching YAL in the secondary English classroom, therefore, risks pigeon-holing adolescents into a contrived existence predicated on despair, trauma, and mortification that YAL, by its very nature, offers little incentive to overcome.

Rising Action: Cultural Narcissism and the Problems with YAL as a Pedagogical Tool

In 1985, Jane Tompkins published her groundbreaking *Sensational Designs*, in which she attempted to see literary texts not as works of art embodying enduring themes in complex forms, but as attempts to redefine social order. Texts that scholars have historically marginalized because of the presence of, for example, stereotyped characters, Tompkins revives in her book because "the presence of stereotyped characters, rather than constituting a defect in these novels, was what allowed them to operate as instruments of cultural self-definition" (p. 17). While Tompkins focused her critical gaze on more classical texts, her notion of cultural self-definition realized through a body of literature parallels the current discussion over contemporary YA literature. As I have already discussed, a recurring trope in YAL—as well as captivity narratives—rests in the notion that the plotlines function in response to some sort of traumatic event where anything, no matter how small or seemingly inconsequential, can evolve into everything. Even though conflict of some form exists in virtually all narratives, YA literature is distinguished from non-YAL in that the traumatic experiences which serve as the watershed moments in the texts situate the characters in a wilderness setting in which they are held captive by a socially constructed set of conventions or mores. While Rowlandson's captors employed threats of physical harm or death, YAL's savage threatens the adolescent with a more psychological or cognitive peril. In Puritan times these captivity narratives relayed a duality of voices: the saga of the captives themselves and the attempts of the local minister to explain the experiences and ascribe some greater social, moral, or theological meaning to the trauma. One sees a similar occurrence in teaching YA.

As Tara Fitzpatrick (1991, p. 2) argues, reading captivity narratives with attention to their several voices allows us to recuperate a moment in the production and transmission of what have become central American arche-types: "the imperiled but chosen pilgrim alone in the wilderness bracing the savage 'other.'" If YA books serve as modern-day captivity narratives insofar as their chosen pilgrim braces not the savage Indian Other but rather society's pigeonholing them into the savagery of the adolescent circumstance, then I argue that teaching YAL creates a *dualistic captivity* in which the teacher simultaneously assumes the roles of both the Puritan minister proclaiming the "lessons" from the experiences of the pilgrim (the book) *and* the savage Other by holding the students captive under a set of established academic/ social expectations. This conflating of the preacher/teacher roles resonates with Lasch's (1979, p. 7) idea that America has become a nation of therapeutic sensibility wherein "people hunger not for personal salvation, let alone for an earlier restoration of the golden age, but for the feeling, the momentary illusion, of personal well-being, health, and psychic security."

"Mental health"—not personal fulfillment—has become the new goal sought by Americans, with therapy offering the means of achievement. Thus, teachers, parents, and politicians must now adopt a therapeutic persona in order to aid in the acquisition of mental stability. And this focus on acquisition, Lasch argues, is precisely the problem. As Rochelle Gurstein (2006, p. 13) notes, Lasch considers therapeutic authority "especially pernicious on account of its subtly totalizing reach." Whether it is the disruptive student whose parent or teacher sends him to a psychiatrist, or the juvenile offender whose judge sends him to a social worker, a culture cultivated by therapy and not authority, Lasch contends, "legitimates deviance as sickness" and "simultaneously pronounces the patient unfit to manage his own life and delivers him into the hands of a specialist" (1979, p. 185). Furthermore, this abdication of authority —the repeated relocation of the child to different captors—results in the incessant search for stability and order, thus perpetuating the captivity which results from the constant crossing of foreign frontiers.

Lasch's brand of cultural narcissism involves not the self-involved egocentrism typically associated with psychoanalysis but rather stresses that today's "narcissist" incessantly seeks validation of self-worth from others. As the polar opposite of Tom Wolfe's idea of the "me decade," in which self-indulgence, hedonism, and selfishness ran rampant, Lasch's brand of narcissism involves *anything but* a strong sense of self. When once the rugged individualists—the Thoreau-like or Emersonian transcendentalists—viewed the world as an empty wasteland waiting to be shaped by their own agency and unique design, today's narcissists view the world as a mirror. Thus, one's identity is contingent solely on the surrounding environment—meaning, of course, that it is subject to change with a corresponding change in setting. This notion reflects a shift in the national conscience from being a culture of character to one of personality. Because mirrors focus only on the present, thus negating the past and rendering the future useless, Lasch fears we are "fast losing the sense of historical continuity, the sense of belonging to a succession of generations originating in the past and stretching into the future" (1979, p. 5). This perspective offers yet another explanation for the absence of parents in YA books: as links to the past, they simply serve no purpose in a nation of mirrors.

When parents or other authority figures *are* present, however, Lasch observes that they "conceal their power behind a façade of benevolence. Posing as friendly helpers, they discipline their subordinates as seldom as possible, seeking instead to create a friendly atmosphere in which everyone freely speaks their mind" (1979, p. 181). As mentioned above, parents and teachers succumb to the therapeutic ethos insofar as they wish to be "friends" with their kids rather than authority figures. This refusal to recognize, as Gurstein (2006, p. 13) writes, "the legitimacy of their child's desire for punishment—their desire for clearly defined and enforced limits"—manifests itself both in the content of YAL and in the act of teaching this material in the classroom. Classroom assessment further problematizes the teaching of YAL by insisting that a grade be awarded which signifies the student's "comprehension" of a given text. When knowing a grade will ultimately reflect their progress in class, students often sacrifice their true opinions or experiences with a respective text in favor of their perceived expectations of the teachers. Because of the therapeutic nature of the pedagogy surrounding YAL, students know that in order to survive a given unit, their grade will be based on their ability to "respond" to the text, confessing their innermost anxieties and concerns regarding their fictional teenage experience mirrored in the narrative.

In order to avoid the dangers of assuming the role of "savage Other," as I have already discussed, teachers in modern schools act as friendly mediators between the students and the lessons intended for a given assignment. Arendt contends that the acts of promising and forgiving are essential prerequisites in maintaining the integrity of a social system (see Jacobitti, 1991). Thus, when teachers move from supportive, caring ally of the students to disciplinarian and "grader," the promise of friendship is compromised and replaced by the realization that a teacher, above anything else, must remain in control of the classroom. As a result, violation of the teacher's unwritten promise of consequence-free confessions has the potential to create not only a social instability within the classroom but a fracturing of the ideal identity formed by the student. The once iconic, sanctified, or idolized teacher has now evolved into the savage Other once again. While this transition can and does occur in any academic discipline, the ramifications of its occurring in the classroom reading YAL remains one of my fundamental concerns. As the Indians fed Mary Rowlandson dog meat to enable her to survive, teachers must feed students grades so that they may survive academically. Still, I wonder how teachers can maintain their role as instructors while avoiding their role as captors. Is this even possible? If, as St. Augustine argued, identification is a moment of recognition that links a person to someone else (Woodward, 2003, pp. 17–20), then the link forged by the bond of teacher and student is destroyed by the application of grades and classroom discipline.

The dualistic captivity resulting from teaching YAL manifests itself further when considering the lack of YAL characters who may potentially serve as role models for their readers. If the presence of ideals in literature allows for admiration and growth on behalf of the reader, the lack of ideals in YAL allows very little room for spiritual transcendence. Instead of reading of teenagers whose outlook on life or strong moral compass provides readers with an admirable figure, again YA characters often mirror the perceived turbulence of the teenage years. Thus, as opposed to stressing moral certitude, YA literature often emphasizes moral ambiguity. This focus on the actual and everyday again resonates with a burgeoning emphasis on "seeing myself in my surroundings." Ironically, while seeking verisimilitude, our perception, our relationship to our surrounding environment, becomes blurred to the point where we question the validity of the external world. What Lasch (1979) notices in factories and classrooms is especially poignant in the contemporary classroom. He argues that this blurred subjectivity is more prominent in today's office setting than in yesterday's factory because work has lost its tangible quality and has become abstract and impersonal. The intense subjectivity embedded in YA pedagogy renders the student captive under a socially induced shell of protective irony.

With reality shows infiltrating virtually every television network and academic success no longer considered socially admirable, Americans have done away with the deification of the exceptional. For example, when once statues displayed our heroes as almost caricatures of themselves engaged in god-like poses and served as larger-than-life beacons of respect and commanders of adoration, now we fashion our heroes simply as just one of the guys. Purdue University graduate Neil Armstrong, for instance, recently had an academic building dedicated to him on Purdue's West Lafayette campus. Fifty years ago, the statue in front of the building would have been taller than any human being, more than likely depicting Armstrong in full NASA uniform, perhaps crafted as if in stride on the Moon. In 2007, however, the unveiled statue depicted a life-size sculpture of Armstrong as a student at Purdue, seated on a bench, gazing at the sky.

Rather than seeking spiritual transcendence or self-aggrandizement, YAL characters often find themselves seeking nothing more than peace of mind. Like the constituency of their readership, these characters' search for mental health is confounded by the fact that the harsh conditions of their world constantly militate against it. Thus, both readers and characters are held captive not by the Others of an alternative race but by their present circumstance itself. However, similar to Rowlandson's literary realm, where the antagonistic bond between society and savagery is a fabrication based on fear, ignorance, and the perversion of Christian social mores, the negative perception of the Other in YAL does not derive from innate qualities of the Other but rather is created through society's insistence that adolescents be pigeonholed in a world of chaos and doubt.

Beginning with the Industrial Revolution in the 19th century, Americans underwent a dramatic shift in terms of their methods of self-identification. When once American workers had a direct and autonomous investment in their labor, with the rise of machines came the rise of dependence on the Other: factories, companies, bosses, and, yes, machines themselves. You no longer defined who you were, for a person now may simply construct one part (as opposed to the complete entity) of the greater whole. Consequently, this severing of the autonomy of American laborers was the catalyst for a nation-wide identity search that, I argue, still exists to this day. As Americans, we experienced a unique position of essentially being *required* to forget our past unless we wished to live in the wake of the British throne. However, with this cutting of our national umbilical cord, combined with the detachment of producer from product, came the rise in cultural narcissism that writers like Tom Wolfe and Chris Lasch so adamantly detest. Still, Lasch goes to great lengths to point out that it wasn't simply the rise of American industry that caused the brand of narcissism that permeated Wolfe's "me decade" of the 1970s, but virtually every major institution, including work, the mass-culture industry, the state, family, and school.

To this point, I realize that I seem to have painted YAL in an over-whelmingly negative light. I wish to clarify, as I will again later, that I am not now, nor have I ever been, against the idea of *reading* young adult literature, for it indeed has a purpose. It can provide companionship for a socially alienated adolescent and escape from a chaotic life, establish shared interests among friends, and serve as a source of exploration and creativity. Plus, it is reading, after all! No, what I question is the practicality and overall value of *teaching* YAL in the secondary classroom as a replacement for texts that traditionally either have gone unnoticed due their perceived inaccessibility to students or occupy the literary canon. Furthermore, my concerns lie in Rakow's (1991) claim that, in addition to needing books to feel better about themselves, teenagers need adult guidance in evaluating writing and relating texts to themselves. Such a notion appears, to me, to undermine the integrity and cognitive capability of teenagers and ascribes for them an identity incongruent to the one they most likely possess. To say that teenagers cannot possibly comprehend the essence of a given text's nuances mirrors the Puritan belief that suggested Indians could not possibly grasp the sophistication present in a civilized, Christian society. Ironically, while advocating the teaching of YAL so that students may grow and learn, we are in turn arresting their develop-ment and retarding their escape from adolescence. Puritan racism has evolved into our ageism.

While Don Wolfe (1958, p. 143) notes that in the 1950s, teachers of litera-ture tended to assign *outside* reading that gave students insight on particular problems, in today's schools it appears as though we have juxtaposed this notion of outside therapeutic reading with classroom assignments intended to foster the development of the students' identity through pedagogical therapy. If, as George Herbert Mead posited, "society shapes self shapes social behavior" (cited in Burke & Stryker, 2000, p. 285), then what kind of identity do books predicated on adolescent trauma and taught by non-medical bibliotherapists produce? Arguably, the identity formed by adolescents in response to the teaching of YAL in schools ignores the key but important aspect of ideal iden-tity. As Conroy and de Ruyter (2002) argue, while compromising aspirations rather than realities, ideal identity makes a major contribution to the definition of self-identity. However, the presence of ideals on the educational spectrum has been replaced, or at best marginalized, by the focus on the "realistic" depiction of the teenage experience. Even though this maneuver was no doubt conceived from an altruistic desire to help the students, I argue that such a pedagogical compromise ultimately jeopardizes the capacity to which teenagers may seek an escape from the troubled and ambiguous identity we have ascribed for them. In other words, what incentive do teenagers have to embrace the challenge of self-improvement if the books we teach them in class only validate their angst-filled lot in life?

Ironically, the assumed victim status—this glorified impotence—of the teenage students is reinforced by the content of YA novels themselves, which, again, often depict teenagers experiencing victimization resulting from traumas in their lives. YA texts perpetuate the notion that being a teenager *necessarily* involves a unique and paralyzing level of struggle whose only remedy is a therapeutic discourse between student and teacher. However, attempts at bibliotherapy in the classroom only hinder the potential for spiritual growth—albeit in the form of an actual education—by confining the student to an ideology which maintains he/she is a victim of his/her own circumstance as a teenager. Students can be helped only as far as the limitations of their captivity allow. As Joan F. Kaywell (1997, p. 91) notes, "because we are teachers of English and not therapists, we are in the business of improving students' literacy more than we are in saving their lives." However, Kaywell continues that, in some ways, by improving students' reading and writing abilities, we are saving them from themselves.

But from what aspect of themselves are we saving them, and at what cost? "Teenagers," argues Susan R. Rakow (1991, p. 48), "need young adult books to help illuminate and validate their own experiences." In a world that often leaves teenagers feeling alien, Chris Crowe (2002) contends that YAL allows students to feel as though their experiences have value and that, contrary to a salient belief among students, this value is not an illusion. I would extend Crowe's position to argue that certain YA texts enhance a teen's sense of individual agency through the realization that while the characters in the book may suffer, the reader may use these fictionalized people to carve his or her own path in life—one that doesn't involve suicide, drugs, or rebellion. In other words, recognizing the dangers in emulating characters' actions, readers may develop into more socially savvy citizens. This agency, however, often gets stripped when YA books are assessed not on the lengths to which they are absorbed by the students, but by grades, projects, or lectures. More troubling, perhaps, is the realization that the Ben Franklin model of self-improvement, the quintessential means of success throughout the first two centuries of our nation's existence, has been overshadowed by a bastardized version of the Protestant work ethic that preaches self-preservation over improvement, and personality over character.

What Lasch (1979, p. 53) dubs "one of the most important underpinnings of American culture," the Protestant work ethic, stood as the standard against which American citizens gauged success and virtue during the centuries of our nation's infancy. The self-made man, the corporeal manifestation of the American dream, owed any and all of his success to habits of industry, sobriety, moderation, self-discipline, and avoidance of debt. Always looking toward the future, the self-made man's public reception rested on admiration by his fellow man, esteem, and public appreciation for his accomplishments. These attributes contributed to the self-made man's character but, unlike the culture of personality, did not define his identity. In our age of what Lasch (1979) terms "diminishing expectations," Americans no longer get as excited about the merits of the dusty Protestant work ethic: our emphasis is on the here, the now, and the greatest potential for instant celebrity. Seeking envy instead of admiration and recognizing that nothing succeeds like the appearance of success, 21st-century Americans no longer care if they made what they have so much as they have it made! However, in the case of YAL, nothing demoralizes quite like the appearance of demoralization. Adolescents are primed no longer to value their connections with the past and are taught that buying now, paying later, is the way to go. The present—their presence as adolescents—is therefore the ultimate captor. For, no matter how hard one struggles, the present can never be escaped. Why, then, strive for anything better?

Since YAL perpetuates this idea of the eternal adolescent, it only makes sense that the characters and the readers display behaviors pervasive in the era of diminished expectations. Since YAL tends to contain first-person narratives in the form of an adolescent narrative voice, these texts frequently walk a fine line between self-analysis and self-indulgence (Lasch, 1979, p. 18). What was meant as a means to give teenagers a voice has evolved into a YA culture of confessions in which the contemporary American's exhibitionist impulse discovers a new home as ink on a page. The implicit message of the YA narrator begging, "Listen to me," when brought into the classroom, becomes the student anxiously saying, "Hear my thoughts!" Hurled against this cultural backdrop, it seems as if everyone has a story to tell which, by its nature, is considered intrinsically valuable. Thus, proponents of YAL subconsciously capitalize on this created identity produced by teaching that adolescence is essentially traumatic and mortifying but also ultimately perpetuate the burgeoning voyeuristic impulse governing much of the media to which our teenagers are exposed. By "voyeuristic impulse," I'm referring to the tendency to seek pleasure not only from the exhibitions of others but from their misfortunes or struggles. What the Germans call "*Schadenfreude*" I call teaching YAL.

What Really *Is* YAL?

Recently I had a discussion with my college freshmen about why they enjoyed reading YA books. (Not to my surprise, most of them declared they preferred reading YAL over those "boring, old books" they *had* to read in other classes.) The most common answer was that YA texts offered stories and plotlines that resonated with their own experiences. As an exercise in deconstruction, I then asked the class to describe the traditional plot structure of YA novels. After further explanation, we produced the following timeline of events.

Most YA stories begin with some sort of watershed event, usually in the form of a traumatic experience. This event often occurs within the first chapter, if not pages, of the story and can involve anything from the death of a friend/parent/ other relative to the beginning of high school, a breakup, a national tragedy— and the list went on. From this watershed moment, the main character usually finds himself/herself in unfriendly or unfamiliar surroundings. More often than not, this results from a physical relocation of the character (a family move, journey to high school, prison, etc.). The characters face obstacles, often in the form of external conflicts with other characters, but conditions slowly begin to improve. The characters may falter a little, but they keep on struggling. In the end, my class decided, the character faces a choice: he/she can assimilate to the cultural conventions of the new environment; reject those conventions; or socially/spiritually/physically die. No one suggested that the character might somehow be rescued or saved in the end, which seems to indicate that my students felt as though the protagonist's captor was adolescence itself, not the condescending, treacherous clutches of his/her new climate.

If adolescence is indeed the captor, it makes sense that an escape from captivity is impossible, for, unless the book is told from the perspective of an adult gazing back on his/her childhood (as very few YA books are), it is implausible to suggest that a character can simply *grow older* in a matter of moments. Still, if the circumstances resulting from one's age—and not society —ultimately hold the character captive, how does that confound my equating YAL's adolescence with Mary Rowlandson's Puritanism? Can it be said that her *religion* held her captive in the same manner as a YA character's *age* does? Is it reasonable to posit that both the Indian savages *and* her religion held her, albeit in different ways, under a system of control? How, then, does this relate to teenagers?

Having, merely a few days prior to the above discussion, completed sections of Mary Rowlandson's narrative, the class (after some prodding from me) quickly picked up on the connections between the YAL timeline we had agreed upon and the plight of our Puritan protagonist. "So what?" a colleague of mine later argued. "It doesn't matter if YA lit *is* modern-day captivity narratives. The kids love it, so why not teach it?" Fair enough. After all, education *is* about conceding to the desires of the students . . . right? But this dialogue with my colleague led us both into a discussion about whether plotlines in YA books are *essentially* different from those of non-YA texts. Is there an experience unique to teenagers—besides, of course, being a teenager at the time of reading the book in question? Of course, puberty and perhaps the statistical prevalence of eating disorders among teenagers come to mind, but how much of YAL is devoted to those? And, more importantly, by what means is that attention paid? Can it simply be argued that the "unique experiences" depicted in YAL are really microcosms for universal experiences? In other words, does the prom become just another social function—like, say, a wedding or an office party— and can teenage breakups translate into adult divorces? Depression is depression and suicide is suicide, so what is so unique about the plots of YA texts? More importantly, why do we insist they have something to offer in the classroom that more rhetorically sophisticated texts do not?

Perhaps the tenet of YAL that people stress as its greatest appeal is the presence and focus of adolescent characters in adolescent situations. Yet the presence of young adult characters in a novel does not necessarily qualify a text as YAL. Nor is the qualification of YAL contingent solely on the presence of young characters. Certainly, YA books exist with adult protagonists, although I concede that with characters of similar ages to their readers comes more likelihood that a young adult will read a given text. In other words, two people who are 16 are thought *automatically* to have more in common than a person who is 16 and someone who is 30. Personally, I find several problems with using age as the quintessential means of identification. In essentializing similarities as a product simply of age, we ignore several other fundamental aspects of one's identity, such as race, gender, religion, sexual orientation, familiar status, and socioeconomic class. To say we should teach YA books merely because the characters are young adults themselves ignores the possibility that perhaps race may trump age to the degree that a reader may sympathize with any given character.

The hyper-emphatic means by which YAL stresses age as the be-all and end-all of bonds further confounds characters' ability to recognize the merit of the Other. As do virtually all forms of the captivity narrative, YAL perpetuates a salient fear and aversion to that which is *not me* by implying that anything that fails to reflect a character's present circumstance (i.e., characters of different ages, races, religions, sexual orientations) warrants marginalization. Thus, the plots of YA texts remain essentially unaltered from Rowlandson's day, when the unfamiliar bore the scarlet "E"—for enemy—while similarities ultimately provided the key to social cohesion. While obscurity and ambiguity both play an integral role in characters' decision-making, the social roles embedded in a YA text are nothing if not clearly defined according to conceptual binaries.

Literarily speaking, characters like J.D. Salinger's Holden Caulfield exemplify the salient ambivalence embodied in teenagers. The female protagonist of Libba Bray's *A Great and Terrible Beauty* (2003) represents budding feminine morality in 1890s London, but also experiments with devilish magic, rejection of authority, and thoughts of suicide. However, in and of itself, moral ambiguity is not a terrible thing. Indeed, many argue, and I would agree, that an intriguing plotline may very well function on the grounds of a morally ambiguous character. And whoever said plot is the most important aspect of a story anyway? In contrast to YA texts, Shakespeare, for example, offers sophisticated rhetoric, opportunities for historical contextualization, and one heck of a key to open virtually any other literary door. Furthermore, aside from YAL containing much less sophisticated prose, the moral ambiguity of YAL characters is rarely resolved in the end, which consequently leaves the readers without a character to whom they may look for inspiration. Thus, characters devoid of moral conviction become the inspiration.

Our good intentions notwithstanding, we must approach the teaching of issues such as depression and suicide with a degree of humility. Despite the prevalence of similar traumatic events in adulthood as well as in adolescents, teenagers certainly lack the life experiences needed to engage in these conversations on the intellectual level comparable to that of adults (which is not to say they cannot articulate it in their own terms). While many of today's youth require some form of guidance in making their way through the trials of teenage turmoil, perhaps we, as teachers, ought not to strive so vigorously to be their instructor, doctor, and savior. As one survey of English teachers indicates, instructors can feel reluctant to bring such issues into the classroom. Rather than faulting them for their apprehension, I applaud them for their humility. One Duluth teacher noted, "I am very leery of anyone 'blundering in' armed with good intentions and very little training. The psychological implications could be tremendous . . . I don't think we should deliberately set out to teach about suicide—could be Pandora's box" (Swing, 1990, p. 78). To what measure does our role as facilitators of development extend? If, as many teachers speculate, contemporary YA fiction romanticizes trauma to the degree that it may provide role models who, rather than serving as saints or icons, reflect a life of anguish and struggle, wherein lies our hurry to bring this material into the classroom? Wolfe (1958, p. 143) contends that any literature may be useful insofar as it has the ability to initiate cogent discussions on these troubling issues. However, I stipulate that the main ingredient lies not in the strength of a given text's prose, but in the competence of a given text's teacher.

At what price do we so anxiously bring YAL into the classroom without first considering *how* and *why* we are doing it? Again, I declare I have nothing against the reading of young adult literature, merely the hasty nature with which we assign it to our students and expect them to respond with the same exuberance with which they read it in their spare time. Since we see and hear the promising effects of YAL on teenagers, we assume that the genre will translate well into the classroom and, with proper instruction, will contribute better to the development of intelligent young thinkers than classical/non-YA texts would. However, this assumption dares to essentialize what it is to be a teenager and, worse, what it means to capture the teenage experience in ink. Even so, perhaps my deepest concern with the teaching of YAL lurks in the notion that young adult literature undermines the value of the teacher's role. With discussion questions and lesson plans in the back of ever more YA books, how is the status of teachers evolving both inside and outside the classroom? Can (and should) YA books teach themselves? Wherein, then, lies our responsibility for facilitation and the fostering of students' identities? I fear that when our quizzes and exams fail to contain similar questions compared to those in the "questions for discussion" found at the back of modern YAL, a sort of cognitive dissonance will form in the students' psyche whereby they will be forced to choose loyalty to the text or the teacher. Because the teacher provides a grade that the text does not, inevitably students will declare loyalty to the teacher and consequently will sacrifice learning the lessons for which the author may or may not have written the text.

It appears as though authors now write books so that they may undergo some sort of literary discussion. I have yet to determine, however, whether these authors intend their lessons to be discussed in a classroom dominated by a teacher and mandated by a set of academic standards and social expectations. Still, to second Wolfe, a good teacher can make any text useful to students. In modifying Pascal's wager[1] for the existence of God into something applicable to teachers, we may find the combinations of good/bad teachers and YA/non-YA texts look something like Table 10.1.

Based on this framework, not only may YA literature fail to live up to the rhetorical sophistication of other, more complex non-YA texts, but, with improper instruction, teaching YAL may potentially be *more* dangerous than teaching other texts because of its exposure of complicated issues to a naïve and untrained readership. One wonders if the issues facing teenagers, though they may not differ conceptually from the struggles of their adult counterparts, warrant a place in the classroom for no other reason than to make the students feel as though their interests matter. In his article "Hidden Intellectualism," Gerald Graff (2006, p. 145) notes that "real intellectuals turn any subject, however lightweight it may seem, into grist for their mill through the thoughtful questions they bring to it, whereas a dullard will find a way to drain the interest out of the richest subject." Thus, with cogent instruction, a student may write of baseball with the same academic zeal with which another may write of Byron. I take Graff's message to heart. Of course, YAL has the potential to provide great benefits for students. As Chris Crowe (2001a) argues, it's a shame that when the literary canon opened up to include marginalized and neglected texts, it didn't simultaneously consider adopting YAL into its ranks as well. Many English teachers remain loyal to teaching canonical texts because success in standardized tests relies on a breadth of knowledge in this area, so YAL often gets overlooked when picking books for a curriculum. Still, I wonder if the risks are worth the reward in this dispute of teaching Hester Prynne or Harry Potter.

Traditionally, the argument against teaching YAL stems from the dual ideas that YA texts are not classics and that they corrupt the young. Even Chris

Table 10.1 Pascal's Wager

Spanke's Wager	YA Texts	Non-YA Texts
Good Teachers	Good teachers will utilize YA texts as a means by which certain themes, struggles, and ideas related to teens will be validated, thus leaving the students aware of the complexity not only of their own lives but of the rhetoric of fine literary study.	Similarly, good teachers will use non-YA texts as a means by which the same themes, struggles, and ideas related to teens are no longer perceived as unique but universal, thus allowing the students to enter into the greater conversation of humanity and not feel isolated within the confines of adolescence.
Bad Teachers	Bad teachers will use YAL as a means to treat students for their problems of adolescence. Their efforts at healing will be confounded by their pedagogical duties, and the resulting cognitive dissonance will cause greater damage to the fragile minds of these teens by making them feel as though they are victims of a contemporary captivity predicated upon the tensions of their own circumstance.	Bad teachers will bore students by teaching non-YAL as a means to understand the world around them. Due to their lack of motivational abilities, few students will engage in the reading, causing test scores to drop and YAL to be considered a viable substitute for these otherwise antiquated texts.

Crowe (2001b), a YA author and an avid proponent of YAL as a literary genre, acknowledges that YA novels fall short of the depth and artistic development of the great works of the literary canon, and that some YA books may have negative effects on certain teenagers. Why, then, do we dare cross the line between reading YAL for fun versus reading it for a grade? Is it because it is easier both to read and to teach? Do we *really* think the students will like it more? Surely we don't suppose it will shield bad teaching by replacing the duties of the instructor with preconceived quizzes and discussion questions.

I would now like to reiterate that, when it comes to reading YA books, I say, "Let them eat cake . . . but no food in the classroom." If we truly believe YAL has something more to offer students, perhaps we should turn the lens back on ourselves as teachers and examine our motivations for teaching and the assumptions we have about our students.

Denouement; Why Do We Teach?

We must remember why we wanted to teach in the first place and refuse to be replaced by these pedagogical supplements but instead rise up and declare loyalty to education, to growth, and to the confrontation of our fears of the unknown Other or difficult material. In 1984, Don Gallo (1984, p. 34) declared his hope that, twenty years from then, the academic interest in YA literature would have grown YAL into an area that "is more widely taught in our [secondary and elementary] schools than it is now." Interestingly, long before the unprecedented rise of interest in YAL in the last few years, Gallo realized that, sometimes, "those of us who are enthusiastic about YA think all YA books are marvelous, when far too many recent titles are published to meet the demand for popular topics and good writing does not seem to be a consideration" (p. 31). In the new millennium, Michael Cart (2003) sees a drastic difference between the YA literature read by Gallo in the 1980s and the books teens read today. Cart writes, "today's writers are freer than ever to experiment, to flex their creative muscles, to employ themes, tools, and techniques that were previously considered taboo in a literature that had once been identified by constraints and too often fashioned according to formula" (p. 113). I find Cart's aversion to formulas ironic considering that even "cutting-edge" YA texts fall within the rubric of traditional captivity narratives or at least subscribe to conventional plotlines found in all genres of storytelling.

Nevertheless, Cart does have a point. "Kids are buying books in quantities we've never seen before," he said in a recent online article (Goodnow, 2007). "And publishers are courting young adults in ways we haven't seen since the 1940s." The topic of young adult literature can (and should) no longer be dismissed by the academic community. As teachers, we must not only accept but embrace the fact that ever more of our students are seeking out this material and we must develop ways to address this reality. However, as I have argued in this chapter, as the popularity of YAL rises, so too does the potential danger resulting from the improper instruction of a YA text. Students may find themselves in some sort of inescapable captivity predicated upon the identity society creates for them. The accessibility of the prose of YA texts, though intended for entertainment or private self-discovery, may limit the lengths to which students are willing to venture for self-improvement. The absence of role models in YA texts may leave some students resistant to changing their own situation, thus rendering a nation of arrested adolescence . . . or arrested adolescents. However, above all, teaching YAL can limit the capacity for challenge and discovery through recognition of the validity of the Other and may undermine the value of good teachers. In the end, kids need *teachers* to teach them. We should not underestimate the value of the bonds formed between teachers and students, nor should we risk the destruction of those bonds. The type of relationship that exists between a teacher and a student can never exist between a student and a mere page with ink on it, irrespective of all the discussion sections in YA books.

Epilogue

If Increase Mather created a dualistic voice for Mary Rowlandson by serving as both the printer and preacher of her captivity experience, then, logically, as a teacher himself, Mather also created a dualistic captivity for Rowlandson. Though her narrative typified the captivity genre, its publication and spiritual resonances pigeonholed her in a world of chaos and confusion in which she spent the remainder of her Puritan existence. When her civilization successfully bartered for her in 1676, her return to normalcy was met with prayers of thanksgiving and praise. But a part of her never *really* left those woods. A part of her remained held captive by the conflation of the haunting memories of her past circumstance and the reality of her newly formed role as Puritan heroine. As teachers, we must take heed of the lessons of Increase Mather and approach teaching young adult literature with an air of caution lest we desire to create a captivity for our students from which they may never escape. While, in time, they will triumph over the wilderness of their own adolescence, Rowlandson teaches us that maladjustment comes with malnourishment. We must feed our students the knowledge that they need now, so that they may embrace their return to normalcy with confidence and courage to relay their story to the world. After all, in the age of confessions, everyone has a narrative to write.

Note

1 French philosopher Blaise Pascal wagered that it is better to "bet" on the existence of God than it is to bet against Him. In short, his wager suggests that if you believe in God, then His existence will grant you entry into heaven; whereas His lack of existence means your "loss" of the bet is finite and therefore negligible. On the other hand, if you do not believe in God, then His existence means damnation in hell; whereas, again, His lack of existence means your "loss" of the bet is finite and therefore negligible. Clearly, the stakes are far worse for not believing in an existing God than believing in a God who does not exist.

Bibliography

Beaman, A. (2006). YA Lit 2.0: How technology is enhancing the pleasure reading experience for teens. *Knowledge Quest*, 35 (1), 30–33.

Bray, L. (2003). *A great and terrible beauty*. New York: Random House.

Burke, P.J. & Stryker, S. (2000). The past, present, and future of identity theory. *Social Psychology Quarterly*, 63 (4), 284–297.

Cart, M. (2003). Bold books for innovative teaching: A place for energy, activity and art. *English Journal*, 93 (1), 113–116.

Conroy, J. & de Ruyter, D. (2002). The formation of identity: The importance of ideals. *Oxford Review of Education*, 28 (4), 509–522.

Crowe, C. (2001a). Young adult literature: AP and YA? *English Journal,* 91 (1), 123–128.

Crowe, C. (2001b). Young adult literature: The problem with YA literature. *English Journal,* 90 (3), 146–150.

Crowe, C. (2002). Young adult literature: Defending YA literature: Voice of students. *English Journal,* 92 (1), 114–118.

Ellis, D. (2001). *The breadwinner.* Toronto: Groundwood Books.

Fitzpatrick, T. (1991). The figure of captivity: The cultural work of the Puritan captivity narrative. *American Literary Review,* 28 (4), 1–26.

Gallo, D. (1984). What should teachers know about YA lit for 2004? *English Journal,* 73 (7), 31–34.

Gallo, D. (2008). Censorship, clear thinking, and bold books for teens. *English Journal,* 97 (3), 114–118.

Goodnow, C. (2007). Teens buying books at fastest rate in decades: New "golden age of young adult literature" declared. Online: http://www.seattlepi.com/books/306531_teenlit08.html.

Graff, G. (2006). Hidden intellectualism. In G. Graff and C. Birkenstein, *They say, I say* (pp. 142–148). New York: W.W. Norton.

Gurstein, R. (2006). "The culture of narcissism" revisited. *Salmagundi,* 150, 13–24.

Jacobitti, S.D. (1991). Individualism and political community: Arendt and Tocqueville on the current debate in liberalism. *Polity,* 23 (4), 585–604.

Kaywell, J.F. (1997). Young adult literature: Using young adult realistic literature to help troubled teenagers: Something new, tried, and true, and recommended nonfiction. *English Journal,* 86 (5), 91–95.

Kestler, F.R. (1990). *The Indian captivity narrative: A woman's view.* New York: Garland.

Kolodny, A. (1993). Among the Indians: The uses of captivity. *New York Times Book Review,* 98 (1), 1–10.

Lasch, C. (1979). *The culture of narcissism: American life in an age of diminishing expectations.* New York: W.W. Norton.

Myracle, L. (2004). *ttyl.* New York: Amulet.

Naidoo, B. (2002). *The other side of truth.* New York: Amistad.

Newman, A. (2003). Captive on the literacy frontier: Mary Rowlandson, James Smith, and Charles Johnston. *Early American Literature,* 38 (1), 31–65.

Rakow, S.R. (1991). Young adult literature for honors students? *English Journal,* 80 (1), 48–51.

Slotkin, R. (1996). *Regeneration through violence: The mythology of the American frontier 1600–1800.* New York: Harper Perennial.

Sturma, M. (2002). Aliens and Indians: A comparison of abduction and captivity narratives. *Journal of Popular Culture,* 36 (2), 318–334.

Swing, G. (1990). Choosing life: Adolescent suicide in literature. *English Journal,* 79 (5), 78–82.

Tompkins, J (1985). *Sensational designs.* New York: Oxford University Press.

Vanderbeets, R. (1972). The Indian captivity narrative as ritual. *American Literature,* 43 (4), 5548–5562.

Wolfe, D. (1958). New trends in the teaching of literature. *Review of Educational Research,* 28 (2), 140–147.

Wolfe, T. (1976). The "me" decade and the third great awakening. *New York*, 23 August, 26–40.

Woodward, G.C. (2003). *The idea of identification*. New York: State University of New York Press.

Chapter 11

Perspective Giving and Taking in the Secondary English Class

Considering the Case of Erin Gruwell

Jeanne Smith Muzzillo

Perspective taking, or experimenting with different points of view in the English language arts classroom, occurs through literary studies and composition instruction. Both teachers and students, however, experience the intellectual and emotional phenomena of perspective taking in the classroom. Consider the challenges and demands that must occur when attempting to see as the "other" in the following scenario:

> A first-year English language arts teacher, let us call her Ms. Smith, skipping lunch, tackled 5th-period freshman English with all the verve her coffee could induce. Both Ms. Smith and the students were attempting to enact at least two identities. The day's lesson called for students to create dialogue. Students were asked to "become" a character from *Romeo and Juliet* and "speak" with their counterparts. Although they were novice writers, they attempted to enter Shakespeare's world, using contemporary language but projecting character traits they discerned. Ms. Smith was also adopting perspectives, those of her students and that of an imagined, composite ideal teacher. Perhaps Erin Gruwell comes to mind, although *The Freedom Writers Diary* as a text did not exist when this teacher was trained. Frankly, if Ms. Smith had had the energy at the end of the day, she [I] might even have patted herself on the back for her ingenuity and that of her student writers.

Such a scenario, however, begs the question: to what end and at what costs do we attempt perspective taking in the classroom? It is possible that even such a simple activity as previously described is problematic on three levels: unanticipated cognitive and affective demands; unexamined ethics of requiring identification with another; and (for the teacher) unrealistic perspective goals that can reinforce notions of teachers, particularly women, as necessarily altruistic.

Barnes-Holmes, McHugh, and Barnes-Holmes (2004) explain that perspective taking is undergirded by relational frame theory, meaning that our constructed understandings derive from relational functions established in our verbal communities. So if I tell you that A is the same as B, and that B is the same as C, what can you derive? This sameness that you perceive in that context is relational responding because of the context influence. It is also termed *arbitrary* because society sets up the context—Bness or Aness can be changed as the community suggests. For example, even before the play begins, the freshmen accept that a "Romeo" is a romantic wooer of women.

We can appreciate the complexity of altering perspectives by attempting to follow Barnes-Holmes, McHugh, and Barnes-Holmes's five intellectual steps. Step One: you hold in your hand (most likely) a printed text. For *simple visual* understanding you know that you can see only this side of the text; you cannot know with certainty what someone else, someone facing you, can see and know. In Step Two, *complex visual,* you comprehend that even if the reader nearest to you can see the text, she or he may quite possibly see it differently from the way you do. *Seeing leads to knowing* at Step Three. When this text is closed, you know that you cannot see/know that someone has placed a dollar bill within as a bookmark. If you had seen such an act, you know that you know and that the dollar is there. As you progress in sophisticated thinking, with Step Four you can *predict*. If you saw me earlier mark the journal page with a dollar, your true belief born of seeing allows you to predict that a dollar is available.

So far we are dealing with seeing experiences that do not disrupt our reality much. But what if, as in Step Five, I (playing the role of teacher here) ask you to predict based upon a *false belief*? In view of my students, I place the projector remote control in my box of gum. While they see me do this, students also hold prior schemata that dictate the proper places for gum and remotes. I violate these. If, however, I ask them later to predict where I'll find the remote, they will all do so accurately. This is not the final difficulty, though. Sometimes reversals are required. If Dromio of Ephesus has a gold chain and Dromio of Syracuse has some coins, and Dromio E. exchanges chain for coins with Dromio S., then Dromio of Syracuse goes to Ephesus and Dromio of Ephesus goes to Syracuse, where is the chain? Somewhat of a challenge, isn't it?

Perspective Taking in Teachers' Lives

I have been describing a unidirectional phenomenon: teachers instruct → students read about others → they attempt to understand the world through the eyes of the specified other person. What further confounds the English language arts (ELA) classroom, though, is that the teacher herself is also constructing other ways of seeing. Professional identification requires both teachers in training and veterans to enact the perspective of Teacher.

In preparation for this chapter, I surveyed a group of pre-service elementary and secondary teachers, undergraduates in elementary education and secondary language arts training. We had read Nikki Grimes's *Bronx Masquerade* (2003), and I was very curious about their perspective taking in a professional sense. *Bronx Masquerade* is a fictional collection of poetic student voices. The presentation of the poems is alternated with student autobiographical short essays that relate and provide segues from one student to the other. "Readings" of the poems are commented upon by the student voice of Tyrone. Students in the *Bronx Masquerade* are writing poems based on classroom study of the Harlem Renaissance led by their teacher, Mr. Ward. What is interesting in Grimes's work is that Mr. Ward does not contribute to the collection explicitly. My presumption was that my education students would identify with the adult figure and take his perspective on what happened in the resulting compilation. I was mistaken. My students mirrored the amount of interest Grimes displayed for the teacher—little. I speculate that the kind of teaching in this fictional setting was what Freire (1970/1993) would have seen as "liberatory." While the teacher was originally a catalyst, the students took over further impetus and responsibility for their own craft and production. There is little room for adult ego. A side note: the teacher in this text is male. Is this a barrier to the students' (primarily female) identification?

What Happens When Hollywood Enters, Stage Right?

However, when I mentioned *The Freedom Writers Diary*, my teachers in training became very animated. They loved the book and the movie. To understand what happens, a little back-story may be helpful. The text is formatted as a compiled, composite diary of 150 high school students in Los Angeles, starting with contributions from freshman English. There they meet the real-life Erin Gruwell. She is a first-year hire, delighted to be in her own classroom. Faced first with failing students for whom a successful day was one which they survived physically, she decides to work three jobs and to buy a set of paperback readings that focus on diversity and acceptance. She works with Anne Frank's diary and that of Zlata Filipović. She includes Wiesel's *Night* and Strasser's *The Wave*. Her students are inspired both by her compassion and enthusiasm and by the poignancy and relevance of the readings. They begin to write their own journals, sharing when they opt to. Eventually named "The Freedom Writers," they become activists for social change. Through their diary entries, readers learn a great deal about the horrific events experienced by young people in Los Angeles and presumably elsewhere. The appeal of the story is that we also learn about the resilience and dignity of youth. The diary was first published in 1997.

Perspective taking enters this reading immediately. I coded the text for instances where readers would need to engage the role of Ms. G, the teacher.

One difference between this precursor and a similar experience with *Bronx Masquerade* is that Ms. G does include an entry from time to time, but only (ostensibly) to mark the passage of semesters. She becomes a focal point, not because of her textual contributions but because of her importance in the daily lives of the writers.

Level One: readers see Ms. G for themselves. She smiles back at us wreathed by the faces and embraces of her students. She is an attractive young white woman (Freedom Writers, 1999, cover illustration).

Level Two: readers see that others see Ms. G differently. "Within the next week, she has managed to fit me into her class. She plays reading and vocabulary games to help us learn, and she listens to our questions. She actually cares. She talks to us on a level I can understand" (pp. 71, 58). Interestingly, the students don't write about Ms. G's appearance other than her mannerisms a few times and the constant invocation of whiteness.

Another perspective level occurs when the Freedom Writers see that others in their school community do not see Ms. G as they do. They come to know that some of the staff see her as making them look bad. Already this is a complex relational frame, because Ms. G was surprised herself when she had to write that teachers did not see her as helping, but as a saboteur.

Level Three: somewhat seen already. Seeing leads to knowing. Readers know by seeing that Ms. G knows:

> The Capulets are like the Latino gang, and the Montagues are like the Asian gang. What? . . . The next thing I know, she's comparing these two families to rival gangs in this city. At first I was thinking, what the hell does this bitch know about gangs? But the real trip was when she actually named them. I didn't think she knew about all the shit that happened up in Long Beach. I just thought she left school and drove home to her perfect life.
>
> (p. 33)

Not only the reader processes knowing by seeing. The Freedom Writers provide numerous vignettes about the importance of witness perspective. An obese girl is especially devastated by an attack because her friends impassively watched. A Latina girl suffers great conflict in deciding whether to testify about a Latino killer whose crime she saw. Almost every writer shares the indelible images of witnessed cruelties.

Level Four: true beliefs and predictions about teachers can be constructed by readers of *The Freedom Writers Diary*. Ms. G bucks the school system to champion her students. Ms. G listens. She is resented. She seemingly has no outside private existence. She is resourceful and inventive. She is ultimately accepted and loved by her students. Perhaps they are dependent on her (she moves up with them through grades). Ms. G is recognized by the outside community. She reaches celebrity–hero status. It must be said, though, that much of the notoriety is not from the students but from the outsiders to whom her story appeals. Does this depiction sound familiar? One slight problem might be in imagining the future when stardom is already achieved.

The student writers from L.A. also construct very important lessons: seeing, forming beliefs so strong that they take it on the road to others, and predicting that peace will reap rewards. The students read of the Holocaust and of Bosnia. They are exposed to countless examples of insane dehumanization from historical accounts and from meeting survivors. They form beliefs that differ from the negativity bred in their neighborhoods. For some reason, their new beliefs and predictions are that violence begets violence and that first one form of violence must stop to break the cycle.

Using Level Five understanding and predicting based on false beliefs, readers will predict about teachers and teaching from a false belief. One student is very excited that Ms. G asks them to draw in class. He/she is a graffiti specialist. The writer says:

> I went to school, but I never really hit the books. My teachers always said, "I'm here to help," but when the time came to start helping they were never dependable, so what I do at school is what I do out on the streets. I ditch my classes, hide from the staff and go to the restroom to kill it. Who cares if I get caught? My mom won't do anything and my father is always too tired to give me a lecture.
>
> (p. 21)

My student teachers in training do not believe the writer's false belief. They predict that some of the teachers were sincere, that the speaker rejected the adult's offers. They predict that Ms. G will be the super teacher who may change the false belief, just as *they* may someday accomplish if only they are worthy.

Adult readers see the falseness of other bizarre rationales offered by writers early in the diaries. A sorority pledge is abused and humiliated publicly in crude and inexcusable ways. She reacts this way:

> Then I started to cry. Not because of the smell or my stained clothes, but because there was no way out. I guess everybody in high school drinks, though, so it's not too bad. I'll get used to it. I hope. I guess now that I look back, it was worth it.
>
> (p. 20)

She predicts belonging and eventual enjoyment of some form; adult readers predict loss of esteem and a downward spiral.

Professional Interaction with Students

Given the complexity of these perspective readings, it behooves us to think again about teacherly classroom expectations and the ethos involved. Can a reader be compelled to take the perspective of another? Can males and females exchange perspectives? Can/should a teacher subvert his or her established identity in favor of a socially constructed professional version? If we say that the Freedom Writers gained strength and community by perspective sharing with the Holocaust texts, then we must also acknowledge that the pre-service teachers will construct potentially unreasonable notions of teacher conduct. Adopting this perspective suppresses the teacher's own needs and daily challenges. The text's Ms. G's non-teacher life is not depicted.

To explore Ms. G as a fleshed-out character we turn to the movie version of *The Freedom Writers Diary*. Film is also the best way to see the double reverse scenario I postulated earlier. Soon after school begins, we see self-imposed segregation among the student body. Life on the street is devolved to nihilism. Clear lines of racial demarcation exist. After a fight and an ugly caricature is shared, audiences see Hillary Swank scold the kids into new seats. For some reason they comply. Director Richard Lagravanese then shifts the gaze from one student to the other as they each *see*. It is important to note, though, that at this point the kids are glaring to assert maintenance of their own separate power. They are clearly not even at the second level of perspective taking.

The critical scene occurs when the Latina character (not named in the diaries) takes the witness stand. In a double reverse perspective, she sees both her gang members, including the shooter who claims to have been protecting her back in the shooting (untrue, by the way, as she was not in danger), and the falsely accused black man's wife and child. In that moment, she takes the gang perspective (protect our own—or else) and the child's perspective of losing her father to social injustice. Whether the teen would have spoken the true perspective is not clear if it were based only on what is right by social standards, but because she has been in the child's place as a result of her own father's incarceration she knows who will be left holding the brick. She knows that all the doubling and swirling issues still leave the burden on another little girl.

Exercising Perspective

We can compare that sequence of reasoning to a secondary school vignette described on the NCTE website for national standards that postulates both the existence and demise of a fictional great aunt. The students are asked to bring to bear a number of source materials to create letters with which to fill the aunt's trunk. Such an activity certainly requires role and perspective taking. Writers must engage Step Five and reversals. As I searched within the NCTE document on national standards (IRA/NCTE, 1996), I found perspective used in a number of specialized meanings. The goals regarding perspective can be associated with:

- adopting roles (such as for writing as a movie director), view (as in what can be seen from this other's stance), prior understanding or already held world views,
- critical thinking skills (as in identifying someone else's perspective but not necessarily adopting it),
- and most commonly—respect (as in first understand what someone's experience and worldview might be and then consciously or subconsciously compare and contrast it with one's own; then, vitally, accept the other's perspective as being as valid as one's own).

Interestingly, I found about as many referents to teachers and researchers themselves on perspective. ELA contributors and patrons own up to their own lenses and experiences. They are explicit in recognition of Otherness in perspective and work with perspectives as foundational throughout the guiding documents. Teacher contributors, however, rarely question but often invoke projecting how students will *do* and or *react* to an activity or idea. Though the instructors may be decades older than the learners, they surprisingly accept that their prolonged experience with young people allows them to think and feel as a teen might. But what specifically do standards say? Again from national statements of ELA desired outcomes:

- Students adjust their use of spoken, written, and visual language (e.g., conventions, style, vocabulary) to communicate effectively with a variety of audiences and for different purposes.
- Students develop an understanding of and respect for diversity in language use, patterns, and dialects across cultures, ethnic groups, geographic regions, and social roles.
- The capacity to hear and respect different perspectives and to communicate with people whose lives and cultures are different from our own is a vital element of American society.

(IRA/NCTE, 1996, pp. 3, 29)

Certainly teachers are aware of the underlying thought processes, empathy, and adaptation required before anyone can evaluate and respond to a "variety of audiences." They understand the inscrutable nature of each individual's "understanding" of diverse peoples. What I am suggesting here, though, is that those same teachers may have grown so used to the loftiness of these goals that they don't fully appreciate the view from the ground any more. The cognitive demands of perspective taking are great.

What Am I Worried About?

I worry that in *The Freedom Writers Diary*, perspective taking is oversimplified. It is really exceedingly complex and ungovernable when exercised. Ms. G doesn't just push perspective on her students. She also found money, energy, time, and enough good fortune to fulfill the expectations she created. There was a tipping point somewhere in the process that allowed these students to construct a hopeful message from "witnessing" atrocity. But without the other supports in place, they might have been devastated through the empathic taking on of the world's hurts.

- I worry that we quite possibly trivialize the gaps that lie between us and create an artifice of "color blindness" that obviates true understanding of our own heritage and comparative understanding of others'.
- I worry that depictions of teachers contribute to the setting of impossible teacher–personhood paradoxes, especially when viewed by our novice colleagues.
- I worry that standards at both state and national levels call for imposed perspective taking. And I question the ethics and the pragmatics of compelling or requiring a captive audience to do so.

And, lastly, I worry that you may misremember my message. It is not that perspective taking is unworthy. In fact, I believe it is the innate ability in humans that keeps us alive. Part of the take-home message is cautionary, however. We must be mindful of perspective-taking tasks in their design, in their complexity of undertaking, in their appropriateness as assessments, and in the consideration of the Other's sensitivities.

Conscious Design

Later he would be named one of our most distinguished valedictorians, but I recall him standing before my desk with arms full of books, sincere concern upon his face. He was describing conflict with another ELA teacher and the writing assignment requiring him to defend the notion of an oversoul (the class had been reading Emerson, 1841). To write the essay, James was compelled to adopt the perspective of an advocate for the idea, do research and synthesize his findings, and to write persuasively about its correctness. Although naturally disputatious, the legitimacy of the oversoul was the least of James's concerns. "I already hold foundational beliefs that preclude my acceptance of the oversoul. I want to preserve them. I asked Ms. X if she could tell me what would happen to my beliefs if I do the preparation and write this paper. She couldn't say." I saw James's point. He wanted reassurance that his teachers had some specific knowledge about the effects they may instigate. Further, James was defending his grade and overall class standing. What options did he have? The paper assignment and the class were required. Ultimately, James felt secure enough in his own resolution and willingness to accommodate ideas where merited to write the paper, but what happens with novice learners armed with few defenses? Teachers may argue that if a student's prior knowledge and beliefs are so tenuous as to be influenced by a composition for class, they were never unassailable to begin with. But is implanting a notion, such as the oversoul, the actual objective of teachers in the first place? I maintain that the ELA teacher had simply hoped students would operate on the highest levels of Bloom's taxonomy, that they would exert their minds and strengthen their rhetorical arsenal. I do not demand full accountability for every thought learned, but I maintain that James deserved a purposeful and thoughtful answer; if for no other reason than that he was essentially coerced into action.

When perspective-taking events are chosen for a classroom community, purpose is critical. Purposefully linking activities and outcomes at least elevates lessons from hopeful to conscientious. Perspective-taking "activities" in ELA classrooms are likely to fall into groupings, so discussion now turns to how instructors can answer my worries listed above. The groupings include: social and affective, gender, race, and generation. The expression *generation* here is meant to convey perspectives associated with age, particularly as institution-alized by roles of teachers and students (even though beginning teachers may be quite close to their older students in age).

Social and Affective Perspectives

For social scientists, perspective taking can be defined as the "ability to recognize, articulate, and coordinate the internal states of others" (Marsh, Serafica, & Berenboim, 1980, p. 141). It is developmental. Each of us graduates from simple, to sequential, to simultaneous abilities by around the age of ten (Shantz, 1975). Optimally, we can recognize others' perspectives and co-ordinate them at the same time. One of the problems with group instruction, then, is that not all class members are developmentally at the same stages. The difficulties we see among students' social problem-solving testify to the fact that they may be struggling to understand the views of others. In fact, it may well be that students in transitional phases may be more susceptible to instruction and change than students who have cemented perspectives, a state often associated with maturity. The important issue for educators is first to elicit some indicators of students' social and affective perspectives. Before using perspective-taking activities as means of assessment especially, teachers can learn about individuals' readiness.

To learn about students' *social* perspective taking, teachers can present pictures that include a variety of persons, then ask learners to generate a story including the persons as characters. Next, the student plays the role of each of the characters and retells the story from the perspective of each. In ascertain-ing students' *affective* perspective-taking potential, educators can borrow an emotionally laden scenario from the class's reading material (for example, the passage detailing Scout tucked within a rolling tire crashing smack into Boo Radley's porch) and ask students what the children (and maybe the Radley household) may be feeling. The two exercises will present ELA teachers with a baseline for variety, quantity, and appropriateness. During the process, students' willingness to participate in these personal ways is also glimpsed. After all, if later perspective-taking compositions are impoverished, it may be more a function of resistance than of ability. Responses to the social and affective perspective-taking "trials" should not be used in such a way that students are penalized for paucity. They should be used as comparatives subsequently and as formative for other activities.

Race + Gender + Identity: Ways to Prepare for Perspective Taking

Anticipating another perspective pitfall, Comfort (2000) suggests that student writers who successfully and consciously embrace mimetic writing (adopting the perceived scholar's perspective) are also erecting barriers to their own writerly identity. If a rhetorical strategy is meant to emphasize acquiring the voice of another rather than cultivating one's own, then an imposed perspective may need no adjustment. However, instructors may be able to foster each, and not at the expense of either voice. Particularly, the further the student writer is in personal traits from perceived "scholar" traits (white males), the more troubling adopting *his* perspective will be. The felt need to adopt the iconic perspective could obviate the personal language and identity formation teachers hope to encourage. After all, language "constructs the person who knows as much as it defines what one knows" (Comfort, 2000, p. 543). As teachers exalt the taking on of another's perspective, even if it is some version of the student's peer, the other perspective is privileged over the young writer's own perceived subjectivity.

In her writing courses, Comfort's students read essays by black feminist authors. The selections often contain self-revelatory passages where the personal is woven within a more detached perspective. This personal juxtaposition allows the writer: a) respect for her or his own perspective; b) a comparative understanding; and c) more complete discussion of the content matter. Comfort's close reading of the following passage isolates another positive outcome of the strategy: a third perspective is possible. In this piece by June Jordan, her perspective blends purposefully with that of Mike Tyson:

> I am more than twice Mike Tyson's age. And I'm not stupid. Or slow. But I'm Black. And I come from Brooklyn. And I grew up fighting. And I grew up and I got out of Brooklyn because I got pretty good at fighting. And winning. Or else, intimidating my would-be adversaries with my fists, my feet, and my mouth. And I never wanted to fight. I never wanted anybody to hit me. And I never wanted to hit anybody. But the bell would ring at the end of another dumb day in school and I'd head out with dread and a nervous sweat because I knew some jackass more or less my age and more or less my height would be waiting for me because she or he had nothing

better to do than to wait for me and hope to kick my butt or tear up my
books or break my pencils or pull hair out of my head.

(Comfort, 2000, pp. 545–546)

In this passage (and the rest of its whole) we can see that perspective taking
allows for some person who is black and may be male or female to emerge; the
racial identification seems to trump gender differences in this case.

Comfort advocates that writers be taught ways not only simply to try on
another's skin but to examine oneself in relation to others. Writing instruction
can help students to

> see more circumstances that invite writers to invoke personal statements,
> to use specific kinds of words, images, and signals that construct a personal
> perspective; to see how distinctions between spiritual and secular, or
> between blackness and whiteness, can be manipulated for various reasons;
> and to learn how these discursive actions taken by essayists make
> considerable difference in how readers think about a given topic.
>
> (p. 558)

Educators may take the author literally by encouraging the conscious weave of
explicit perspective by attending to pre-writing notes, placement and quantity
of personal interjections, and through editing activities designed to map the
subsequent messages created by readers when compared to student writers'
intentions.

Horace Hall's *Mentoring Young Men of Color* (2006) reminds educators of
what they already know—male students of color may be loath to express the
perspective of others. This particular group of students already spend their
classroom hours dealing with the discourse of teachers and authors who may
represent oppressive groups to them. Taking on such perspectives might not
only be an exercise in "selling out," but might be beyond the empathy and
writing skills they possess. Here is where a resource can help. Because teachers
cannot wholly abdicate their power and therefore become entirely neutral
readers in the estimation of young writers, they can learn more about students'
beliefs and experiences through a third party. Through conference with
mentors in school programs and in the community, teachers may uncover and
build upon authentic student voices. One student involved in Hall's mentor
program REAL wrote, "REAL is a medium of expression for the previously
unexpressed" (Hall, 2006, p. 100).

More importantly, Hall's emphasis on art-based mentorship and affect
in writing establishes self-knowledge for participants. In fact, Hall reports that
during his pilot mentor program, relying on activities that didn't cultivate
and encourage such voices yielded a disappointing experience for both young
members and mentors. When participating male students wrote and performed

poems and songs or designed and created T-shirts, they reported feeling invested in the program. Composing in a safe (in this case, single-gender), respectful environment, then sharing their compositions, these students are much more ready to risk the taking on of others' perspectives. Teachers who have heard and seen authentic productions unhindered by censure of grades and assessment can adapt their classroom exchanges with writers and readers. They can avoid the pitfalls of students' own "blame game" and attendant perspectives, building personal agency "in redirecting their power, confronting their pain, transcending their rage, and organizing themselves to create a better, more constructive way of being" (Hall, 2006, p. 24). Teachers can also avoid thinking they know these young men simply by the dismal statistics with which they are often described.

Moving from self-knowledge to the actual language choices made by perspective takers can be accomplished with explicit language study and role-playing. Judith Baker (2002, p. 53) begins the process by asking students to create complete descriptions of how they speak with family and friends. A partial list includes a name for the type of English you each speak, clipped words, regional words or expressions, style-setting language, other languages mixed in with English, double negatives, use of swearwords (when and why), use of your hands, eyes, and other body language. Once students are fully aware of respect for their home language and that language is indeed a matter of choice, they attempt role-playing responses to specified scenarios. Here is one of Baker's examples:

> Son (played by me) returns home at Christmas from his first semester at college and his mom greets him in her own home language. College student responds in a more formal manner, using a few words his mom does not fully understand, and which sound somewhat alien to the rest of the family assembled for the holiday. Students, playing the mother and family, had a wide variety of responses, some positive, some more negative. "You better take that mess out of this house. You're not better than nobody here." "I'm so proud of you talking so educated. This is why I saved money for college, and I hope the rest of you all children listen real close."
>
> (p. 57)

The way Baker honors the languages of the home and "streets," as some of the students termed it, provided a safe environment in which students could try on perspectives of others and anticipate further interactions. The author plans further explorations and investigations into students using languages of their future professional selves. Borrowing the perspectives, exhibited through the associated language, of their high-interest fields, students in Baker's classes avoid the "worry" I expressed earlier—that of being coerced into conflicted speech and writing. The answer here is choice.

The same kind of self-knowledge must strengthen teachers' notions of their professional selves as well. To resolve my own concerns about novice teachers and their unexamined ideological perspectives I turn to bell hooks, Janet Alsup, and Gary Howard. The three scholars are related in their advocacy for purposeful teacher identity work. One approach used by hooks (1994) is discovery through reflection and illuminating discourse with Ron Scapp. Both Scapp and hooks feel that their original professional goals (having not been necessarily to teach) help them avoid inflexible or defensive notions about change and adjustment. Novice teachers often fail to acknowledge their own physical selves, believing that traits such as youth and gender can only detract from their intellectual goals. Scapp and hooks make these observations:

> hooks: . . . as a Black woman, I have always been acutely aware of the presence of my body in those settings that, in fact, invite us to invest so deeply in a mind/body split so that, in a sense, you're almost always at odds with the existing structure . . . But if you want to remain, you've got to remember yourself—because to remember yourself is to see yourself always as a body in a system that has not become accustomed to your presence or to your physicality.
>
> Scapp: Similarly, as a white university teacher in his thirties, I'm profoundly aware of my presence in the classroom as well, given the history of the male body, and of the male teacher. I need to be sensitive to and critical of my presence in the history that has led me there.
>
> (p. 135)

Dialogue such as the above excerpt serves as an excellent beginning, especially for veteran teachers, but more engagement in identity discourse is needed for new educators.

Alsup (2006) found that pre-service teachers can reveal, scrutinize, and negotiate realistic and durable notions of teacher selves through the construction of metaphors. English education students created these metaphors by snapping photos and engaging in *borderland* discourse about what the pictures represented. Students willing to negotiate in these shifting landscapes seem to fare much better than students who persist in non-negotiable, fixed ideas of self; thus, she calls for recognition for bi-discoursal professionals (p. 195). Novice teachers who anticipate the purposeful construction of their teacher selves will be more resistant to the impossible expectations raised by pop culture teacher depictions. Exposed to these images, they can adopt perspective taking selectively, looking for practical self-improvement but only insofar as the changes can translate into their contexts. Beginning teachers won't be attempting to channel Erin Gruwell; their own perspectives can be respected and sustaining.

Lastly, and most pointedly, Gary Howard's heuristics for racial self-identifying offer ways to know our own heritage and perspectives before we attempt to impose them (or others) on students. In fact, his recommendations would benefit teachers and their students if they transacted them together. Howard (2006) allows white readers to see the effects and mechanisms of their own privilege, but does not leave them mired in guilt. Having traveled our own heritage and current culture, we can find ourselves represented on his map of "white identity orientations" (p. 104). Scope is difficult to generalize for each of our journeys, but sequence often follows in these modalities of growth: thinking (constructing truth, whiteness, and dominance) leads to feeling (self-awareness, emotional response to differences and to discussions of racism) leads to acting (approaches to cross-cultural interactions, teaching about difference, and leadership) (p. 104). Perspective taking holds the greatest promise when any of us acts as a *transformationist*—but we rarely can make a leap to action without steps of recognition first. In essence, the messy work transacted in Erin Gruwell's classroom by both herself and her students is multicultural education as espoused and designed by Howard. Such work takes time and commitment, but persistence and frequently revisiting multicultural themes make safe perspective taking possible.

Embracing My Perspective

So, yes, I have worried and still do. But as I share my worries with you, I begin to disarm them too—urging all teachers to be mindful of the demands and ethics of perspective giving and taking. *My* perspective is optimistic. In being mindful, each of us is at least halfway to excellence. Trying, adapting, being purposeful in design, all can and will yield the kinds of activities and effects to which most ELA teachers aspire (me sharing their perspectives). As understanding and taking others' perspectives keeps us alive as perceptive and reactive beings, as virtually all topics are fair game in English language arts texts and discussion, we can ill afford to take them or leave them.

References

Alsup, J. (2006). *Teacher identity discourses: Negotiating personal and professional spaces.* Mahwah, NJ: Lawrence Erlbaum.

Baker, J. (2002). Trilingualism. In L. Delpit & J. Kilgour (Eds.), *The skin we speak* (pp. 49–62). New York: The New Press.

Barnes-Holmes, Y., McHugh, L., & Barnes-Holmes, D. (2004). Perspective-taking and theory of mind: A relational frame account. *Behavior Analyst Today*, 5 (1), 140–145.

Comfort, J.R. (2000). Becoming a writerly self: College writers engaging black feminist essays. *CCC*, 51 (4), 540–559.

Emerson, R.W. (1841). *Essays and English traits.* New York: P.F. Collier.

Freedom writers. (2007). Directed by Richard Lagravenese. Paramount Pictures.

Freedom Writers with Gruwell, E. (1999). *The freedom writers diary: Their story, their words.* New York: Broadway Books.

Freire, P. (1970/1993). *Pedagogy of the oppressed.* New York: Continuum.

Grimes, N. (2003). *Bronx masquerade.* New York: Penguin Young Readers Group.

Hall, H. (2006). *Mentoring young men of color: Meeting the needs of African American and Latino students.* Lanham, MD: Rowman & Littlefield Education.

hooks, b. (1994). *Teaching to transgress: Education as the practice of freedom.* New York: Routledge.

Howard, G. (2006). *We can't teach what we don't know: White teachers, multi-racial schools.* New York: Teachers College Press.

International Reading Association and National Council of Teachers of English (IRA/NCTE). (1996). *Standards for the English Language Arts.* Newark, DE and Urbana, IL: International Reading Association and National Council of Teachers of English.

Marsh, D., Serafica, F., & Barenboim, C. (1980). Effect of perspective-taking training on interpersonal problem solving. *Child Development,* 51 (1), 140–145.

Shantz, C. (1975). The development of social cognition. In E.M. Hetherington (Ed.), *Review of Child Development Research* (pp. 257–323). Chicago: University of Chicago Press.

Part III

Why Are Teens Reading YAL?

The final section of this collection addresses the question of why various types of teen readers might choose to read YAL. While this issue was also explored in Part I of the book, in which chapter authors explored the various ethnic, racial, and socio-cultural memberships to which contemporary US teens belong and how these memberships might lead to certain reading interests, this section takes a second look at the question through the eyes of researchers. What follows is two chapters that report on qualitative and mixed method research studies investigating the question: "Why do teens read YAL?"

Through action (or teacher) research and collaborative projects between classroom teachers and university researchers, we can learn a great deal about why teen readers choose YAL for independent reading—perhaps over other types of literature, including adult fiction, classical literature, or nonfiction. These chapters ask the relevant questions. When are young adults too old to read YAL? What is it about the characters and plots of YA narratives that draw adolescent readers? How do (or should) teen reading choices affect teacher behavior? And finally, and perhaps most importantly, to what extent does reading YAL affect teens' cognitive and emotional growth, real-world choices, and literal behaviors, all of which influence their burgeoning identities and self-concepts? These questions are explored in the section that follows, and the last chapter leaves the reader with some final thoughts to consider.

Chapter 12

The Appeal of Young Adult Literature in Late Adolescence

College Freshmen Read YAL

Gail Zdilla

Cara[1] is excited about turning 20 years old. Her sophomore year of college is coming to a close, and she is ready to be treated like an adult. Despite the fact that her parents pay for her tuition, room and board, car insurance, and cell-phone bill, Cara feels that she is no longer an adolescent. She has ideas, opinions, and values of her own and is capable of making important decisions. On top of a heavy course load, Cara has managed to do well in a part-time job for the university and handles her money wisely. While many adults would look at Cara's current stage in life and consider her still to be a dependant, Cara would argue that she is in control of her life and is, therefore, an independent adult (personal communication, March 1, 2007).

"Generation Next" is a common term for 16–25-year-old Americans who have grown up online, seen school shootings devastate their country, witnessed the collapse of the Twin Towers, and watched a highly controversial war take place overseas. These same young people are also the most educated generation in American history, yet they are not "growing up" as quickly as their ancestors did.

On January 3, 2007, Scott Simon, the host of National Public Radio's *Talk of the Nation*, interviewed Judy Woodruff about her Public Broadcasting Service documentary titled *Generation Next*. During the show, Simon and Woodruff took calls from listeners and discussed some of the traits of Generation Next. One particular section of the exchange focused on how college students are becoming more dependent on their parents because they cannot afford the lifestyle they would like to have (Goodwin, 2007). Parents are just a cell-phone call or e-mail away, so many college students keep in close touch with their families and look to their parents for guidance while they are pursuing degrees. Being out of the house does not necessarily mean living on your own any more.

What does all of this mean? The period of adolescence is expanding into the early 20s for many young people. As Amy Pattee (2004, p. 244) points out, youth is "a representation of 'how a society thinks about itself.'" Adolescence traditionally has been defined by developmental and cognitive changes, but this is no longer the case as our cultural conception of adolescence has redefined this period of life. Continued dependence on parents in order to meet their needs marks many 20-somethings as not quite ready for the demands and responsibilities of adulthood. Unless children are earning their own living, they are not perceived to be adults in American society today.

Rationale

> No book is really worth reading at the age of ten which is not equally (and often far more) worth reading at the age of fifty . . . The only imaginative works we ought to grow out of are those which it would have been better not to have read at all.
>
> (Lewis, 1966, p. 15)

The extension of adolescence is affecting the marketing and readership of young adult literature (YAL):

> Since adolescents' thoughts center on their sexuality, relationships with peers and adults, and future roles and values, YAL can give readers a chance to experience vicariously their concerns, doubts, and dilemmas— to confront the stages of their development through the printed word.
>
> (McBroom, 1981, p. 76)

Sylvia Engdahl (1975, p. 49) says, "Times have changed since publishers labeled insipid mysteries and school romances 'ages 13 and up.'" YAL is seeing improved quality in characterization and complexity of plots and is even addressing more mature, and often emotionally difficult, issues. As a result of these changes, books published in the last ten years as YAL are now considered more appropriate for 14–21-year-olds (Yampbell, 2005). Books such as Alex Sanchez's *Rainbow Boys* (2003), Patricia McCormick's *Cut* (2002), Julie Anne Peter's *Luna* (2004), John Green's *Looking for Alaska* (2006), An Na's *The Fold* (2008), and Elizabeth Scott's *Living Dead Girl* (2008) push the boundaries of YAL with their sexual content, references to drug use, violence, and other topics that are typically considered to be appropriate for adult audiences only.

Since this shift in the target audience for YAL has occurred, I was interested to see if older adolescents are actually reading YAL or if they have moved on to adult literature. Are contemporary YA books able to meet the interests of college students? If so, then what is the appeal of these novels?

For four years, I taught 15–18-year-olds English and journalism in a suburban public high school in New Jersey, and many of them selected YAL to read on their own. While my male students would tell me what they were reading, a bit about the plots, and what they thought of their books, I had lengthier conversations with my female students about the fictional pieces they were choosing to read. I remember Mya telling me that she loved YAL because the stories were about people her age and she could relate to them. Is this the case for college students, too? Are they able to identify with the characters and storylines in contemporary YAL?

There must be some reason (or even multiple reasons) why older adolescents and even many adults are deciding to give YAL a try. The Harry Potter books, the Inheritance Cycle (*Eragon, Eldest,* and *Brisingr*), and the *Twilight* series are perfect examples of how YAL is crossing boundaries; children, adolescents, and adults eagerly read these books cover to cover. In fact, four months before it was to be released, countless adults preordered J.K. Rowling's *Harry Potter and the Deathly Hallows* (2007) and helped it to be number one continuously on the bestsellers' list on Amazon.com. If these books are being read by people of all ages, then other YAL books may also be crossing age categories.

In the spring of 2007, I taught Reading in Middle and Secondary Schools for seventeen special education majors at a major Midwestern university. During a couple of our conversations in class, we discussed how YAL can be used in secondary classrooms and what books we could suggest to teenage readers. As we shared ideas, I thought of the questions I had about what college students read in their spare time. Were they really picking up YAL books and reading them? If so, why? Since I had students who were candid about their reading experiences and willing to help me learn more about today's typical American college student, I decided to conduct an action research project. But first I needed to learn more about the history of YAL and the current trends in this genre.

Research Questions

The following are questions that will be considered in this chapter:

1   What is young adult literature?
2   Who is the intended audience for young adult literature?
3   What are late adolescent college students reading?
4   Why have late adolescents chosen to read about certain subjects?

Literature Review

What is young adult literature? This question has been answered, debated, and revisited over and over again by literary critics, writers, publishing companies, librarians, teachers, and parents. While many would agree that it is simply what teenagers are reading at the moment, most want a more concrete and strictly defined understanding of what is considered YAL. After all, there should be guidelines, right? Impressionable teenagers are the target audience of these stories, and society dictates that they need adult supervision showing them right from wrong. Adolescents should read material that is safe for them—no violence, inappropriate language, sex, or material that is too mature for them to handle. On the other hand, YAL should focus on issues to which teenagers can relate. If it ignores the interests of teenagers, then what is the point of having a specific category of books for adolescent readers? So, what is appropriate subject matter for teenagers? And who makes this decision?

In American society today, YAL seems to be most often defined by adults for their specific purposes. Literary critics look at the depth of characters and the quality of the story for adolescent readers. At the same time, parents want to see stories that their children will enjoy but will also teach lessons. Classifying books as YAL is a difficult task, yet publishing companies do so all the time. Even though authors have been writing for children for hundreds of years, YAL constantly changes based on the needs and values of the current society.

Literature has been used for centuries to guide young people's behavior and help mold them into responsible adults. Despite the fact that YAL has evolved over time, the genre still exhibits characteristics of its ancestry. In the Middle Ages, books showed young adults how they were supposed to act and what they should emulate (Bushman & Haas, 2006). Teaching the Christian faith and didactic literature was the primary emphasis of the 17th century. By the mid-19th century, domestic novels and series, such as Louisa May Alcott's *Little Women* (1869), had emerged. Formula fiction dominated YAL in the late 19th century and into the 20th (Bushman & Haas, 2006). Following the publication of S.E. Hinton's *The Outsiders* in 1967, many noticed a turning point in YAL. Donald Gallo observed that authors began to focus on "the realities of teenage life and offered readers an honest view of the main characters' hopes, fears, and dilemmas" (Herz & Gallo, 2005, p. 10). This trend continued throughout the 1970s, 1980s, and 1990s, and YAL experienced significant growth in popularity (Yampbell, 2005). Today YAL encompasses thousands of titles. Browsing through the YAL section of bookstores and libraries and the lists published by the Young Adult Library Services Association (YALSA) gives an idea of just how broad this genre truly is.

So YAL books have been around for many years, yet how were/are YAL books classified?

After researching contemporary trends in YAL, Herz and Gallo compiled a comprehensive list of characteristics of young adult fiction:

- The main characters are teenagers.
- The length of the average book is around 200 pages, though it may be as brief as 100 pages or (as in the case of the Harry Potter novels) as long as 900 pages.
- The point of view is most often first person, and it is usually that of a teenager.
- The narrator is most often the main character.
- The story is usually told in the voice of a teenager, not the voice of an adult looking back as a young person (as it is in Harper Lee's *To Kill a Mockingbird* (1960) or John Knowles's *A Separate Peace* (1959)).

- The language is typical of contemporary teenagers, and the vocabulary, unlike that of adult classics, is manageable by readers of average ability.
- The setting is most often contemporary, but also can be historical, futuristic (as in science fiction), or imaginative (as in fantasy); it takes place most often in the United States but is occasionally set in foreign countries.
- The books contain characters and issues to which teenagers can relate.
- In a majority of the books, parents play a minor role or are "the enemy."
- The plot and literary style are uncomplicated but never simplistic, though the plots of a few books are quite complex (for example, those of Robert Cormier, M.E. Kerr, Chris Lynch, and E.R. Frank).
- The outcome of the story is usually dependent upon the decisions and actions of the main character.
- The tone and outcome of the novels are usually upbeat, but not in all instances. (Since 2000, there has been an increase in the number of darker, grittier novels for and about teens.)
- With the exception of complicated plotting, all the traditional literary elements typical of classical literature are present in most contemporary novels for young adults—well-rounded characters, flashbacks, fore-shadowing, allusions, irony, metaphorical language—though they are used less frequently and at less sophisticated levels to match the experiential levels of readers.
- The very best YA books can be as appealing to adult readers as they are to teens.

(Herz & Gallo, pp. 10–11)

These characteristics show the complexity of YAL and just how difficult it is to define this genre in simple terms. Despite the variety of content and styles it encompasses, YAL does serve a significant purpose: it offers a transition from children's literature into the world of adult literature. This is the one category of literature that is written for or about young adults (Bushman & Haas, 2006). Sylvia Engdahl (1975, p. 49) points out that "the present adult market demands fiction of a kind that adolescents lack experience and emotional maturity to cope with. Critically-acclaimed novels frequently treat themes in which adolescents are not even interested." YAL tailors to the stage of life adolescents are experiencing. According to Joyce Stallworth (2006, p. 59), contemporary YAL is "an electrifying genre for getting today's young adolescents reading and exploring who they are." Teens are able to try out new experiences vicariously through the stories they read. Learning about other cultures and history is possible through the eyes of characters teenagers recognize. As they have questions about the world around them, adolescents explore, and YAL offers this outlet for them to test their values. They can take on characters' roles, grapple with the plot, become completely engaged in the story and even escape reality for a while.

After looking at how YAL has developed as a genre and what it tends to include, another question surfaces: who is reading YAL? While the response to this question may seem obvious to some—"adolescents"—others may be quick to reply, "Okay, then define 'adolescence.'" Some have said YAL is considered appropriate for early adolescent readers, 10–14-year-olds (Engdahl, 1975). More often, though, contemporary YAL is intended for 12–20-year-olds (Bean & Moni, 2003). This genre has become more like adult literature, with its increasingly complex style, form, and content (Kåreland, 1999). Examples of this newer, more complicated type of YAL would be M.T. Anderson's *The Astonishing Life of Octavian Nothing, Traitor to the Nation* series (2006, 2008), Walter Dean Myers's *Monster* (2001), Neal Shusterman's *Unwind* (2007), and Neil Gaiman's *Stardust* (1999).

Since the intended audience for YAL has shifted to older adolescent readers, does this mean that high school and college students—rather than upper elementary and middle school readers—are picking up YAL in libraries and bookstores? Is YAL now considered inappropriate for younger adolescents? Within the past ten years, some authors have focused their writing on tough issues, such as domestic violence, rape, drug addiction, suicide, sexuality, cults, and so on—difficult topics for younger teens. But these are not the only YAL topics that are thriving today. Attempting to fit in with friends, frustrations with parents, and finding one's own identity are still among the popular plot sequences found in YAL. However, it is impossible to ignore the new material that is placed on library and bookstore shelves simply by dismissing it as material for older readers. As Cat Yampbell (2005, p. 351) writes, "Young Adult Literature has broken nearly every boundary of acceptable subject matter in trying to address real-life problems and intrigue teen readers." There are opposing forces that compete for control of YAL. Marc Aaronson (2001, p. 88) explains,

> To the world at large, a teenager is a potential consumer whose desires and hormones are fair game. To parents, a YA book is a manual for living, a kind of mini-Bible that serves as a babysitter for older children. What space is there between these poles?

YAL publishers continue to journey into new and potentially dangerous subjects. Why? Because controversy sells. According to Yampbell (2005, p. 350), "liberals and conservatives continue to battle over the age appropriateness of subjects such as relationships, sex, drugs, and death." Stephen Chbosky's *Perks of Being a Wallflower* (1999), Philip Pullman's *His Dark Materials* trilogy (1995–2000), Cecily Von Ziegesar's *Gossip Girl* series (2002–2007), and Alvin Schwartz's *Scary Stories* series (1981–1991) have all been challenged in recent years. Adults try to shelter teenagers from this sort of material, but that merely tends to make them more interested in what these books have to offer.

In Herz and Gallo's (2005) characteristics of YAL, they highlight the fact that adults are also reading books from this genre. The main reason for this is probably the blurred line between what is considered YAL and what publishing companies label as "adult." At the beginning of the 21st century, publishers began to reformat YAL books into trade size (Yampbell, 2005). The idea was that these books would transcend the boundaries of age and could be marketed to a larger audience. Teens and adults alike would be more likely to buy books that looked like those typically found in the adult section. Publishers also encouraged bookstores to stock YAL in adult literature. Again, the marketing scheme was that YAL books would have a better chance of being picked up by more people if they were in both sections of bookstores. Publishing companies have been successful when promoting YAL in these ways, but the content, writing styles, and storylines also appeal to older readers. Stallworth (2006, p. 60) says, "Today's young adult problem novels illustrate different viewpoints and portray characters involved in realistic problem solving."

The world of YAL is broad and offers opportunities for a wide range of readers (ability and age-wise). But while adults attempt to sort through and label books as YAL, the ones who really know the most about why adolescents read what they do are the adolescents themselves.

Methodology

In order to gain a better understanding of late adolescent college students' reading interests, I carried out an action research study with some of my students who were enrolled in Reading in Middle and Secondary Schools during the spring 2007 semester. All of the students who participated knew that they would not be rewarded or punished academically for taking part. Fifteen students, all sophomores aged 19 or 20, completed a reading interest survey. Of these students, there were thirteen females and two males. Two weeks after the survey, six students volunteered to join a conversation about their reading experiences. Then one female student was selected for an hour-long, one-on-one interview.

Since I wanted to learn about what types of books college students were reading, I created a one-page, short-answer survey (see Appendix 12.1) for my students to complete. I was also curious what thoughts they had about YAL, so I included a couple of questions about their experiences with the genre. I chose to ask my students questions on individual paper surveys so that they could take their time with their responses and not be influenced by their peers while they answered the questions. The survey was administered at the conclusion of our class session on Tuesday, March 6, 2007.

After I looked over the surveys, I talked with six students (two males and four females) about some of the responses that stood out to me. This gave me more information about what they wrote and allowed them to discuss their ideas about YAL openly.

The student selected for the one-on-one interview was chosen because of her age (19 years old) and her particular experiences with reading from childhood through late adolescence.

Discussion of Collected Data

As I evaluated the results of the reading survey, the small group discussion, and the one-on-one interview, I observed that college students read a variety of material for many different reasons. Some of my students admitted to reading and enjoying YAL, while others said that they tended to gravitate toward adult bestsellers or adult nonfiction. My students were honest and open about their reading interests, and they created a fascinating picture for me.

Out of all the data I collected, what was most interesting to me was that several of my students said they read YAL because the main characters are their age or close to their age and/or they can relate to the situations in the stories. Amanda said she enjoyed reading YAL because she "can relate to a lot of the situations." When I asked her if she could clarify what she meant, she explained that many YAL books focus on struggles in friendships or setbacks that seem to occur when growing up. Cara also said she enjoyed reading about girls her age and their experiences with friendships and dating. Overall, my female students agreed that they could find similarities between themselves and the female characters they found in YAL: "YAL seems to grow up with you some-how. I can find people my age in these books and see what they're doing—how they're handling their lives. It's kind of cool," commented Laura. An interest in the story was a big pull for my students. Being able to identify with the characters or the storyline somehow was also crucial.

Seth and Tony agreed with their female counterparts, but added other reasons for picking up YAL to read. They both thought that YAL contained a lot of "quick reads," which seemed appealing to them. As Seth said, "I don't have much time to read, except for what is required for classes. That's why I like YAL—I can get into it, absorb it, and then finish it in just a couple hours." Tony echoed this response and added that he really enjoyed being able to understand the writing style and vocabulary in YAL. The other students agreed that this was helpful to them, too. A couple of them elaborated by saying that the stylistic flow of YAL writing was natural or what they were used to using/hearing. Rachel compared YAL to reading Shakespeare by saying that "the language has to be current and the story has to be something which we can understand in our world today." All agreed that the stories that had universal themes or were centered on relationships were probably the ones that would last beyond their generation and be read for many years.

Laura had written on her survey that her favorite books were Dan Brown's *Da Vinci Code* (2003), J.K. Rowling's Harry Potter series, and books by Eric Carle. These were just a few of the titles she said she remembered at the time of the survey. When we talked about reading interests in class two weeks later, Laura added to her list of favorites Stephen Chbosky's *Perks of Being a Wallflower* and Ann Brashares's *Sisterhood of the Traveling Pants* series (2001–2007). I asked her if she noticed that the titles she mentioned were considered YAL. Laura admitted that she looked through her bookshelves after she took the survey to refresh her memory of books she really liked. This sparked a new topic of discussion about the books my students always enjoyed rereading.

I noticed a pattern in book titles my students shared as their favorites. Most of the books they reminisced about were either YAL or children's literature. Seth commented that the books he liked were ones that he had read and exchanged with his friends: "I still think of my friends from high school when I reread [Thomas T. Hecht's] *Life Death Memories* [2004]. We were all really interested in World War Two, and this one was powerful." Even though my students were now sophomores in college, they said that the books they read in high school had made quite an impact on them and were typically the ones they wanted to read again.

Seth boldly admitted that he had enjoyed going back and reading books that were assigned in his high school English classes. When I asked him why he wanted to do this, Seth replied, "I guess I felt guilty for not taking them seriously." A couple other students shared this sentiment and said that they too had gone back to the books they were assigned in high school and gave them a second chance. Some students told me that they had read the novels when they were in high school, but they had a different perspective looking at them a second time. Cara noted that she always seemed to enjoy the books she was assigned in middle and high school. In fact, some of them were still among her favorite books: "I remember one book—*Night* [1960] by Elie Wiesel . . . It was very real . . . pulled me in." While the titles my students shared seemed to be typical of the high school English canon, they did bring up more contemporary reads, such as Christopher Paolini's *Eragon* (2003), Chinua Achebe's *Things Fall Apart* (1958), Sandra Cisneros's *The House on Mango Street* (1984), Laurie Halse Anderson's *Speak* (1999), Christopher Paul Curtis's *Bud, Not Buddy* (1999), Walter Dean Myers's *Monster*, and Mary Pipher's *Reviving Ophelia* (1994). When I asked them about these titles, I discovered that these pieces were read either as self-selected reading projects or in elective English courses. The more traditional reads, such as John Steinbeck's *Of Mice and Men* (1937) and F. Scott Fitzgerald's *The Great Gatsby* (1925), were found in their required English classes. Several students commented that the books assigned in their regular English classes must have been selected because they were considered classics in our culture. They recognized that these titles were somehow important to history.

Each of my students admitted that their reading interests had not changed very much since their high school days. The topics and categories of books they gravitated toward in their early teen years were still among the areas they searched for today. Some noted that they read certain books because their friends or relatives suggested the titles to them. Most of the group said that they preferred just searching bookstore shelves for topics or covers that interested them. Cara was currently reading Kim Izzo and Ceri Marsh's *The Fabulous Girls Guide to Etiquette* books (2001–2004). This series is classified as YAL, but Cara says it discusses situations that young adults of all ages would understand. She said, "I know it sounds strange to read kinda self-help books. But it's interesting to see how to handle sticky situations . . . like work or social situations." None of the students seemed embarrassed to admit that they would read YAL. They felt that people should be encouraged to read what interests them, no matter how the books are categorized in a library or bookstore.

My students were confirming what I had previously thought: an interest in the setting, characters, and/or plot is essential if they are going to stick with a book, and active readers cross categories/genres. Being able to connect to the story is important to my students. And they are not afraid to look throughout libraries and bookstores to find what they like. The group of six students who said that YAL titles were among the books they enjoyed the most comprised the students who earned the highest grades in my course. This may just be a coincidence, considering these students were also the ones who seemed to read the widest assortment of books; however, it might also say something about the seriousness of contemporary YA readers.

After surveying and talking with my students, I was able to learn more about what college students are reading in their spare time. I was surprised to see just how many of my students claimed still to enjoy YAL. Maybe YAL is just a bridge for them as they enter adulthood, or maybe it is a category they will revisit throughout their lives.

Implications

Learning about what my students were reading and hearing about why they selected the books they did was a helpful experience for me as a teacher. A lot of the titles they said they really enjoyed were books to which they had been introduced by their middle and high school English teachers. English teachers obviously have an impact on what adolescents read. What they are exposed to in school often become areas of interest adolescents continue to have as readers.

It is my hope that I will encourage my students to explore many categories and genres as they discover what types of books appeal to them. Some of my students may enjoy YAL, while others may find adult fiction or nonfiction books more to their liking. Being able to have conversations about reading and sharing experiences with books in my classroom will help support my students as readers and give them ideas for future reading endeavors.

I will continue to share YAL in my English classroom and allow my students to select material to read from these texts. This category of books covers so many topics that are relevant to adolescents today and offers a wide array of opportunities. YAL allows teenagers to test their convictions, escape reality for a while, and explore the world around them. As Gail Gauthier (2002, p. 75) says, "The YA audience is unique. We need to acknowledge that and find a way to deal with it in order to create a literature from which our teenagers can expect to gain a satisfying 'sense of comradeship among equals.'"

Appendix 12.1

Name: _____

Reading Survey

Directions

Please respond to the following questions as honestly and with as much detail as you can. If you would like to skip any of the questions, simply leave those responses blank.

1 Name some of your all-time favorite books (approximately two to five of them).

2 What books have you read for leisure in the past two years?

3 Do you enjoy reading books that are categorized as Young Adult Literature? If so, which books have you enjoyed the most?

4 Why do you enjoy reading Young Adult Literature? (*Please skip this question if it does not apply to you.*)

5 What types of books or specific titles do you think belong in the Young Adult Literature category?

Note

1   All names have been changed for confidentiality.

References

Aaronson, M. (2001). *Exploding the myths: The truth about teenagers and reading.* Lanham, MD: Scarecrow Press.

Achebe, C. (1958). *Things fall apart.* London: William Heinemann.

Anderson, L.H. (1999). *Speak.* New York: Farrar, Straus & Giroux.

Anderson, M.T. (2006). *The astonishing life of Octavian Nothing, traitor to the nation.* New York: Candlewick Press.

Anderson, M.T. (2008). *The astonishing life of Octavian Nothing, traitor to the nation.* Volume II: *The kingdom on the waves.* New York: Candlewick Press.

Bean, T.W. & Moni, K. (2003). Developing students' critical literacy: Exploring identity construction in young adult fiction. *Journal of Adolescent & Adult Literacy,* 46 (8), 638–648.

Brashares, A. (2001–2007). *The sisterhood of the traveling pants.* New York: Dell Books for Young Readers.

Brown, D. (2003). *The Da Vinci code.* New York: Doubleday.

Bushman, J.H. & Haas, K.P. (2006). *Using young adult literature in the English classroom* (4th edn). Upper Saddle River, NJ: Pearson.

Chbosky, S. (1999). *The perks of being a wallflower.* New York: Pocket Books.

Cisneros, S. (1984). *The House on Mango Street.* Houston, TX: Arte Público Press.

Curtis, C.P. (1999). *Bud, not Buddy.* New York: Delacorte Books for Young Readers.

Engdahl, S. (1975). Do teenage novels fill a need? *English Journal,* 64 (2), 48–52.

Fitzgerald, F.S. (1925). *The great Gatsby.* New York: Charles Scribner's Sons.

Gaiman, N. (1999). *Stardust.* New York: Avon Books.

Gauthier, G. (2002). Whose community? Where is the "YA" in YA literature? *English Journal,* 91 (6), 70–76.

Goodwin, S. [executive producer]. (2007). *Talk of the nation.* January 3 [Radio broadcast]. Washington, DC: National Public Radio.

Green, J. (2006). *Looking for Alaska.* New York: Speak Press.

Hecht, T.T. (2004). *Life death memories.* Piscataway, NJ: Transaction.

Herz, S.K. & Gallo, D.R. (2005). *From Hinton to Hamlet: Building bridges between young adult literature and the classics* (2nd edn). Westport, CT: Greenwood Press.

Hinton, S.E. (1967). *The outsiders.* New York: Viking Press.

Izzo, K. & Marsh, C. (2001–2004). *The fabulous girls guide series.* London: Corgi.

Kåreland, L. (1999). Two crosswriting authors: Carl Sandburg and Lennart Hellsing. In S.L. Beckett (Ed.), *Transcending boundaries: Writing for a dual audience of children and adults* (pp. 215–237). New York: Garland.

Lewis, C.S. (1966). On stories. In *Of other worlds.* New York: Harcourt, Brace & World.

McBroom, G. (1981). Young adult literature: Research: Our defense begins here. *English Journal,* 70 (6), 75–78.

McCormick, P. (2002). *Cut.* New York: Push.

Myers, W.D. (2001). *Monster.* New York: Amistad/HarperCollins.

Na, A. (2008). *The fold.* New York: Putnam Juvenile.

Paolini, C. (2003). *Eragon.* New York: Alfred Knopf.

Pattee, A.S. (2004). Disturbing the peace: The function of young adult literature and the case of Catherine Atkins' *When Jeff Comes Home*. *Children's Literature in Education*, 35 (3), 241–255.

Peter, J.A. (2004). *Luna*. New York: Little, Brown.

Pipher, M. (1994). *Reviving Ophelia: Saving the selves of adolescent girls*. New York: Putnam.

Pullman, P. (1995–2000). *His dark materials*. London: Scholastic Point.

Rowling, J.K. (2007). *Harry Potter and the deathly hallows*. New York: Arthur A. Levine Books.

Sanchez, A. (2003). *Rainbow boys*. New York: Simon Pulse.

Schwartz, A. (1981–1991). *Scary stories to tell in the dark*. New York: HarperCollins.

Scott, E. (2008). *Living dead girl*. New York: Simon Pulse.

Shusterman, N. (2007). *Unwind*. New York: Simon & Schuster Children's Publishing.

Stallworth, B.J. (2006) The relevance of young adult literature. *Educational Leadership*, 63 (7), 59–63.

Steinbeck, J. (1937). *Of mice and men*. New York: Covici Friede.

Von Ziegesar, C. (2002–2007). *Gossip girl*. New York: Little, Brown.

Wiesel, E. (1960). *Night*. New York: Hill & Wang.

Yampbell, C. (2005). Judging a book by its cover: Publishing trends in young adult literature. *The Lion and the Unicorn*, 29 (3), 348–372.

Chapter 13

1 Female Reader Reading YAL

Understanding Norman Holland's Identity Themes Thirty Years Later

Janet Alsup

I have been interested in the reading and study of young adult literature for several years, beginning during my own undergraduate education at the University of Missouri-Columbia when I had the privilege of taking a young adult literature course with Professor Ben F. Nelms. Over the last few years my interest in young adult literature has shifted from the literary and pedagogical to include a psychological dimension—namely, the possible intersections between the reading and study of YA and the cognitive, emotional, and psychological development of adolescent readers. I continue to wonder if the reading of YA novels affects adolescents' self-perceptions and self-concepts. How do the narratives, whose authors often directly state that they are seeking to mirror adolescent life and enable young people to "relate" to characters and events, influence the burgeoning identities of these young people and perhaps even affect their actions in the real world? If the reading and study of YA literature does result in emotional and behavioral change in young readers, what does that mean for the teacher of literature?

The chapters in this collection have addressed various aspects of these questions, ranging from how reading books can influence social–emotional development, to the range of cognitive responses teen readers can have to the genre of YAL, to why the age range of YAL readers seems to be widening. However, the questions of whether and in what ways reading young adult literature affects the real lives of teens might simply be unanswerable in the end. All teens are different—just as all classrooms and cultural contexts are different. How can the social–emotional–moral–cognitive effects of reading YAL ever be summarized or placed in a neatly answered package when there are so many different readers and ways of reading? The very desire to engage in such definitive analysis nearly contradicts what many of us believe about response-based literature teaching and individual reader response. But, having raised these quandaries, I continue to believe it is important to literary pedagogues to understand as deeply and widely as possible how and why teen readers respond to YA literature and to what extent this response leads to both emotional and cognitive growth.

As I wrote in the Introduction to this volume, there continues to be a great need for educational and literary scholars to study the genre from a critical, research-oriented perspective. While many articles and books assume the effectiveness of literature to improve *both* students' reading skills *and* their self-concepts, very few studies or analyses reinforce these assumptions with empirical data or theoretical support. One exception is the work of Norman Holland. In 1975, over 30 years ago, reader-response theorist and psychologist Norman Holland conducted an interview-based research study with five university student readers reading classic short stories which he described in a book-length report, *5 Readers Reading.* Holland found that each of the readers re-created and understood the texts based on his or her own "identity themes," or the reader's individual values, fears, joys, and beliefs. For example, if a reader had life-changing experiences with a father figure (or lack thereof), then the role of Emily's father in the William Faulkner story "A Rose for Emily" became important to understanding all of Emily's behaviors, and, ultimately, the story's overriding theme. Holland hypothesized that since a reader demonstrates a "deep and essential unity in his personality" (p. 53) that affects how he/she reads a story, individual readings can be understood by understanding these so-called identity themes. In short, you cannot "separate the act of reading from the creative personality of the reader" (p. 123).

While I agree that individual readers certainly read stories and novels in different ways, I am skeptical about the idea of a singular "identity theme" which guides a person's life and, by association, his or her reading. I tend to believe in a multiplicity of identity or subjectivities which emerge or recede based on the context in which a person acts. Such multiplicity in expression of identity might be particularly true when speaking of adolescents, who are at a time in their lives when they may be experimenting with various identity expressions or enactments and whose brains are still developing, guiding their abilities to respond to various cognitive and emotional stimuli which they encounter. I am also curious about whether Holland's findings are applicable to the reading of *young adult* literature, in addition to classic texts. Holland's readers were somewhat older than what most of us would label "adolescent"; they also read canonical short stories which might be taught in a college class-room, not YA texts written for adolescents about adolescent issues and concerns. As authors in this text have wondered, does reading about characters and situations which attempt to mirror a reader's own life change the reading experience? Does it make the experience more powerful and poignant, or does it make it an exercise in extreme self-absorption?

Interested to see how adolescent readers reading YAL might respond in a similar situation, I planned a small empirical study exploring the reading habits of three young adult readers reading YA texts, inspired by Holland's landmark text. In the remainder of this essay, I will discuss this study I conducted with adolescent readers of YAL and describe what I learned about their reasons and methods for reading YAL, focusing in particular on one female student. In conclusion, I provide suggestions for how the classroom teacher might utilize what I learned in my study in secondary school classroom teaching of young adult literature, as well as suggestions for further research.

The Study

In the spring and fall of 2008, I conducted survey research with two groups of adolescent students and interviews with three adolescent readers in an attempt to answer questions about who reads YA, why they read it, and what happens to the readers psychologically and emotionally during the reading process. I summarize my survey findings first, discuss the interview findings second, and then draw some initial conclusions about this empirical component of the research.

I distributed 100 surveys to university freshmen, ages 18–20, and 96 surveys to eighth-graders at a local middle school (the survey is reproduced here as Appendix 13.1). Students completed these surveys, and I analyzed the answers, with the following results.

University Surveys

Sixty women and forty men completed the university surveys. Sixty-seven percent of the women and 30 percent of the men said they currently read YAL. Of those who said they read YAL, a majority of the women said they read it either because it is "relatable" (13 out of 40 respondents) or because "the books talk about the same problems that they have and they therefore find it interesting" (15 out of 40 respondents). Half of the men who read YA said they did so because the books are about "topics that interest them" (6 out of 12 respondents). Very few said it was because it was relatable, in contrast to the female readers (2 out of 12 respondents).

Middle School Surveys

Of the 96 surveys completed by eighth-grade language arts students at a local middle school, 50 of the respondents were female and 46 were male. Of the female respondents, 84 percent said they currently read YA, while only 59 percent of the boys currently read the genre. As with the college-level respondents, there were more female readers of YAL represented in my surveys than male. The female readers of YAL gave the following reasons for reading it:

1   "interest"/"motivation"/"escape" (52 percent)
2   "relatable" (29 percent)
3   readily available in school or required for school assignments (19 percent).

Of the male readers of YAL, the following reasons were provided:

1 "interest"/"motivation" (63 percent)
2 "relatable" (19 percent)
3 required for school (15 percent)
4 unknown (3 percent).

As you can see, the older and younger readers of YAL provided many of the same reasons for reading it. However, in both age groups, more females reported the importance of being able to "relate" to the characters and events in young adult books.

Interviews

Of the 196 participants who completed surveys, I asked three female respondents to meet with me for two interviews during the spring semester of 2008. I asked these female readers to read a young adult novel, write between three and five journal entries during their reading in which they responded to various aspects of the book, and then talk with me about their reading experiences. The readers chose one of two young adult books I selected because of their contemporary themes related to mainstream teenage life as well as the extent to which they seemed to encapsulate the traditional characteristics of the YA genre. The two novels I selected were *Anything but Ordinary* (2007) by Valerie Hobbs and *The Plain Janes* (2007), a graphic novel by Cecil Castellucci and Jim Rugg.

Anything but Ordinary is a novel about two teens, Winifred and Bernie, who date throughout high school but take different paths after graduation: Wini attends a university and Bernie takes a job in a tire shop. Wini is taken in by the homogenizing college culture and changes her identity to fit in with the crowd; Bernie realizes he has made a mistake giving up Wini and follows her, seeking a reunion. The novel explores issues of teenage identity and how to be oneself in a culture that often urges sameness.

The Plain Janes is a graphic novel about an extraordinary teen named Jane who begins a secret club called "P.L.A.I.N."—People Loving Art In Neighborhoods. The club goes around the city engaging in random and anonymous acts of art such as swathing objects in wrapping paper or putting bubbles in a fountain. Jane and her "girl art gang" eventually have to stop their "attacks" because local law enforcement sees them not as acts of beauty, but as vandalism. However, Jane and her friends are forever changed by their independent acts of artistic expression.

I will describe the response of one of the three readers, Bonnie (a pseudonym), who chose to read *Anything but Ordinary*. (On a related note, I had a hard time convincing the girls to read the graphic novel because, despite its leading female character, they viewed graphic novels as a boy's genre.) The quotes come from my two interviews with Bonnie, an 18-year-old freshman, during which I asked her the following questions about her reading habits and experiences, how she reacts to books and integrates them (or not) into her real life, and her specific response to the novel of her choice:

- Tell me about yourself as a reader. If you read, why do you read? If not, why not?
- What young adult literature can you remember reading? Why did you read it? When did you read it?
- Do you still read young adult literature? Why do you think this is?
- How is young adult literature different from other things you read?
- Why do you think literature is taught in schools? How do you think it is best taught?
- Tell me about the book we are reading together. Do you like it? Why or why not? What does it make you think of? Remind you of? What kinds of feelings are you having reading it?
- Note some key entries in your reading log and discuss why they are important or interesting.
- Note some key passages from the novel and discuss why they are important or interesting.
- Do you think reading is an active experience or a passive absorption of ideas?
- Have you ever been influenced by anything you have read to change your opinions or actions? If so, can you tell me about this experience?
- Tell me the story of your experience reading this book.

Here are some of Bonnie's responses to these questions in her own words (all emphasis is mine):

- "It helps when I read if *I can connect* to the characters and sort of *put myself in their shoes*. It's a lot more fun to read."
- "I think the characters seem to be based round certain conflicts that teenagers deal with on a day-to-day basis in school. Whereas something that I would read for literature class would be more complex, more to deal with life after high school and college. *I guess I haven't really read a lot of stuff other than YA books.*"
- "I think I really got into the book *because I could relate it to my own life* because my boyfriend and I started dating toward the beginning of the summer after our senior year. He's in New York, and I'm here. *It was easier to connect with the characters because I'd sort of been in a similar situation.* Matt and I have realized that even though it is a book, it can work."

As you can see, Bonnie seems to see the value and pleasure of reading YAL to be mostly in its connection and relatability to her own life experiences and concerns. Both in my reading and in my survey study, *realism* (usually meaning similarity to the reader's own life experiences), *relating*, and *connecting* were important to adolescent readers who used these words on their own—I made a point never to use these words in any of my questions about the texts. I wonder why these words so often arise when teens talk about books (and even movies and TV shows). Is it because English teachers are using them so much in class when we lead literary discussions? Are they symptomatic of that self-absorbed, but not necessarily self-assured, "me" generation described in Jean M. Twenge's (2006) *Generation Me: Why Today's Young Americans are More Confident, Assertive, Entitled—and More Miserable Than Ever Before?* Do they result from Oprah Winfrey pseudo-psychological culture in which everyone should self-analyze and determine how one responds to social stimuli of all kinds? Going even further than psychological "relating" or identification, Bonnie was also able to connect the events in the book *Anything but Ordinary* to behavioral decisions she has made in her real life: "Matt and I have realized that even though it is a book, it can work [in their lives, as with the characters]." Bonnie and her boyfriend Matt seem to take comfort in the novel, and because its main characters are able to withstand a college-driven separation, they believe that they can as well. In Bonnie's case, the book seems to do what YAL authors and publishers often claim YAL will achieve: help teen readers work through problems in positive, life-affirming ways.

However, it does not seem, at least not in the brief interviews I conducted with Bonnie, that she is engaging in much critical thought, psychological grappling, or thoughtful deconstruction of the literary text she is reading, as is recommended and explored by many theorists cited in the previous chapters, including Deanne Bogdan, David Miall, and Northrop Frye. However, she also reads the novel basically independently, without the assistance of classroom discussion or a teacher as discussion leader. Perhaps Bonnie's emotional/cognitive experience with the novel would have been different had it been guided by a skillful literature teacher and if she had engaged in more discussion about it with either peers or a teacher.

So does Bonnie have an "identity theme," in Holland's sense, and, if so, is her literary experience affected by this theme? Perhaps so. Bonnie is a young female in her first year of college, similar to Wini in *Anything but Ordinary.* Her "identity theme" as a young female college freshman worried about her primary romantic relationship seems to affect her reading of the novel. While she might have focused on other aspects of the novel (independence versus fitting in, peer pressure, psychological changes when one moves from high school to college), Bonnie instead focuses on the issue of romantic relationships, certainly one of the novel's major themes. However, it almost seems as if the notion of identity themes and literary response is not as important when talking about young adults reading young adult literature. It appears a given to say that their positionality, their lived subjectivity, influences their reading of the novel. Isn't that why YAL authors write young adult literature? Isn't that why parents buy it and teachers teach it? Because young people are supposed to like it better, respond to it more fully, because it mirrors or imitates their own time of life? The point is that they can *relate* to it, after all.

It seems to me that if a teacher is teaching YA literature in the classroom, he or she not only must think about how to tap into the identity theme of the student reader in order to understand his/her reading behavior and response, but must figure out how to help the student reader extend his or her identity theme into a new realm—into a new and deeper level of response that enriches the literary experience and stretches the reader's cognitive and emotional response to it. So, the goal is more than just to get students to respond to the text about teens as teen readers; the goal is first to get the response, then to encourage students to grapple with it, wonder about it, and ask questions about it. For example, Bonnie might feel as if *Anything but Ordinary* acts as a narrative encouragement for her and her boyfriend to stay together despite their university-based separation because, like Wini and Bernie, they are meant to be married and live happily ever after. As her teacher or a peer reader, I would encourage Bonnie to think more about this relatively simplistic, one-to-one identification with Wini and Bernie. I could ask Bonnie some questions about the novel, such as: Why do you think Wini and Bernie should stay a couple? What arguments can you think of that support such a relationship? What arguments can you think of that oppose it? Can you think of anyone else, in life or literature, who has made a similar decision and either been glad about it or regretted it?

Like Bogdan (1992), I believe that such critical questions lead to a distancing from the text for the reader—and with YA literature such distancing might be more difficult, yet more important, than even for classic texts. Since the text is designed to be close to a young person's life experiences, engaging him or her in personal or aesthetic response is relatively easy—what's more difficult is the critical distancing, the very critical analysis and re-seeing of the text that allows for cognitive and emotional disequilibrium, resulting in substantive learning. In the Introduction, I called this type of reading experience recognition of the "gap" between the reader's real life and the world created in the text by the author. Such a recognition and analysis of difference can lead to lasting personal growth for the reader.

Louise Rosenblatt (1938/1983) wrote many years ago that the reader first engages in personal response; then, he or she can engage in critical response. She wondered if too many classrooms were engaging in only the critical part of the response continuum, ignoring the personal. I wonder now if the opposite might be the norm in many classrooms. Are we stopping literary study after only the personal response   the easy, one-to-one identification of reader and character? Are we worried primarily about our students "relating" to characters and events and forgetting to encourage them to step back from the text and examine its characters and events critically, through their own personal–cultural lenses and relevant literary (and even historical) theory? If we are turning our literature classrooms into spaces for personal response and identification without the critical, distanced component of literary studies, I fear we might be sacrificing cognitive/emotional growth for superficial student engagement. If this is true, at least in some cases, I do not see such classroom realities as arguments against the use of YAL in schools; in fact, I see it as an argument for increased and continued use of it. However, I also see the need for literature teaching pedagogies that support the thoughtful and thought-provoking teaching of YA literature.

When thinking about a book such as *Anything but Ordinary*, I hypothesize that teachers might change how they teach literature in their classrooms so that adolescent girls (and boys) have a larger repertoire of critical lenses (e.g., feminist theory, post-structuralist theory) through which to read literary texts, whether they are reading them independently or for class assignments. Research has shown that girls who have lower self-esteem are more likely to be influenced by the images and characters in books and movies (Cole & Henderson Daniel, 2005). There is additional research evidence that exposure to certain female images affects young girls' conceptions of what they can be: for example, "laboratory exposure to nontraditional images has been found to highlight the importance of achievement in women's aspirations" (p. 7) and "findings from survey data indicate that greater exposure to thin-ideal media is associated with higher levels of dieting, exercising, and disordered eating symptomatology" (p. 11). It seems that girls draw upon the narratives they experience to make comparisons between themselves and what they could or might be; these comparisons affect their real-world behaviors in varying ways, depending on their level of critical analysis, self-esteem, and confidence. Perhaps if teachers provide girls with more critical tools with which to approach such texts, tools rooted in core beliefs and ideologies recognizing the autonomy and inherent worth of girls and women, they will approach such contemporary young adult literature with stronger, more independent self-concepts and critical reflectivity.

Where Should We Go Next?

Knowing what we currently do about the experiences of young readers with young adult literature, what types of research do theorists of literature teaching need to pursue next? I believe that even larger, survey-based studies with interview components focusing on a sub-group of adolescent readers taking place over the course of several months or even an entire school year are warranted. A larger sample size and a longer period of time during which to interview teen readers about a wider variety of YA books would shed additional light on how the teen reader interacts with the YA novel. Additionally, it would be interesting to follow and learn from readers who are both reading independently and reading for a classroom assignment.

I believe the following research questions, among others, are important as literary and educational scholars continue to learn about the usefulness and challenges of teaching young adult literature:

1   How do the adolescent readers respond to different types of character in YA fiction?
2   How do the adolescent readers respond to different types of narrative events in YA fiction?
3   How do the adolescent readers respond to different narrative settings in YA fiction?
4   How and when do adolescent readers use the words "realistic," "relate," and "identify" when taking about texts?
5   How and when do the adolescent readers separate identification (or relatability) from critical or more distanced response? When they do this, how does this distance change their answers to the first four questions?
6   Are there any differences between written and oral response to YA literature?
7   Can particular behaviors (e.g., school attendance, disciplinary infractions, relationship behavior, making of future plans) be linked to reading experiences? If so, which ones, and how?

While many questions have been explored in this collection, we have much more to learn about readers of YA literature: how they read, why they read, and how the reading experience affects them emotionally, cognitively, and behaviorally. This knowledge has direct implications for how teachers should approach teaching young adult literature, and, hence, for English teacher educators like myself who educate new teachers of English.

Current research has shown that the adolescent brain is developing quickly, and various brain functions originating in the pre-frontal cortex have been connected with emotional and social behaviors, such as altruism, moral decision-making, and conflict detection (*World Science*, 2009). When we ask students to read books about others like them, supposedly having problems like theirs, in a world which is similar to the one they inhabit, we hope to encourage them to identify with others like themselves and, maybe, learn some new coping methods relevant to their own lives. However, let's not forget the value of reading about someone different, someone perhaps a little more difficult to relate to and identify with. Let's think about encouraging and helping teen readers see the similarities in a seemingly dissimilar situation. Thinking across such a gap in characterization and plot might just stimulate that pre-frontal cortex to rethink initial emotional and cognitive responses and modify those that do not seem adequate to the task of understanding others or making difficult life decisions that may have been previously unconsidered or viewed as impossible. Perhaps literary study can change the way adolescents relate to others and approach their life experiences. What more compelling argument could there be for reading and studying young adult literature? I can think of none.

Appendix 13.1

Young adult literature is defined as literature written specifically for an audience aged 11–21. It can be found in the "teen" or "young adult" sections of bookstores and libraries and often centers on teenage main characters in contemporary settings experiencing modern dilemmas.

1 Do you read young adult literature?

2 If you do read young adult literature, *why* do you read it?

3 If you do read young adult books, do you read them for school or for pleasure?

4 If you do read young adult books, please name one YA title you have read in the past year.

5 If you don't read young adult literature, what do you read instead?

6 What is your age?

7 Are you male or female?

Acknowledgement

I would like to thank Purdue University and the College of Liberal Arts Center for Humanistic Studies for its support during the completion of this research project.

References

Bogdan, D. (1992). *Re-educating the imagination: Toward a poetics, politics, and pedagogy of literary engagement.* Portsmouth, NH: Boynton Cook.

Castellucci, C. & Rugg, J. (2007). *The plain Janes.* New York: DC Comics.

Cole, E. & Henderson Daniel, J. (Eds.). (2005). *Featuring females: Feminist analyses of media.* Washington, DC: American Psychological Association.

Hobbs, V. (2007). *Anything but ordinary.* New York: Frances Foster Books.

Holland, N. (1975). *5 Readers reading.* New Haven, CT, and London: Yale University Press.

Rosenblatt, L. (1938/1983). *Literature as exploration* (4th edn). New York: MLA.

Twenge, J.M. (2006). *Generation me: Why today's young Americans are more confident, assertive, entitled—and more miserable than ever before.* New York: Free Press.

World Science. (2009). A seat of wisdom in the brain? Online: http://www.world-science.net.

About the Contributors

Janet Alsup is an associate professor of English Education at Purdue University, West Lafayette, Indiana. Her previous publications include *But Will It Work with Real Students? Scenarios for Teaching Secondary English Language Arts*, co-authored with Jonathan Bush (NCTE, 2003) and *Teacher Identity Discourses: Negotiating Personal and Professional Spaces* (Erlbaum/NCTE, 2006), which won the 2007 MLA Mina P. Shaughnessy Prize.

William J. Broz is Assistant Professor of English Education in the English Department at the University of Texas-Pan American. He was a columnist for the *ALAN Review* and is the author of several articles on YA literature, including "Hope and Irony: Annie on My Mind," which won the *English Journal*'s 2002 Hopkins Award. He taught high school English in Iowa for over 20 years.

Aliel Cunningham is currently pursuing a Ph.D. in English Language and Linguistics at Purdue University. She has an M.A. in Applied Linguistics from Ohio University and has taught English for non-native speakers in a variety of school settings for nine years—both in the United States and abroad. She has reviewed YA and children's literature in the past and has a continued interest in following the developing trends of new genres that explore interactive meta-narratives and their intersection with fantasy literature.

Joy Dangora, originally a Massachusetts native, came to Purdue University to study Elementary Education. She earned her bachelor's degree in 2003 and a master's in Literacy and Language Education in 2008. She is currently a fourth-grade teacher at Happy Hollow Elementary School and a middle/high school coach in West Lafayette, Indiana.

Lisa Schade Eckert earned her Ph.D. in English Education from Western Michigan University in 2002, after a ten-year career teaching secondary English. She is currently an associate professor of English Education at Montana State University. She is the author of *How Does It Mean? Engaging Reluctant Readers through Literary Theory* (Heinemann, 2006).

James R. Gilligan taught high school English in New York for nine years. He left high school teaching to work at Purdue University, where he has taught composition, literature, and education courses. He currently serves as the Student Teaching Placement Coordinator in the College of Education at Purdue, where he is also pursuing a Ph.D. in Literacy and Language with a focus on secondary English education and queer theory.

Nisreen M. Kamel Anati received a B.A. degree in English Language and Literature from Hebron University, West Bank, in 1998, an M.S. degree in Curriculum and Instruction from Purdue University in 2006, and a Ph.D. in Curriculum and Instruction with a specialty in English education from Purdue in 2009. Immediately thereafter she joined the United Arab Emirates University, UAE, as a visiting professor in the Curriculum and Instruction Department.

Nai-Hua Kuo, a native of Taiwan, taught English to middle school students in her homeland using young adult literature. She is currently a Ph.D. student in Literacy and Language Education at Purdue and is continuing to study the many pedagogical uses of YA and multicultural literature.

René Saldaña, Jr. is an assistant professor of Language and Literacy in the College of Education at Texas Tech University. He is the author of several YA books, including *The Jumping Tree* (Delacorte, 2001), *Finding Our Way: Stories* (Wendy Lamb, 2003), *The Whole Sky Full of Stars* (Wendy Lamb, 2007), and *The Case of the Pen Gone Missing: A Mickey Rangel Mystery* (Piñata Books, 2009).

Jeanne Smith Muzzillo holds a Ph.D. in English Education. A veteran secondary school English teacher, she is now an assistant professor in the English Department at Bradley University. In addition to the English teaching methods courses she teaches, Dr. Muzzillo also teaches young adult literature.

Jeff Spanke earned a master's degree in American Studies from Purdue University and is currently teaching English, Speech, and Film Literature at North Montgomery High School in Crawfordsville, Indiana. He has taught literature and writing at the college level and holds an interest in the intersections of literature, psychology, and pedagogy.

Gail Zdilla is a high school English and journalism teacher in Wallingford, Pennsylvania. She has also taught literacy and language classes to elementary students through pre-service teachers in the United States and Indonesia. She graduated with honors from Millersville University in May 2001 and earned her master's degree in English Education from Purdue University in May 2008.

Index

eBooks – at www.eBookstore.tandf.co.uk

A library at your fingertips!

eBooks are electronic versions of printed books. You can store them on your PC/laptop or browse them online.

They have advantages for anyone needing rapid access to a wide variety of published, copyright information.

eBooks can help your research by enabling you to bookmark chapters, annotate text and use instant searches to find specific words or phrases. Several eBook files would fit on even a small laptop or PDA.

NEW: Save money by eSubscribing: cheap, online access to any eBook for as long as you need it.

Annual subscription packages

We now offer special low-cost bulk subscriptions to packages of eBooks in certain subject areas. These are available to libraries or to individuals.

For more information please contact webmaster.ebooks@tandf.co.uk

We're continually developing the eBook concept, so keep up to date by visiting the website.

www.eBookstore.tandf.co.uk